Critical Criminological Perspectives

Series editors: **Professor Reece Walters** Faculty of Law, Queensland University of Technology, Australia

Dr. Deborah Drake Department of Social Policy and Criminology, The Open University, UK

The Palgrave *Critical Criminological Perspectives* book series aims to showcase the importance of critical criminological thinking when examining problems of crime, social harm and criminal and social justice. Critical perspectives have been instrumental in creating new research agendas and areas of criminological interest. By challenging state defined concepts of crime and rejecting positive analyses of criminality, critical criminological approaches continually push the boundaries and scope of criminology, creating new areas of focus and developing new ways of thinking about, and responding to, issues of social concern at local, national and global levels. Recent years have witnessed a flourishing of critical criminological narratives and this series seeks to capture the original and innovative ways that these discourses are engaging with contemporary issues of crime and justice.

Titles include:

Kerry Carrington, Matthew Ball, Erin O'Brien, Juan Tauri
CRIME, JUSTICE AND SOCIAL DEMOCRACY
International Perspectives

Claire Cohen
MALE RAPE IS A FEMINIST ISSUE
Feminism, Governmentality and Male Rape

Marianne Colbran
MEDIA REPRESENTATIONS OF POLICE AND CRIME
Shaping the Police Television Drama

Pamela Davies, Peter Francis and Tanya Wyatt (*editors*)
INVISIBLE CRIMES AND SOCIAL HARMS

Melissa Dearey
MAKING SENSE OF EVIL
An Interdisciplinary Approach

Michael Dellwing
THE DEATH AND RESURRECTION OF DEVIANCE
Current Ideas and Research

Deborah Drake
PRISONS, PUNISHMENT AND THE PURSUIT OF SECURITY

Matt Long and Roger Hopkins Burke
VANDALISM AND ANTI-SOCIAL BEHAVIOUR

Margaret Malloch, William Munro (*editors*)
CRIME, CRITIQUE AND UTOPIA

Erin O'Brien, Sharon Hayes and Belinda Carpenter
THE POLITICS OF SEX TRAFFICKING
A Moral Geography

Maggie O'Neill and Lizzie Seal (*editors*)
TRANSGRESSIVE IMAGINATIONS
Crime, Deviance and Culture

Diane Westerhuis, Reece Walters, Tanya Wyatt (*editors*)
EMERGING ISSUES IN GREEN CRIMINOLOGY
Exploring Power, Justice and Harm

Tanya Wyatt
WILDLIFE TRAFFICKING
A Deconstruction of the Crime, the Victims, and the Offenders

---

Critical Criminological Perspectives
Series Standing Order ISBN 978–0–230–36045–7 hardback
(*outside North America only*)

You can receive future titles in this series as they are published by placing a standing order. Please contact your bookseller or, in case of difficulty, write to us at the address below with your name and address, the title of the series and the ISBN quoted above.

Customer Services Department, Macmillan Distribution Ltd, Houndmills, Basingstoke, Hampshire RG21 6XS, England

---

Vandalism and Anti-Social Behaviour

Matt Long and Roger Hopkins Burke
Nottingham Trent University, UK

palgrave
macmillan

First published 2015 by
PALGRAVE MACMILLAN

Palgrave Macmillan in the UK is an imprint of Macmillan Publishers Limited, registered in England, company number 785998, of Houndmills, Basingstoke, Hampshire RG21 6XS.

Palgrave Macmillan in the US is a division of St Martin's Press LLC, 175 Fifth Avenue, New York, NY 10010.

Palgrave Macmillan is the global academic imprint of the above companies and has companies and representatives throughout the world.

Palgrave® and Macmillan® are registered trademarks in the United States, the United Kingdom, Europe and other countries.

ISBN: 978–0–230–58085–5

This book is printed on paper suitable for recycling and made from fully managed and sustained forest sources. Logging, pulping and manufacturing processes are expected to conform to the environmental regulations of the country of origin.

A catalogue record for this book is available from the British Library.

A catalog record for this book is available from the Library of Congress.

Contents

Acknowledgements

The authors are primarily indebted to James Irving of Sheffield Hallam University and Phil Hodgson of Derby University for their data collection and contribution to the early drafts of this work. We wish to credit their intellectual input during the process of the writing of this book.

We further acknowledge the support of our colleagues both on the wider Division of Sociology under the leadership of Jason Pandya-Wood and our more immediate colleagues in the Department of Criminology at Nottingham Trent University. The lead author has been based at NTU since 2006, and the second author since 1999.

We also appreciate the moral support of our respective families and friends.

Introduction

It is astonishing to the authors of this book that Stanley Cohen's (1973) undoubtedly ground breaking work on vandalism is now over four decades old. Since then, others have endeavoured to review Cohen's typology, for example, Wilson and Healy (1987), who added the notion of 'innocuous vandalism', yet in our opinion the original remains pivotal.

That said, Cohen's work is in need of revisiting, not least because of the rapid development of the consumer society over the past 40 years and the parallel rise of the politics of individualism. The world was a very different place during the early 1970s than it is now in the second decade of twenty-first century. Cohen (1973) observed that most acts of vandalism were (at that time) committed against public rather than private property. Forty years on, with the growth of consumer culture in late-modern societies and with more and more sections of the working class (and indeed the workless classes, which were much smaller during the earlier period) owning more and more commodities such as the motor vehicle and indeed their own homes, it is not surprising that vandalism (or criminal damage as we shall discover later in this book) has been increasingly targeted at private property. We will commence our discussion by revisiting the year of 1973 so that we can locate Cohen's important contribution within its cultural context.

That was the year that was – 1973

The year of 1973 was a landmark year politically as the United Kingdom, Ireland and Denmark entered what was then referred to as the European Economic Community (EEC), later to become the much expanded European Union (EU). This was all taking place at the same time that the Provisional Irish Republican Army (IRA) was conducting a major bombing campaign on the mainland and in particular London, with Whitehall and the Old Bailey symbolic targets. Ironically, the House of Commons was to vote against the restoration of capital punishment by a margin of 142 votes.

The country was in even more economic turmoil than is usually the case in United Kingdom. In May, more than 1.5 million workers went on strike in support of a Trades Union Congress (TUC) 'day of national protest and stoppage' against the Government's anti-inflation policy, which involved significant cutbacks in the public sector and an unprecedented wage freeze. These are policies with which we are, again, very familiar at the time of writing, although the levels of support from a now emasculated trade union movement are much smaller today. Things came to a head in December of that year when, in response to Western support for Israel in the Yom Kippur War, the Arab-dominated Organisation of Petroleum Exporting Countries (OPEC) eventually quadrupled the price of crude oil, thus instigating a worldwide 'oil crisis'. It was in this context – and because of significant coal shortages caused by regular industrial action on the part of the miners – that the electricity consumption reduction measure famously known as the 'three-day week' was introduced in the United Kingdom. The average salary for UK workers was £2263, with the average house price around £9000. According to the National Travel Survey (2007), car ownership in the mid-1970s was just over 40 per cent. This figure was to almost double by the twenty-first century, which is significant when we come to consider the motor vehicle as a specific cultural target for the vandal (RAC Foundation, 2014).

In the United States, the country's involvement in the Vietnam War was coming to an end, with the signing of the Paris Peace Accords. Domestically, there was no escaping trouble for President Richard Nixon with the aftermath of the Watergate Scandal and the so-called Saturday night massacre leading to calls for his impeachment. Meanwhile, the American Psychiatric Association removed homosexuality from its list of mental illnesses.

In terms of popular culture, the Yorkshire-based television comedy series *Last of the Summer Wine* was first screened, thus instigating decades of Compo chasing the wrinkly-stocking-clad Nora Batty! The music world was well and truly rocked by the release of Pink Floyd's iconic album *The Dark Side of the Moon*, and Elvis Presley's *Aloha From Hawaii* television special was seen around the world by more than one billion viewers.

In the world of sport, heavyweight champion Smokin' Joe Frazier was lifted off his feet and sent to second-round oblivion against the huge and seemingly indestructible George Foreman in a fight which saw the former's promoter Don King utter the appallingly unashamed line, 'I came with the champion and I left with the champion' as he departed with the man who would later make millions through selling barbecue grill products. Long before he waved that infamous glove at us on the golf course after his controversial acquittal for murder in a case which divided America, O.J. Simpson became the first running back in history to rush for 2,000 yards in a season for the Buffalo Bills. Back at a packed Wembley stadium, Ian Porterfield's winner made huge underdogs Sunderland unlikely FA Cup winners over Don Revie's mighty Leeds United.

So 1973 was indeed a very different world to that of today, and as we will argue, a newer and more culturally informed consideration of vandalism is needed for the second decade of the new millennium. It would, however, to borrow the words of the Tenpole Tudor Song, be a mistake to 'throw the baby out with the bathwater' by completely overlooking Cohen's (1973) typology. Cohen made a fantastic original contribution to knowledge, not least because of two things. Firstly, he acknowledged the patterned nature of vandalism, and secondly, his work located the social practice of the vandal in terms of specific subcultural contexts.

Cohen's typology of vandalism

Cohen (1973) identified six major categories of vandalism, namely (1) *acquisitive* – in which the vandalism is incidental in the process of material acquisition; (2) *ideologica*l – in the sense that the act is motivated recourse to a wider belief system, with people acting upon so-called principle; (3) *tactical* – in which acts are conducted in pursuance of achieving some personal advantage; (4) *vindictiv*e – in that the act is committed as a mode of revenge for real or perceived wrongdoing against oneself; (5) *malicious* – in which acts are generically anti-social rather than specifically targeted against an individual victim; and (6) *play* – in that such acts are carried out ordinarily by children who are keen to explore the axiomatic 'boundaries' as far as their engagement with property is concerned. We will reflect and build upon this typology throughout this book.

Cohen's work (1973: 23) was clearly innovative in describing vandalism as 'institutionalised rule-breaking', and he was perhaps the first academic to observe that vandalism is *patterned* behaviour – arguing that 'some patterning in the physical characteristics of the target is also apparent' (ibid.: 50) – in that its forms and specific styles are repeated generation after generation. In this sense the social practice of vandalism involves a form of 'ritualism' (ibid.). He cites the examples of 5 November Guy Fawkes Night celebrations in the United Kingdom and the routine destruction of property on Halloween night in the United States. This is significant in that vandalism is often censured as being random or sporadic. Take, for example, an article which appeared in the *Washington Post* in 1992, entitled '3 Arrested in Random Vandalism; Teens Blame Boredom for Actions, Police Say' (Redding, 1992). In this case, damage to both cars and houses committed by three youths, is presented as being a sporadic outburst. Likewise, an article in the *Miami Student* newspaper in February 2010 (Miami Student, 2010) made reference to 'sporadic' vehicle vandalism on the college campus. Cohen (1973) was the first criminologist to make the point that, far from being 'random' and 'sporadic', much vandalism is often patterned, repeated and as we will see highly predictable.

Cohen's (1973: 50) second major contribution which we aim to build on, was to assert the subcultural nature of vandalism in that 'vandalism is almost always a group rather than an individual offence'. This is of massive importance as it already takes us way beyond the realms of black letter law, whereby it is only ever individuals who are culpable for damage and are prosecuted separately. Hopkins Burke (2005: 105) observes that there are many different deviant subcultural theories, but they all share the conviction that 'certain social groups have values and attitudes that enable or encourage delinquency'. Taken collectively, the deviant subcultural tradition is of paramount importance to the study of vandalism because it tells us that such acts are *meaningful* to those who commit them. This is hugely important as vandalism is often censured as being 'mindless'. For example, the South Ayrshire Council censured the vandalism of signs intended to educate dog owners in Ayr as 'mindless' and 'wanton' (South Ayrshire Council, 2013). Similarly, in March 2010, a 17-year-old teenager from Jaywick was given an Anti-Social Behaviour Order (ASBO) by the Harwich Magistrates Court for anti-social behaviour and so-called 'mindless vandalism' (Clacton Gazette, 2010). Cohen taught us that very often what appears to be 'mindless' and 'meaningless' is in fact, when taken from the viewpoint of the detached observer, invested with meaning for the vandals themselves.

Revisiting vandalism through a cultural criminological lens

It is worth speculating as to why four decades on, the work of Cohen on vandalism remains quite simply 'the best there is'. The answer possibly lies in the rise of right realist or populist conservative criminology which infused criminological discourses from the early 1980s and which is still popular in today's times of austerity in the second decade of the new millennium. Cohen was writing at a time in the early 1970s when the neo-Marxist revival across the social sciences was in full swing and radical criminology was in many ways at its peak, evidenced by the publication in that year of the seminal text *The New Criminology*, by Ian Taylor, Paul Walton and Jock Young.

The Americans had just gone through the horrors of the Vietnam War in the 1960s, and the abuses of power with President Nixon and the Watergate scandal meant that people were seeking to challenge the proverbial 'system' – and with a desire to challenge came the belief that one must first understand. It was in that context that Cohen's work in many ways represented the last serious intellectual attempt to *understand* vandalism. Back in the 1970s, it was still acceptable for academics like Cohen to try and understand vandalism because criminal justice practitioners still held on to the belief that the rehabilitative ideal carried some possibilities. There was a conviction that the psychological outlook and the social conditions of the vandal could be changed and that if that were to occur, then desistance could occur – so there was merit in attempting to *understand* vandalism.

With the onset of the Reagan and Thatcher administrations in the United States and United Kingdom, the 1980s witnessed a return to the rational actor model of criminal behaviour in the form of rational choice theory (see Cornish and Clarke, 1986). The vandal was no longer the victim of circumstance, but rather *chose* to engage in his (and it was normally his) destructive and anti-social activity. The politics of individual self-responsibilisation took over, and there was nothing left to understand. The always anti-social and never politically progressive acts of the vandal were now open to censure as being 'mindless' and 'moronic' by an invigorated realism of the Right (see Wilson and Herrnstein, 1985; Hopkins Burke, 2014a).

There is clearly a need to revisit the issue of vandalism because we live in a very different world from that when Cohen conducted his research and wrote his seminal work. Cultural criminology is alive and receptive to the contested 'reality' that we inhabit, what is often described as a 'postmodern' world or the 'postmodern condition' (Hopkins Burke, 2014b). This is a world in which objective truths are increasingly challenged and rejected, a world in which reality and truth are fragile, negotiable and socially constructed. Cultural criminology follows the postmodern perspective and rejects the previously dominant modernist approaches to attempting to understand the world based upon making assumptions about the 'progress' offered by science and rationality which followed the Enlightenment period.

Having acknowledged the primary contribution made by Cohen (1973) we must now address the inherent problems in producing ANY typology of vandalism.

Problems with typologies

Cohen offers us a useful typology which enables us to appreciate the sheer diversity of social practices subsumed under the catch-all notion of 'vandalism'. It was nevertheless a product of its time in the early 1970s. Whilst 'sociologists of deviance' such as Taylor, Walton and Young were preaching a 'new criminology' (1973), practitioners still believed in the ideals of rehabilitation for offenders. The political 'New Right' was still lurking in the political shadows, while associated criminological ideas around risk management and actuarialism had not yet come to the fore. It was a world of certainties in which people still believed in the pursuit of objective truths. This links with one of the problems of this earlier typology when viewed from the perspective of today, in that it tends to objectify the act of vandalism. It tends to assume there is one singular truth or rationale behind the act of vandalism itself. The typology is itself distinctively objectivist. There is one and only one meaning that the act of vandalism can have. This is distinctly problematic when viewed through the lens of a postmodern social order. In reality, meanings and motives for vandalism are multiple. Where does 'play' vandalism stop and 'malicious' vandalism begin, for instance? Moreover, this earlier typology ignores the possibility that the act of vandalism may have completely different interpretations from the point of view of the 'offender' and the 'victim'. This is clear from the following conversation.

A female in her twenties described her experiences as a member of a family who were the only Asians on the street. She described how what started off as racial harassment and incidents with cigarettes being pushed through the letterbox then began – according to her quite understandable *perception* – to escalate in intensity when the car windscreen was vandalised:

> Our neighbours were hosting what you'd basically call a Chav house party. They pretty much had some kind of party every weekend. Soon enough, the house party turned into a street party. We heard a loud bang in the middle of the night and the next day woke up to find that a bottle had been thrown through the car window – there was glass everywhere. It could just have been an accident or high spirits during the party but I think it was intentional. We'd had trouble before – out of all the cars in the street, why did our car get damaged? – It's just too coincidental.

The point drawn from the above quote is that what for the offender(s) *may* have been a prank or even an accident, is for the victim perceived to be something entirely different – namely an act of vindictive vandalism with distinctly racial undertones. What is the 'truth' behind the act of vandalism described above? For Cohen, this act would have to fit in with one of his six types: (1) acquisitive; (2) ideological; (3) tactical; (4) vindictive; (5) play; or (6) malicious. It is a central component of modernist thought that things need to fit neatly into categories, and has long been a criticism of traditional positivist social science (see Foucault et al., 2001). Social practices such as vandalism cannot belong in more than one category. Yet, on reflection, there are multiple possible meanings of this act, and they certainly are open to contestation. It may have been committed in the spirit of 'high jinks', in which the alcohol was flowing and the music at the party was banging away, with a bottle being carelessly tossed out of a window into the night sky, with the car being hit almost by accident. At the other extreme, it may have been a deliberately calculated and targeted act of vindictive vandalism aimed at one particular family in the street purely because of the colour of their skin. The point is, the 'truth' will never be known, as is so often the ambiguous case where vandalism is concerned. It is thus worth at this point offering some thoughts on the methods which have informed this piece of work.

A note on methodology

This work is clearly located in a qualitative tradition of study. The authors attempt to develop a reflexive and culturally informed criminological perspective which rejects positivist epistemologies underpinned by cause and effect and multivariable analysis. Our work involves a triangulation of both secondary and primary data sources. Whilst we have included the usual academic books and journals, these secondary data sources have relied heavily on the Internet to provide empirical examples of various modes of vandalism and anti-social behaviour. Whilst we acknowledge the problems of utilising Internet-based sources in terms of reliability and verification, we were also keen to acknowledge that engagement with this mediated form of technology provides us with good research material. This has provided us with a range of examples from both across the United Kingdom and around the world in which to test the strength of this new updated typological model which we develop in this text. Indeed a leaning towards Internet-based sources is becoming increasingly common in a postmodern world where people are more likely to identify with each other as members of virtual communities of interest rather than real communities which are fixed geographically in time and place.

As well as secondary data sources, we have engaged in primary data collection. As well as the self-reflections of the authors, this has taken the form of conversations with 'key informants' in the field. Rather than attempt to select a random or systematic sample of so-called 'vandals' from probation reports or prison records, which may have been both ethically dubious and certainly pragmatically difficult, we have once again rejected all claims to positivistic science by relying on a small volunteer sample of key informants who were purposefully sampled due to convenience. We make no apology for this as we feel that the insight gained from a variety of sources, including police officers, social workers, environmental protesters and those who have gone on to desist from their anti-social practices, adds considerable insight. Had we attempted to generate a large sample of unwilling and 'captive' interviewees (in the literal as well as the metaphorical sense of the word), our insight would have been limited. The conversations we have captured do not provide us with a direct window of light into social practice, but what they can do if employed appropriately, is to provide a degree of phenomenological insight into 'what actually goes on'. We felt that our decision to use key informants to speak to rather than to generate some random sample with ambiguous claims to representativeness, was far more beneficial as our respondents were talking to us of their own volition and many were well motivated to actively engage with our project because they were not coerced into doing so.

It would have been ethically and practically impossible to conduct research with current offenders. First, to interview those under the age of criminal responsibility about their potential misdemeanours would have led these authors to be accountable to a plethora of institutional ethics committees (see Ferrell et al., 2008) which might well have stopped us anyway or at least place impossible restrictions upon our practice to have made the project undoable. Second, to have attempted to interview offenders motivated to vandalise through hatred of minority groups would have been illuminating, but may have risked creating moral outrage as we may have risked the accusation that we were offering the 'oxygen of publicity' to such offenders. Any ethnographic attempt to understand the 'position of the other' on this matter may not have been tolerated by the aforementioned ethics committees in light of the 'zero tolerance' policy which purports to exist where sensibilities risk being offended on issues of race and diversity in today's society. This type of ethnography, whilst by no means impossible, arguably had its peak in the 1970s and is perhaps best evidenced with reference to the covert work of Fielding (1981) on Far Right groups. This sort of work is extremely difficult to conduct nowadays because of the requirement to secure written consent from research participants. Despite using an example of the US practice of 'institutional review boards' (TCU, 2007: 7, 10), this is best articulated by Ferrell et al. (2008: 164), who argue that 'they (ethics committees) reserve especially harsh consideration for proposed research that might put subjects "at risk of criminal or civil liability", or for research involving "vulnerable populations" (including prisoners)'.

Having offered some rationale with regard to method, we now end this introductory chapter with an outline of the structure of the book.

Book structure

Chapter 1 on cultural and political contexts asserts the need for a discussion informed by cultural criminology on the most common of all criminal offences by arguing that both vandalism and anti-social behaviour have been repoliticised by recent political and policy discourses.

Part 2 suggests that vandalism is a culturally created artefact and that for it to be fully understood, it is necessary to locate the actions in the context in which they occur. Thus, Chapter 2 begins by examining the type of vandalisms which orthodox criminology has chosen to fetishize, namely the 'exploratory' and 'drift' vandalisms of children and adolescents. In beginning to offer a more critical perspective, Chapter 3 argues that the conventional vandalisms of the young are far from 'sporadic' and 'random', but rather that they are highly patterned and to a certain extent predictable due to the targeting of certain cultural objects such as the motor vehicle. Chapter 4 develops the idea that conventional vandalisms of the young become normalised in certain contexts depending on the type of people who engage in its social practice.

Part 3 discusses 'cultural criminology and vandalism', and the chapters move away from the conventional vandalisms of 'exploration' and 'drift', reminding the reader that some 'anti-social' vandalisms are driven by the drive for material acquisition ('collateral vandalism'). In continuing the links to strain theory, Chapter 6 moves on to explore how a rise in profoundly 'anti-social' hate vandalism can partly be explained by the material conditions generated by a double-dip economic recession.

Part 4 discusses 'cultural criminology, the anti-social state and the pro-social vandal. This section of the book rejects the orthodox criminological view that the private individual is to be the locus of the blame for 'anti-social' vandalism and asserts that the state has the capacity to act in a malevolent and profoundly anti-social way in its vandalism of the environment, and yet this is very rarely censured as 'vandalism'. Chapter 8 moves on to consider that many vandalisms committed by individuals and collectivities can actually be 'pro-social' in attempting to challenge the 'anti-social' practices of the state.

Part 5 begins to draw the book to a conclusion by exploring the possible futures of vandalism. Chapter 9 assesses the impact of mediated communication on vandalism, arguing that the late-modern focus on virtual as well as real geographical communities fundamentally challenges the way in which we must assess the vandalisms of both the present and the future. Chapter 10 continues its focus on the future by developing a more international perspective on vandalism and anti-social behaviour, looking at likely future trends through an informed cultural criminological lens.

So without further ado, we now move Towards a Cultural Criminology of Vandalism and Anti-Social Behaviour as our starting point.

Part I

Political Context

1
Towards a Cultural Criminology of Vandalism and Anti-Social Behaviour

All of us will have broken something on many occasions in our lives – it could be in a domestic context like a plate or a vase. It could be in a social context, like a glass. Accidental damage aside, evidence suggests that at some point or other in our lives, many of us will have also wilfully broken something. It is the shift from the former as in the 'accident' to the latter in terms of intentionality, which signifies what we term 'vandalism' in our culture. We begin this chapter by asking what this term actually means and by tracing where it actually comes from.

The origins and history of the notion of vandalism

It is important to trace the genealogy of the term vandalism, as this kind of 'archaeological method' advocated by Michel Foucault (1969) encourages us that an understanding of the past can forge a healthier and more rounded comprehension of the present.

As we observed in the introduction to this text, the work of Stan Cohen (1973) remains highly influential for those seeking to understand our subject matter. Over 40 years ago, he observed that the notion of vandalism derives its meaning from an East German tribe known as the Vandals, who during the fourth and fifth centuries CE invaded Western Europe and destroyed cities. Cohen (1973: 33–34) commented that 'they were traditionally regarded as the great destroyers of Roman art, civilization and literature and their actions were associated with a general barbaric ignorance'. It was thus Renaissance and Early Modern writers who were keen to censure the vandals, and historian Lisa Jardine (1998) reminds us that the artists of the Renaissance period were patronised by the ruling elites and that any artefact critical of those in power would be unlikely to be bought.

In the year 406, the Vandals moved from their homeland in Pannonia – in present-day Hungary – and travelled along the Danube, but met resistance from the Franks when they reached the Rhine. Having defeated the Franks in a bloody battle, the Vandals invaded Gaul (now France) and in 409, they crossed into the Iberian Peninsula (Spain) via the Pyrenees, later moving into North Africa in 429. The infamous 'Sack of Rome' occurred in 455, with Pope Leo the Great begging King Genseric of the Vandals merely to pillage the city rather than to murder, rape and commit arson. The Vandals duly obliged and departed with the spoils of the Temple in Jerusalem booty, which had been brought to Rome at the beginning of the millennium by Titus. Interestingly, regardless of their label as the masters of destruction, it is thought by some that the original Vandals were actually no more destructive than comparable invaders in existence in ancient times (see Cohen, 1973). It was simply what invaders at that time in history did, and this is interesting in terms of an assessment as to how and why the label of the vandal has survived many centuries and endures in postmodern times.

The Romans unsuccessfully retaliated against the Vandals in 460 with attacks from both their Western and Eastern empires, and by 470 they had signed a peace treaty signed with the Vandals in Constantinople. The Vandals were subsequently heavily defeated by the Berbers in two major wars in North Africa between 496 and 530, and the Vandal King Gelimer surrendered to the Romans in 534, effectively bringing an end to the Vandal Empire.

In an interesting shift from a focus on a subculture of people to that of property, Cohen (1973: 34) notes that during the nineteenth century, the term 'vandalism' came to refer to the planned destruction of medieval buildings in order to make way for ones which were representative of the new Churchwarden Gothic era, and observes that:

> It is not clear when the term 'vandalism' became used to describe destruction of property in general. Its etymological connection with the destruction of aesthetic objects is obviously too restrictive to cover the range of behaviour conventionally described as vandalism. Nevertheless, the original connotations of the term should not be lost sight of.

The above connotation has recently resurfaced in our present-day culture with the Prince of Wales reportedly bemoaning the apparent 'madness' of seeing heritage buildings abandoned to 'arsonists and vandals'. Prince Charles is reported to have made these comments to distinguished guests who appeared at the reopening of the English Heritage managed Kenwood house on Hampstead Heath in December 2013 (see Furness, 2013; Wright, 2013).

Whether we are talking about medieval buildings in the nineteenth century or former stately homes in 2013, what is significant is that from the former period onwards the notion of the vandal was no longer used merely to refer to a specific tribe of people, but rather to describe a social practice – namely that of property destruction. This observation is worthy of further reflection because as we have seen, the original Vandals were a force to be reckoned with in terms of colonial expansion. Thus, they murdered, raped, pillaged and looted. These original connotations all seem far removed from the label of the modern-day vandal, for example, the so-called 'feral child' of the socially excluded housing estates so beloved by popular media reports. In writing for the Daily Mail, for instance, Harriet Sergeant (2009) wrote how a generation of so-called 'violent, illiterate' young men were 'living outside the boundaries of civilized society' and could as such be labelled as 'feral youths'. Nonetheless, this can all be taken too far, for exactly who, outside the esoteric academy, makes any connection between the present day 'vandal' and a once to be feared buccaneering, force of colonial expansion?

Therefore, our first point requiring cultural criminological analysis is that the contemporary understanding of the term vandalism differs radically from its original meaning. Having established this, we now turn to an exploration of what is understood by the notion of vandalism in contemporary society.

What is vandalism in contemporary society?

A good starting point is to take a look at black-letter law. A glance at the statute book tells us that there is no such offence as vandalism, which is a term used more as a label or a censure (Sumner, 1994) and possibly a catch-all term for something else. The correct legal term is of course 'criminal damage', and this unambiguously refers to 'crime':

> Criminal damage refers to crimes where any person without lawful excuse intentionally or recklessly destroys or damages any property belonging to another. Activities resulting in non-permanent damage (i.e. that can be rectified, cleaned off or removed at no cost) such as letting down of car tyres should not be classed as criminal damage, nor should accidental damage.
>
> (Home Office, 2006a)

In a strict legalistic sense, according to case law if no damage in fact occurs, then no liability for criminal damage can arise (see for example *A [a Juvenile] v R* [1978] Crim LR 689). Black letter law can, however, only take us so far in that there is ambiguity with judgment, and police officer discretion is required in order to decide what actually constitutes 'permanent' or 'non-permanent' damage. Whilst letting down car tyres might constitute non-permanent damage, it may actually represent more of an inconvenience for the car owner than having their wing mirrors broken. The former temporarily incapacitates the car owner and might mean a missed hospital appointment or a later appearance at work, whereas the latter does not mean the car cannot be driven. In practice, therefore, 'damage' may not be strictly defined by the legislation, and is thus not limited to permanent damage. One such example may be the smearing of mud on the walls of a police cell by a suspect, which may be classified as criminal damage even though technically it can be removed. In practice, therefore, what constitutes damage is a matter both of fact and degree, and it is for the court, using its common sense, to decide whether what occurred is damage (Crown Prosecution Service, 2011).

There is nevertheless legal recognition that some forms of criminal damage are significantly more serious than others, and this begins to give us a clue as to the fact that vandalism is diverse. Criminal damage may not just desecrate property, but can in certain cases endanger human life. To this end, the Criminal Damage Act 1971 prescribes a maximum sentence of life for arson or criminal damage that endangers life and for any threat/possession with intent to commit criminal damage involving explosives. Indeed, few would dispute that these are serious offences worthy of significant sanction. This is, however, once again an ambiguous area, particularly when what we will define as 'political' acts of vandalism are considered. The waters are muddied in the sense that, as we shall see later, members of organisations such as Greenpeace, for instance, may claim that their protests, although dangerous, are morally justifiable as they are carried out for the purpose of the wider social good, environmental concerns and sometimes to prevent what are perceived to be potentially greater long-term harms to humanity.

There are much tougher sentences for racially and/or religiously aggravated offences of criminal damage, but whether an offence is judged to be religiously or racially motivated depends on (a) the perception of the victim and (b) the awareness of the police officer(s) investigating in terms of their appreciation of current legislation and good practice. An offender may receive a maximum prison sentence of 14 years when the offence of criminal damage is racially motivated or religiously aggravated, and there is a 10-year maximum sentence for all other forms (see Crown Prosecution Service, 2011). As we shall see later in the book, some forms of vandalism are regressive and aimed at undermining attempts at diversity, inclusion and multiculturalism, and considered deserving of the full weight of the criminal law. These are what are collectively known as Hate Crimes, and what we term 'hate vandalism' is a subcomponent of this.

The 'seriousness' of vandalism is invariably related to the cost of the damage rather than taking into account motivations of the offender, which is a fundamental underpinning of criminal law, taking us back to the utilitarian philosophy of Jeremy Bentham and John Stuart Mill (Hopkins Burke, 2013). It is not so much the intention of the perpetrator that is important but the damage they cause to the victim or society. Thus, if the cost of damage in value terms exceeds £5,000, the maximum penalty is six months in prison and a £5,000 fine. If the value is less than £5,000 the maximum sentence is three months in prison or a £2,500 fine (see Crown Prosecution Service, 2011). The Criminal Damage Act of 1971 has in some respects been complemented by more recent legislation such as The Anti-Social Behaviour Act 2003, which introduced £50 Fixed Penalty Notices for offences relating to minor graffiti and flyposting, with clearly some ambiguity existing here as to what constitutes 'minor' in such cases and the impact of the damage on the wider community.

The above being taken into account, a cultural criminological perspective on vandalism, however, rejects a narrow legalistic conception of how the criminal justice system deals with acts of 'criminal damage'. Whilst the criminal justice system does arbitrate on the level of seriousness of the offence of property damage which has been committed, a dry black-letter legalistic approach says very little about the sheer diversity of social practices which can be subsumed under the label of vandalism. Vandalism, as we shall see, covers a diverse range of social practices.

The diversity of vandalism

There is considerable diversity in the acts that are included in the black-letter legalistic category of criminal damage including arson. This is important for us to acknowledge because 'fire starting', for example, is materially different from, say, tagging a bus shelter. The definition of arson favoured by the British Crime Survey is 'deliberate property damage caused by fire to a person's home or vehicle' (Nicholas et al., 2007). This again warrants criminological attention in that we might ask ourselves whether the sort of person who knocks a wing mirror off a car as a drunken prank is the same as one who would deliberately sets fire to a school to cause millions of pounds worth of damage. Some might think not and consider these to be completely mutually exclusive acts at the polar ends of a seriousness spectrum, but others might note a linkage with a 'one thing leading to another' syndrome located in the context of a spiral of decline or increased activity (see Knights, 1998).

Unlike some forms of damage, arson is a serious criminal offence as it has been estimated that more than half of all fires which cause property damage are started deliberately, with the wider costs to the economy amounting to £2.2 billion a year. Despite the creation of an Arson Control Forum, with an annual budget of £4million, a typical week sees arsonists start 21,000 fires. As well as damage to property, these vandalistic acts can lead to the far more serious eventuality of injuries (estimated at 55 per week), with an average of one death per week (Daily Mail Online, 2013). As with simple property destruction, we again find that arson, far from being random and sporadic, is remarkably patterned, and it is this patterning which provides us with one of the golden threads of this book. It is estimated that approximately 50 per cent of arson is targeted at cars (usually stolen), with other targets including garages, sheds and schools. Over one in five fires in homes are started deliberately, and on an average day, 17 schools will be targeted. The Association of British Insurance estimates arson costs over £1million per day, with 'direct losses' being related to property damage, emotional suffering due to injury/loss of life, health service costs, fire service response, environmental costs and lost production. Additionally there are 'indirect costs' related to fire protection, for example, smoke alarms and prevention activity by the Fire Service (Home Office, 2013).

The peak period for fire starting is between 7 p.m. and midnight, which, at first sight, might suggest a rational actor model motivation with people choosing to commit these acts under the cover of darkness, while a predestined actor model suggestion might be that offenders are more likely to be drunk during the more conventional 7 p.m. until 11 p.m. pub drinking hours. As a cultural criminologist, the late Mike Presdee (2007), reminds us that fires have more of a visual effect at night and that there is something seductive about the partaking of acts of transgression under the blanket of the hours of darkness, demonstrating the compatibility, rather than exclusivity of these theoretical approaches. Detection rates for arson are low, 8 per cent compared to 24 per cent for all other criminal damage offences, probably because fingerprint and even DNA evidence can be easily destroyed in the flames, which also suggests torching a crime scene to be a very rational criminal action (see Association of British Insurers, 2009).

In further considering the diversity of acts of vandalism, it should be noted that the category 'criminal damage' also includes the very ambiguous notion of 'graffiti'. Thus, what some consider an artistic and creative process offering a social commentary through both image and word is not allowed for in a criminal code, which does not recognise such a diverse form of expression. At its simplest form graffiti involves images, lettering, scratchings, scrawlings, paintings and/or markings on property. It derives from the Italian word *graffiato*, or 'scratched', and its origins can be traced to Ancient Greece and the Roman Empire, for example, with figure drawings on walls, ancient sepulchres/ruins. There is evidence of Viking graffiti in Rome and Ireland, as well as Chinese graffiti on the Great Wall of China. Cohen (1973: 29) observes that 'graffiti are hailed as legitimate and amusing forms of self-expression', but we might be less charitable if the graffiti is ugly, offensive and on our own property. Black-letter law aside, and again from a cultural criminological perspective, we might ask ourselves whether the 'tagging' of a bus shelter or a grave is the same thing as a work of art produced by the revered (in some quarters) graffiti artist Banksy? Indeed, we might well ponder – as some clearly do – whether Banksy has the (human or civil) right to paint his murals on your property without your consent in the name of art and, furthermore, are you some awful philistine because you object? According to Jeff Ferrell (1996: 5), the importance of disaggregating different forms of graffiti which are unhelpfully subsumed under the label of vandalism is paramount:

> (T)hose who shape public perceptions of urban graffiti-local and national media, anti-graffiti campaigners, and others – intentionally and unintentionally muddy the boundaries between types of graffiti and graffiti writing, confusing one with the other in their condemnations of all graffiti as vandalism and crime.

In his study of hip-hop graffiti in Denver, Ferrell observes how *Life on Capitol Hill* repeatedly referred to graffiti artists by means of the derogatory censure 'graffitiodiots'. Paige (1989), a well- known talk show host in the United States, has referred to graffito artists as 'gauche graffiti goons' and 'spray-can cretins' (cited in Ferrell, 1996: 137), and in so doing graffiti is censured and denied status as an activity of artistic pursuit. Ferrell (1996: 138) noted how in July 1988, the *Rocky Mountain News* equated graffiti with other different sprees of vandalism (see also Pugh, 1988), and according to the author (1996: 138), 'the effect, of course is to lock graffiti into the context of vandalism, to tie it to activities like window smashing and cemetery desecration'. So we have in effect the lumping together of people who smash up bus shelters, start fires by pouring petrol through letterboxes and those who use a spray can to perform a work of art. The criminal law apparently allows little room for acknowledging the diversity and motivations which lie behind these totally different social practices, although we might add that these apparently disparate acts do have something significant in common. All are criminal damage, and they are so because, for the simple reason, they are damaging someone's property without their permission, regardless of how aesthetically pleasing the outcome might be to some observers. As cultural criminologists, however, we have to be more ambitious in our attempts to understand the sheer diversity of social practices alluded to above, and our starting point is an attempt to understand vandalism through popular cultural depictions. By exploring these popular cultural depictions we can begin to see how certain stereotypes of who vandals are and what vandalism actually is have taken root in our culture.

An understanding of the vandal through popular culture

If there are two fictional figures who occupy prime spots in the public consciousness when the notion of 'the vandal' is brought to mind, it has to be Dennis the Menace and The Smasher. The comic strip *Dennis the Menace* first appeared in *The Beano* on 17 March 1951, featuring Dennis as the archetypical 'naughty schoolboy', along with his Abyssinian wire-haired tripe hound, Gnasher. The 'uncontrollable' youngster has historically been presented as taking pride in causing chaos to those with whom he comes into contact through his insubordination and disdain for the rules made by those in authority. Armed with catapult, peashooter and water gun, Dennis would add excitement to the drudgery of his day through minor acts of vandalism and incivility.

In an interesting commentary on how the morality of crime is often made to play out in depictions of transgression (see Sparks, 1992), Dennis would very often be made to get his proverbial 'comeuppance', thus reinforcing the message that ultimately 'crime never pays'. In more recent years the Dennis the Menace character has been subject to more commodification through the medium of television, with a series being launched in 1996 and once again in 2009. The character has taken on an even further satirical twist in recent years with the magazine *Private Eye* inventing the character often referred to as Beano Boris or alternatively Boris the Menace, widely assumed to be a parody of the Mayor of London, Boris Johnson, who features in greater detail later in this book.

Somewhat reminiscent of Dennis the Menace is the fictional character The Smasher, who regularly appeared in the iconic British comic *The*

Dandy between 1958 and 2004. As we will see later in the book when we investigate what we have termed 'exploratory vandalism', much of The Smasher's antics were assumed to be playful acts of property damage rather than calculated acts of malice. The enduring appeal of this character can be evidenced by his re-emergence in the 2013 *Dandy Annual*.

So as cultural criminologists, taking popular and fictitious depictions of vandals as our starting point is a good one. What can we learn from the depictions of both Dennis the Menace and The Smasher in popular culture? Firstly, vandalism is associated with the young – namely childhood and adolescence. At this point fiction sits well with fact in that figures have shown that around two thirds of those cautioned and/or convicted for offences of criminal damage in Magistrates Courts are males under the age of 18. This basic finding loosely fits with the 'delinquency and drift' thesis of David Matza (1964), which tells us that deviance is often a transitory and passing phase of juvenile development. Offenders tend to 'grow up' and 'grow out of' crime. Secondly, whilst these fictional characters are often profoundly anti-social, we learn through them that breaking things – hearing the sound of broken glass – is often fun. There is a whole history of literature in the cultural criminological tradition which acknowledges the joy of transgression and the fact that transgression itself is an antidote to boredom (see for example Katz, 1988; Presdee, 2000).

The above consideration of vandalism through popular culture is enlightening, but not sufficient for the task of cultural criminology. Our task is now to try and locate vandalism in its wider political context. An understanding of political discourses around vandalism is certainly not the only cultural medium through which we should or will approach the study in the rest of the book, but politics is important for cultural criminologists. This is precisely because cultural criminology draws some of its intellectual inspiration from radical schools of thought across the social sciences (see for example, Taylor et al., 1973). The contemporary development of cultural criminology has some of its roots in the so-called 'new deviancy explosion' of the 1960s and 1970s, which was furthered by organisations like the National Deviancy Conference and the Centre for Contemporary Cultural Studies at the University of Birmingham. As well as taking into account the concept of 'moral panic' (Cohen, 1972), contemporary cultural criminology draws on subcultural and labelling theories (see Ferrell et al., 2008). This is significant because all these aforementioned theories and concepts raise questions about the nature of power in society. More specifically they encourage us to ask questions in this study like the following: Whose interests are served by classifying certain property into 'publicly' and alternatively 'privately' owned? Who has the power to label an act as vandalism? How is vandalism packaged and presented as being a political problem? These are questions which require the framing of political context, and it is to that which we now turn.

Political context

To frame the political context of vandalism in 2015, one has to consider also the notion of 'anti-social behaviour'. This is because, rightly or wrongly, the two concepts have become inextricably intertwined in recent years. On its web page 'Building a Better Bournemouth', for example, Bournemouth borough council lists vandalism as a subcategory of the much broader phenomenon of 'anti-social behaviour' (www.bournemouth.gov.uk). Likewise, on its site, Nottingham City Homes lists vandalism as one of 13 subcategories of anti-social behaviour (www.nottinghamcityhomes.co.uk). So what does the notion of anti-social behaviour actually mean?

Anti-social behaviour, or 'ASB' as it is increasingly commonly referred to, is a generic term which encompasses both criminal and non-criminal behaviour and is fundamentally considered to be actions that exhibit a lack of respect for other people and the wider community. The Crime and Disorder Act 1998 (s1[1a]) defined anti-social behaviour as acting 'in a manner that caused or was likely to cause harassment, alarm or distress to one or more persons not of the same household as [the perpetrator]', while the earlier Housing Act 1996 defines it as 'engaging in or threatening to engage in conduct causing or likely to cause a nuisance or annoyance to persons engaged in lawful activities'.

The above being said, whilst the notion of 'anti-social behaviour' is common in political and wider social discourse today, it is worth noting that its entry into the collective consciousness of our society is a relatively recent event, although it is often difficult to imagine that there was ever a time when the term did not exist. Hayes (2012) proposes that it emerged around the mid-1990s in the United States as a catch-phrase of Mayor Rudolph Giuliani as part of his 'zero tolerance' campaign against 'incivilities' in New York City, and argues that New Labour were quick to seize on the growing popularity of the notion of 'nipping crime in the proverbial bud' proposed by that strategy by announcing in their 1997 election manifesto,

> We will be tough on crime and tough on the causes of crime.... We will tackle the unacceptable level of anti-social behaviour and crime on our streets. Our 'zero tolerance' approach will ensure that petty criminality among young offenders is seriously addressed. (Labour Party, 1997)

Following the party's election in 1997, New Labour's White Paper *No More Excuses* (Home Office, 1997) undoubtedly put the spotlight onto anti-social behaviour in the context of its almost revolutionary youth justice strategy, which swept aside the system in place at the time (Hopkins Burke, 2008). The communitarian philosophy contained in the White Paper was translated into the Crime and Disorder Act 1998, in which 'anti-social behaviour' was defined as the kind of aforementioned practices which could cause 'harassment, alarm or distress' to other persons who were perceived to have to endure this kind of behaviour (see Squires and Stephen, 2005: 38). The legislation introduced the now infamous Anti-Social Behaviour Order, or ASBO. Whilst a civil order, if breached, this could result in a jail sentence of up to five years. It established the ASBO conditions which prohibited the offender from entering into defined areas or from committing specified 'anti-social' acts, and breach of this order constitutes a criminal offence, which was widely criticised by widespread liberal opinion. The later Anti-Social Behaviour Act of 2003 amended the 1998 Act and introduced further sanctions such as Child Curfews and Dispersal Orders in order to strengthen and rationalise the communitarian strategy.

The labelling theorists would be interested in the 'net-widening' effects of anti-social behaviour legislation, as Ahmed (2005: 16) points out: 'the issuing of anti-social behaviour orders may satisfy the tabloids but for recipients with mental health and social care needs they can be the first step towards criminalisation'. One of the consequences of the legislative assault on anti-social behaviour, for instance, was the blurring of boundaries between behaviour which may not have previously been criminalised and that which perhaps had been deemed criminal. Squires and Stephen (2005: 32) observe that 'rather than separate entities, it is notable that in the White Paper, "anti-social behaviour" and "crime and disorder" had now become aspects of a single range of behaviours' (see also Squires, 2008).

These developments can be best understood in the context of the communitarianism that emerged as a political philosophy in the United States during the 1980s as a response to what its proponents considered to be the limitations of liberal theory and practice (Hopkins Burke, 2009).

The dominant themes of that philosophy are that the individual rights vigorously promoted by liberals need to be balanced with social responsibilities, and it proposed that unless we redress the balance toward the pole of community, our society will continue to become normless, self-centred and driven by special interests and power seeking (Hopkins Burke, 2013). For Calder (2004) perhaps one of the most recognisable and evocative of the numerous political slogans used by New Labour leader Tony Blair in the promotion of the importance of 'community' was the notion that individual rights were to be equally coupled with social responsibilities. This logic was inspired by the work of Amitai Etzioni (1993), a leading proponent of mainstream communitarianism. In contrast to the traditional liberal idea that members of a society may be simply entitled to unconditional benefits and services, it was being proposed by New Labour that individuals should be increasingly made responsible for their actions. For Blair and his sociological guru Anthony Giddens (1998) the message in terms of 'community' was about the need to reinforce civic obligations. Blair's 'third way' was presented as the binary opposite to the unashamed individualism engendered by Margaret Thatcher's classic statement that 'there is no such thing as society'. For Blair, this was about redefining the role of the state and learning the lessons from the past. He argued (1998: 4) that 'the grievous 20th century error of the fundamentalist Left was the belief that the state could replace civil society and thereby advance freedom'. For Blair, the role of the state would be to facilitate civil renewal and a reinvigorated sense of community life (Calder, 2004). Those who dissented from this ideology have subsequently pointed out that the New Labour agenda would go on to take on a far more authoritarian character than had been previously suggested by Tony Blair when New Labour was in opposition and when he was originally espousing the belief in both 'rights' and 'responsibilities' (see Calder, 2004; Driver and Martell, 1997; Jordan, 1998). Hughes (1998) thus refers to the communitarianism of Etzioni and his acolytes – and pursued enthusiastically by governments both in the United States and the United Kingdom – as moral authoritarian communitarianism. Houdt and Schinkel (2013), go further, and illustrate how authoritarian communitarianism operates in combination with neoliberalism with the emphasis on 'responsibility' in communitarianism compatible with the notion of 'responsibilisation' in neoliberalism, in other words, a neoliberal communitarianism used as a tutelage strategy against the poor and the socially excluded, in particular.

In terms more specific to our debate about vandalism and anti-social behaviour, before he assumed the mantle of Prime Minister, Gordon

Brown, in a speech to the Labour Party Conference in September 2006, reflected on Blair's maxim about rights and responsibilities, observing a 'commitment to a Britain of responsibilities as well as rights demands strict measures to combat vandalism, violence and all forms of anti-social behaviour' (BBC News, 2006a), thus providing further evidence of this automatic association of vandalism with anti-social behaviour. Significantly, the Conservative Party adhered to this line of thinking in the build-up to the General Election of 2010, with Party Leader David Cameron giving a speech which again made explicit the association between vandalism and anti-social behaviour as part of his 'Broken Britain' thesis. The proposed solution was to be a charity-led, cost-cut form of communitarianism, rather than the state-led form – the 'Big Society' – claiming that 'Conservative councils are safer, with lower levels of the crime, anti-social behaviour and vandalism which strikes fear into so many people' (Cameron, 2009). Since the formation of the Conservative and Liberal Democrat Coalition Government in 2010, there has been contested debate over the conceptual boundaries of vandalism and 'anti-social behaviour'. In September 2010, for instance, the Chief Inspector of Constabulary, Sir Denis O'Connor, controversially claimed that police officers did not regard anti-social behaviour as 'real crime' (BBC News, 2010e), but in responding, Home Secretary Theresa May (2010) stated:

> Crime is crime, however it's categorised in the figures – and the public expect us to fight it; Vandalism isn't anti-social behaviour' – its crime. Intimidation isn't 'anti-social behaviour' – its crime. Drug dealing isn't 'anti-social behaviour' – its crime.

The above goes some way towards explaining why, in December 2010, just seven months after his election, Prime Minister Cameron refused to acknowledge the political motivations of those protesting about a rise in university tuition fees, arguing that those who 'smashed up property' should feel the 'full force of the law' (Daily Telegraph, 2010a).

So the conflation of vandalism and anti-social behaviour, as discussed above, represents a repoliticisation of a range of increasingly criminalised social practices. Such is the diversity of social practices which are covered by these two terms, that it begs the question as to whether this conflation inhibits a deeper cultural understanding, whilst promoting censure and condemnation.

So this first chapter began by tracing the origins and history of the notion of 'vandalism'. We then moved on to explore the meanings and connotations which vandalism has in contemporary society. This led to an appreciation of how 'vandalism' is in effect a label which covers a diverse range of social practices, some of which actually bear little resemblance to each other. We then examined popular representations of fictional characters with a propensity towards vandalism as represented in comics and magazines of the like which many of us may have read when we were younger. We argued that these popular and caricatured depictions of vandalism are worthy of cultural criminological attention because they are presented in enduring social mediums in terms of magazines which have not only survived but which have evolved over the decades. These popular depictions of the caricatured vandal do not, however, tell the full story in that an acknowledgement of political context is important in framing a social practice which is criminalised. The conflation of vandalism as a subcategory of anti-social behaviour re-politicises the issue, and some would argue allows for all variety of social practices which can be subsumed under this somewhat unhelpful label to be further censured.

So having started by acknowledging characters like The Smasher and Dennis the Menace, Chapter 2 begins by taking a look at the type of vandalisms which these characters indulged in and the type of property damage which is given primacy by our own criminal law – we move on then to a consideration of what we term the 'exploratory' and the 'drift' vandalisms of children and adolescents.

Part II

Cultural Targets and Vandalistic Contexts

2
Exploratory and Drift Vandalism

In this chapter we consider what we have chosen to term the 'exploratory' and the 'drift' vandalisms perpetrated by both children and adolescents respectively. In beginning to classify and label vandalism, we must acknowledge the original typology which the late Stan Cohen (1973) developed over four decades ago. One of his typologies was 'play vandalism', which is carried out by children and characterised by an apparent lack of overt malice. It is our contention that much vandalism is committed by children in the spirit of mere curiosity and in the spirit of discovery; hence, our term exploratory vandalism. In terms of this conceptualisation, property damage may be incidental rather than intentional.

Empirically, children's vandalism is notoriously difficult to investigate. Thus, two senior police officers spoken to during the course of this research expressed the view that the main age group for the commission of the kind of routine vandalism that we term 'drift' – and which is explored later in this chapter – is committed by those between 17–19 years of age. Although children clearly participate in such activities, it is hard to produce accurate figures of their involvement because many of the culprits are undetected, and those below the age of criminal responsibility are not prosecuted.

It is nevertheless worth considering at the outset that the most common discourse surrounding children and vandalism is not one of children as the protagonists of damage and hurt, but rather as the victims of such activities. This is particularly evident when instances of vandalism occur which are perceived to impact on public services which make provision for the personal, social, and educational development of children.

Children as victims of vandalism

In 2010, the Children's Library in Cheltenham had to be temporarily closed after vandals broke in through a fire exit. Furniture, computing equipment and bookshelves were damaged in the attack, which was described perhaps not surprisingly as 'a mindless act of vandalism that has meant families in Cheltenham missing out on all the excellent facilities in the Children's Library' by the Head of Gloucestershire County Council's libraries and information, David Paynter (BBC News, 2010a). It is significant to note that this undisputed case of vandalism is censured by an authority figure as being 'mindless'.

In actual fact, this act may have been anything but 'mindless'. For example, it could have been a rational response to circumvent circumstances and to provide material gain. The censure of the act as being 'mindless' occurs seemingly because of the perceived 'innocence' of the victims – if not direct victims, then children as victims by proxy. For how could anyone in their 'right mind' seek to willingly deny such children access to their educational development and needs?

In March 2011 it was reported in the national press that vandals had been instrumental in wreaking havoc in a children's playground in Wanstead, East London, causing an estimated £1,000 worth of damage by apparently 'hacking' through a rope seat, ten inches thick (The Guardian, 2011a). Whilst some of the outrage over this act of vandalism was undoubtedly exacerbated by the fact that the new swing had only been installed some 48 hours earlier, there does seem to be something in the discourse of outcry because children's 'playtime' has been desecrated. A regular user of the facilities was parent of four, Elizabeth Canavan, who commented, 'It's such a shame that they've done this as it's a really nice play area, so many children enjoy it down there'. Once again alluding to the perception of such vandalism as 'mindless', mother of two, Wendy Bolton, commented, 'Why anyone would do this is beyond me'. The outrage caused by the vandalism of children's play facilities seems to go way beyond the mere destruction of the object such as the swing or the slide or the paddling pool – it is almost as if the children's right to innocent pleasure has been cruelly snatched from them – an attack on 'innocence' itself.

Similar outrage occurred in Oldham in 2010, with the 'desecration' of a garden which children at Alexandra Park Junior School had spent months building (Oldham Chronicle, 2010). It was reported that the weeding, digging, planting and decorating had gone to waste after three 'hooded louts' had scaled a high fence and smashed up a £200 shed, including the watering cans, while trampling on and ripping up the flowers. What is interesting is the presentation in the article of the 'hard work' and 'innocence' of the children used in comparison with the demonic act of the 'hoodies' – who, along with predatory paedophiles, undoubtedly constitute the focus for one of *the* moral panics of our age (see Young, 2009). In reality, the so-called 'hoodies' themselves may have been adolescents, not too much older than some of their 'victims' and indeed probably former pupils of the school themselves. Furthermore, it would seem that this kind of vandalism is to be more heinous because it does not involve acquisition or material gain. According to an unnamed teacher,

> It's just mindless vandalism. They've destroyed all the hard work that children have put in for months. The shed was not locked as there was no equipment in it so they did not steal anything. They did not have to force open the shed; they just destroyed it for the sake of destroying it. They have ripped it to pieces for the sheer fun of it.
>
> (Oldham Chronicle, 2010)

Inherent in this censure is the assumption that had these 'hoodies' been out to satisfy some material need through theft and which had resulted in what we later term 'collateral vandalism', then their crime would have been more understandable, if not excusable. The fact that these 'hoodies' may have been bored out of their minds and in need of some hedonistic fun is not seen to be worthy of comment, if indeed recognised. It is at this point, that cultural criminological explanations of such acts can be usefully utilised in conjunction with realist criminological arguments. Both 'right' and 'left' realists quite rightly remind us that crime is a reality, and it does have a very real impact on the quality of lives of many of its victims (see Hopkins Burke, 2013; also Hopkins Burke and Hodgson, 2013). This is clearly the case in Oldham, with the exasperated teacher going on to say,

> The children have asked what we can do but all our funds are gone.
>
> They have learned the value of taking care of things and have now had someone come along and show them the opposite.

Realist arguments are clearly significant, not least because in recessionary times the educational sector is grappling with the issue of scarcity along with other public services. Moreover, the public outcry about the victimisation of children at the hands of anti-social vandals is clearly understandable – not least to those of us who are parents – but does seem to be informed by the belief that both as a socially constituted group and as individuals children are not just victims but are fundamentally 'at risk'.

One such notorious example was the vandalism of the Blue Peter Garden Garden back in 1983, which caused distress to the late television gardener Percy Thrower and outraged then presenters Janet Ellis, Simon Groom and Peter Duncan. The 'Whodunit?' mystery was reignited years later when former England football striker Les Ferdinand, who used to live in the White City Estate near the BBC TV centre, admitted that he had 'helped a few people over the wall', whilst appearing as a guest on the BBC Choice programme, *45 Minutes*. There was an implication that fellow England teammate and former Chelsea star Dennis Wise may have been involved due to his friendship with Ferdinand in the early '80s (BBC News, 2000).

Undoubtedly, this form of vandalism is profoundly 'anti-social' as it creates fear, mistrust and indeed disgust amongst communities, let alone the psychological impact it might well have on the children. The vandalism of the Blue Peter Garden is quite possibly an early example of a location's being targeted by youths with the knowledge that their misdeeds would lead to a level of local notoriety and five minutes of fame on the next edition of the show.

Children at risk

The 'children at risk' discourse is at the heart of the public and media censure of vandalism, which is perceived to have a negative psychological impact on them. Back in 2010, for instance, it was reported that 'Children at risk as vandals target Flintshire play park' (Davies, 2010). This report went so far as to suggest that the children's very lives were at risk because of the 'targeted' vandalism of older youths who had seemingly attacked play park equipment. Bolts and screws had apparently been tampered with and removed from the climbing wall. The fear was that children could have been seriously injured had the damage not been discovered earlier. Clearly, criminological realists have a valid point here: There are often *real* victims of apparently innocuous crime. This kind of vandalism surely does not advance any political or ideological cause, as more radical theorists may have misguidedly suggested in the past. Actions which could potentially result in the serious injury or even death of a child cannot in any way be considered politically progressive in this sense. Argoed Community Councillor Ken Houghton referred to the area as being 'plagued' by periodic attacks of vandalism, referring to this incident as particularly 'nasty' and a potential 'booby trap'. Again inherent in the article was the discourse of the ever-present 'risk' with the all-pervasive fear that because the area was a site of repeat victimisation that the 'culprits could strike again', and it does seem a reasonable argument.

The theme of putting the lives of children at risk is present in a case reported by Howard (2006), in which there is a conflation between the 'drift vandalism' – we will discuss in more detail below – and anti-social behaviour, with the clear message given that the latter can potentially cause a fatality. It was reported that groups of youths were congregating around the Mill Meadow area and had engaged in shed break-ins, caused damage and graffiti to picnic tables, as well as what was perceived to be anti-social behaviour in the form of littering. Of most concern in terms of the endangering of children's lives was an incident involving a picnic table being placed on top of a climbing frame and a further four tables being stacked on top of each other. The perceived danger seems to have been related to the potential for unstable and heavy objects to fall and seriously injure young children. Countryside Officer Dave Hughes commented that 'had a child climbed on to the tables before the Rangers found them early the following morning the tables could have fallen and killed them. It took three of us with ropes to safely lower the table from the climbing frame before we could allow anyone to use the play area' (Howard, 2006). This example demonstrates that vandalism can be potentially far more problematic than simply 'anti-social' when it threatens to impact not only on the emotional but also on the physical well-being of people, some of whom are vulnerable minors.

Alongside the complementary twin discourses of children as victims and of being 'at risk', there is another coexisting discourse about the damage that children can often do through their playful acts of exploration.

Children's vandalism

A Freedom of Information request to Fife Constabulary made by the press in 2009 revealed that in Dunfermline, a child as young as four years of age was detected for vandalism. In the following year, a five-year-old was similarly detected in the West Fife Villages policing area (Dunfermline Press, 2011). In Scotland, the age of criminal responsibility was eight years of age at the time (the lowest in Europe), and thus a child under that age could not be charged with criminal offences (although in March 2011, the age of criminal responsibility was raised to eleven). In England and Wales it was ten years of age, and remains so.

Prior to the Crime and Disorder Act 1998, the legal situation for children over the age of ten (eight in Scotland) and under the age of fourteen had been made ambiguous by the long-established rule of *doli incapax*, which had presumed that a child less that fourteen years of age cannot ordinarily know that an act they have committed was seriously wrong. Thus, in order to obtain a conviction in such cases, it was necessary for the prosecution to establish that the child did know the difference, and it would be clearly difficult to establish this in many ambiguous cases of vandalism. Consequently, many such cases were not taken to court.

With the 1998 legislation, the onus of the rule of *doli incapax* was completely reversed: it was now assumed that a child between the ages of ten and fourteen *does* know the difference between right and wrong, and it is now the responsibility of the defence to prove otherwise. The outcome was that far more previously ambiguous cases were to be formally processed by the youth justice system, with a significant increase in the number of convictions (Hopkins Burke, 2008). A former social worker provided us with the following humorous anecdote:

> I can recall around the time the rebuttable presumption was abolished. I was called to an incident at a Children's Home where child M, was sitting on the roof of the Children's Home, exposing himself while pulling off roof tiles and throwing them at the watching crowd of police, residential workers and fire fighters below. This was a fairly common occurrence for M who had previously been removed from other child care establishments and foster carer's for his behaviour. M was 9 years old at the time of this particular incident and his birthday was the following week. Between the profanities being shouted by M, one Police Officer who was aware of M's forthcoming birthday was heard shouting, 'M, why don't you come down...we can do this again next week'. When next week came, M duly obliged instead of his usual ticking off was duly arrested!

In a classic case of 'net widening', the unintended consequences of changes instigated by the Crime and Disorder Act 1998 drew more children and young people into the youth justice system for what had previously been considered non-problematic offences of what we have termed 'exploratory vandalism'. The former social worker explained,

> Because of the way the Children's Home operated, I don't know if it was because of insurance issues, every 'criminal act' committed by a child over 10 suddenly was being reported to the police. This was

> ridiculous and was a clear example of how kids in care were being drawn into the criminal justice system. If your child writes their name on their bedroom wall or deliberately breaks a window or smashes something, I would imagine that as angry as you are the last thing you would want to do is call the police and have them prosecuted. Not so in Children's Homes.... I saw this happen on many occasions with kids in care. The kids would come into the Home as a vulnerable child and leave a few weeks later as a vulnerable child with a criminal record. Most hadn't done anything which in the 'real world' would have been considered worthwhile reporting.

The above example shows that more and more acts committed by children have the potential to be both formally labelled and potentially censured as being 'anti-social', and we can here observe the complex interaction between legislative change and moral panic recognised by labelling theorists. Stan Cohen (1972) observed that moral panics can lead to 'knee jerk' calls for new laws to curb increasingly disapproved of activities, and we can observe that it is these self-same legislative changes that can add further fuel to the flame of moral panic about 'feral' and 'out of control' children. Thus, the *Daily Mail Online* (2009) carried the online shock headline that 'two three-year-old boys investigated for vandalism become youngest criminal suspects in British history', with the report noting that there were some ten children under the age of six who had been investigated for offences, some of which involved vandalism.

Significantly, concerns about the transgressions of children can soon lead to the creation of stereotypical caricatures about their propensity to offend, as the following infamous example demonstrates.

'Rat Boy' – realism or caricature?

The 'adult' comic *Viz* contains the exploits of a fictitious character by the name of 'Rat Boy', whose character is an intended gross caricature of the stereotypical 'juvenile delinquent'. His age is ambiguous, being anything from under the age of criminal responsibility to his middle teenage years. In a clear allusion to the moral panic over the 'Chav' phenomenon, Rat Boy always wears his track suit or shell suit as his normal mode of attire. The still influential (post-)Lombrosian notion that 'criminals' are a visible, identifiable class apart is present in the physical depiction of him as being rat-like with massive ears, a long nose, bucked front teeth and a scampering movement in his gait. He is presented in the comic as being the younger half-brother of the character Tasha Slappa, who is an echo of the simultaneous moral panic over the so-called 'ladette' phenomenon, her name derived from the slang term in popular culture to refer to a young working-class woman with low moral standards who is sexually promiscuous.

Exaggerated sexual promiscuity is presented as being at odds with the ideal of virginal femininity, and in a clear link to the widely fashionable (in some quarters) eugenicist conception that some women are 'unfit to breed', Tasha Slappa is presented as a poor mother whose periodic abandonment of her children and apparent 'drowning' of them in a canal is a clear risk to them. Like Rat Boy, her physical appearance is a caricature of the Chav stereotype, with the wearing of copious amounts of cheap, tacky 'bling' jewellery and her Geordie dialect and dismissive colloquialisms such as 'I divvint give a fuck' clearly fuelled by the notion that she comes from a family of 'inbreds'. Yet, we should note that the comic is produced in Newcastle by self-made working-class entrepreneurs, and there is a clear moral ambiguity about the depiction of these characters, which appears at times to be as much affectionate as it is censorious. Indeed, if anything, it appears to be more of the former.

Rat Boy himself has a reputation for defecating at the scene of his burglaries and acts of vandalism; hence, his caricature as having a permanent piece of faeces sticking out from his backside! Although acts of vandalism using faeces constitute a relative rarity (Hopwood et al., 1996), one person recounted the following incident from his teenage years, followed by what can only be described as an attempt at 'do it yourself' restorative justice, under heavy coercion from his father:

> We walked down the road necking this wine, then smashed up the bottle in the middle of the road. Next me cousin decides to take a shit on the graveyard wall, arse facing the road, I picked up a beer mat or old paper, summthing like that, ran over the road up a driveway and smeared it on a car. Went back for the second log, went back up same drive way and as I was putting it through the letter box heard a loud knock at the window, so I ran off, me and my cousin, got home slept a couple of hours then went to M. rock concert, where we were all chuckin' bottles of piss and all that. When we got home me mum went mad, at me, she'd had a 'phone call from the woman who'd knocked on the window who'd recognised me. Me dad grabbed me by my hair and tried to punch me, I don't really remember much after

that, but did have to write a 'sorry' letter, I mean how do you write that without sounding like you're rubbing it in! (Male: mid-30s)

'Getting away with it'

As the above quote suggests and as 'right-wing' critics argue, restorative justice processes are often seen as 'soft' and 'lenient' on offenders. Rat Boy mirrors these 'weaknesses' and 'fears', as he is presented as a young offender who 'gets away with murder', having a publicly funded holiday in Spain while on probation, and preys on right-wing populist fears that the criminal justice system is simply not punitive enough. Conservative concerns that non-custodial forms of punishment are both 'soft' and 'ineffective' are echoed in the depiction of Rat Boy's eating away at his own leg in order to free himself from his electronic tag so as to successfully continue his criminal reign of terror with yet another burglary spree. His depiction as a vandal is just part of the wider caricature of him as a drug addict who is dependent on the proceeds of his acquisitive crimes in order to fund his habit. This again links into popular fears that if left unchecked, so-called minor infractions and incivilities such as vandalism and anti-social behaviour can lead to much more 'serious' and persisting forms of career criminality, as suggested by 'broken windows theory' (Wilson and Kelling, 1982).

Some have suggested that the cultural caricature of 'Rat Boy' is based on the real life juvenile criminal, Tommy Laws, who was given the nickname 'Spiderboy' by the media because of his ability to scale the heights of drainpipes and roofs in order to make good his escape. Laws, from Wallsend in North Tyneside, had something in the region of 87 previous convictions dating back to his tenth birthday in 1991. While some of these earlier offences were relatively minor acts of vandalism, like the cartoon character Rat Boy, Law's criminality spiralled out of control. In 2002, for instance, he robbed a taxi driver of his takings, and by 2007 he was given an indefinite sentence and ordered to serve a minimum term of five years for robbing an 18-year-old at gunpoint, which is unambiguously serious offending (BBC News, 2007).

Laws was the subject of public outrage back in 2001 when it emerged that he was to be paid by a North Shields-based church charity – The Cedarwood Trust – for his appearance in a short film. The well-intentioned aim of this film was to attempt to deter youngsters from crime, and it was not in any way meant to be a celebration of Law's criminality or to provide further titillation over the Spider Boy phenomenon.

But many felt that this was a complete misuse of public funds and that he had only been included because he was a notorious celebrity (The Guardian, 2001).

Reflections on exploratory vandalism

The most important point to consider when theorising the exploratory vandalism of children is their limited responsibility, and this notion is widely accepted. Commenting on the aforementioned case of the four-year-old in the West Fife Villages policing area, the Scottish Conservatives justice spokesman, Bill Aitken, observed that 'It is deeply depressing that children of these tender years are committing serious offences. These children may be at risk' (Dunfermline Press, 2011). We can observe again this seemingly ever-present notion of even wayward children somehow being 'at risk' to themselves, and once again the allusion to children of such 'tender years' is a clear reassertion of both their 'innocence' and perceived vulnerability.

The way in which the 'responsibility' of a child is defined is nevertheless something which constantly shifts. Pitch (1995) observes that the notion of 'limited responsibility' is socially defined, fluid and changeable over time and context. On the one hand, we have the idea of the vulnerable angelic child being led astray by dark forces beyond his or her control and, on the other, we have the demonising of the 'Rat Boy' phenomenon, which further fuels conservative demands for what David Cameron once called 'tough love' (The Guardian, 2011b).

Explanations for exploratory vandalism often refer to social learning theory. Thus, in commenting on the case of the four-year-old 'vandal' in the West Fife Villages policing area, Dr Cynthia McVeigh, Head of Psychology at Glasgow Caledonian University, observed that the anti-social actions of children could be a result of learned behaviour: 'when you get children acting like this sometimes it is a case that they themselves have been abused or have witnessed crimes being committed' (Daily Mail Online, 2009). It was the work of Julian Rotter (1954) in talking about 'motivational factors' and the desire for 'positive outcomes' which suggested that human behaviour was influenced by environmental rather than merely psychological factors. Albert Banduru (1977) subsequently introduced concepts such as 'close contact' and 'imitation of superiors', which allowed us to more clearly see how the interplay between social and cognitive factors shapes all kinds of behaviour.

Clearly the notions of social learning theory can be legitimately applied to the exploratory vandalism of children, but there are limitations to this perspective. Thus, one of the problems is that because these theories are so heavily underpinned by the notion of 'imitation', we are almost left with a feeling that young people are mere 'puppets on a string' who are unable to make relatively free-thinking choices or even exert their own human agency. This criticism received intellectual justification from the work of Dennis Wrong (1961) and his classic notion of 'the over-socialised conception of man'. By uncritically using social learning theories in an attempt to understand the vandalism of children and anti-social behaviour, there is a real possibility of an 'over anti-socialised conception of child'. There is, for instance, the assumption inherent in Stan Cohen's (1973) original typology that acts of vandalism must be 'exploratory' simply because they are committed by children.

Children's vandalism is not always exploratory and 'innocent'. It is sometimes invested with huge political ramifications. Thus, for example, it was reported by BBC News back in 2006 that three children aged between eight and ten years had been arrested in County Antrim, Northern Ireland, following the serious vandalism carried out on a Catholic school (BBC News, 2006b). In what was thought to be a religiously motivated attack of hate vandalism, over 40 windows were smashed along with the posting of sectarian graffiti on the walls of St Mary's on the Hill Primary School at Carnmoney. In an attempt to minimise the impact of the sectarian vandalism, the school headmaster Patrick Kennedy was at pains to stress, 'I think it's important to keep this in perspective – we are talking about a small minority of children'. By presenting the children as being 'unrepresentative' of those of similar age in the wider Protestant and Catholic communities, Kennedy was hoping to neutralise and depoliticise what was essentially a hate crime, despite his school's appearing to be a target of repeated attacks periodically. Interestingly, in passing public comment on the incident, the senior police spokesperson – district commander Will Kerr – similarly appeared to use the status of the protagonists as mere children to depoliticise the issue and make it appear as if the act were a straightforward act of what he simply described as 'anti-social activity'.

An acknowledgement that this vandalism was indeed more than just 'anti-social behaviour' came from the Mayor of Newtownabbey – Alliance Councillor Lynn Frazer – who explicitly referred to the twin notions of 'prejudice' and 'hatred' in saying that 'people should be setting a positive example for young children, not instilling prejudice and hatred in them'. This re-categorisation of the incident as more than *just* the kind of anti-social behaviour associated with 'exploratory' or drift vandalism was at the same time tempered with the view that the *real* offenders were not the children themselves but adults motivated by political malevolence who were cynically and calculatingly manipulating and exploiting such young 'innocents'. Councillor Frazer stated that 'those who lead young children astray and prompt them into committing sectarian acts are an absolute disgrace'. Social learning theory tells us that the children were being 'led astray' and simply imitating the actions of their elders, but it is worth considering whether some acts of vandalism committed by children are done so with explicit intent and an underlying motivation. Children develop in different stages at different rates of progress, with there being a difference between (a) chronological, (b) biological and (c) social ages, and some acts of vandalism which they commit cannot be automatically labelled as mere 'exploration'.

A common recent political discourse about the anti-social behaviour and vandalism of children is the notion of the 'responsibilisation' (Garland, 2001) of the family. Following the widespread rioting and urban unrest in August 2011, Prime Minister Cameron announced plans to put 120,000 of the most 'troubled families' in the United Kingdom through family intervention programmes. Thus, he said,

> The broken society is back at the top of my political agenda ... I have an ambition, that before the end of this parliament, we will turn around the lives of 120,000 of most troubled families ... we need more urgent action on the families that some people call 'problem', others call 'troubled'. The ones everyone in their neighbourhood knows and often avoids.
>
> (The Guardian, 2011b)

This pledge appears to be a continuation of the kind of New Labour communitarian philosophy advocated by Gordon Brown, who back in 2008 promised to target some 110,000 'problem families' which contained 'disruptive young people'. Official figures nevertheless show how in practice only a fraction of these families (3,518) were being embraced by these intervention programmes two years later. Matt Kavanagh of the Institute for Public Policy Research observed that honouring Cameron's pledge would require an additional £100m a year over the next four years, something which has to be questioned in these recessionary times of public sector austerity (The Guardian, 2011b).

These interventionist ideas are by no means new. Indeed, the underlying principles of social learning theory were evident in the Head Start program launched in the United States in the 1960s as part of President Lyndon Johnson's War on Poverty. Originally introduced as a 'catch-up' summer school programme, today the Head Start program is not only still active but its remit is greatly expanded. It makes provision for comprehensive education, health and parent involvement services to those families with children on low incomes. By the end of 2005, it was estimated that more than 22 million preschool-aged children had participated in the program (NHSA, 2014).

Early intervention programs have been extremely influential with left realists who are keen to change the social conditions which can lead to children's getting involved in criminality, and who were clearly influential with the New Labour governments during the period 1997–2010. One of us has previously referred to these concerted policy initiatives as a 'reintegrative tutelage' strategy with the intended aim of seeking to reintegrate a sizeable and growing socially excluded underclass back into mainstream society (Hopkins Burke, 1999, 2008, 2013). Significantly, contemporary Britain is a very different society from the optimistic post-JFK United States of the mid-1960s following the passage of the Civil Rights Act 1964 by his successor, Lyndon B. Johnson, and his notions of the 'Great Society' or even the renewed optimism of post-1997 'New Labour' Britain with its widespread belief that wholesale interventions in social problems could be successful. There is now a real concern in some quarters that early intervention programmes in Britain are driven by a conservative agenda which is more concerned with identifying, classifying, labelling and 'neutralising' those deemed to be a future threat to the social order, isolating any risk that these groups might pose to mainstream society.

In cultural criminological terms this has echoes of the 2002 science fiction movie *Minority Report,* starring Tom Cruise as PreCrime Captain John Anderton. Set in the year 2054, a specialised police department, 'PreCrime', sets out to arrest people for *future* crimes based on controversial foreknowledge provided by three psychics known as 'precogs'. The film raises the question of whether life is predetermined or whether free will can change the course of events. It also raises the concern relevant to early intervention programs as to who has the right to 'play God' or, as the film asks, are mutated humans with apparent precognition abilities best placed to take the moral high ground because of the assumption that they can prevent future crimes like murders. We must also ask whether this is simply science fiction or whether it contains some potential reality.

In January 2012, *The Independent* newspaper reported that 'a pioneering technique to predict crime before it happens could be imported from the USA to this country' (Morris, 2012), and this prediction came true the following December, when Kent police began 'a trial of a predictive policing model from the USA that assesses several years' worth of crime data and human behaviour to predict the areas in which offences are likely to take place' (Police Oracle, 2012; Statewatch, 2013).

The Gravesend Reporter observed that by taking previous years' crime data and daily updates of location, time and type of crime committed, the software 'creates prediction boxes of precise 500 square feet zones which are listed in priority order as to where crimes are most likely to occur, which is then delivered to the smart phones, tablets and PCs of police officers who use it to make decisions on where to deploy' (Dubuis, 2013). Analysis of other factors is also taken into account. A police officer featured in a *France 24* report observed that 'it's the real demographics of the area – the people, the places, what kind of buildings they are. Taller buildings might mean there's more crime or less – it takes into account everything'. According to the police force undertaking the trial, 'the scheme is a natural extension of intelligence-led policing method pioneered by Kent Police' (France 24, 2013; Statewatch 2013). So science fiction does begat reality, reminding us that the development of electronic tagging was instigated in March 1983 by a district court judge in New Mexico, Jack Love, who was supposedly inspired to act based upon a storyline in a Spider-Man comic whereupon an electronic bracelet is placed on the superhero to follow his movements (Gable, 1986).

In the following section we further explore the assertion that vandalism is not random or 'mindless' and that it is to a certain extent predictable. We will see how certain cultural objects tend to be the preferred targets of vandals if not by conscious rational choice, then at least subconsciously as routinised forms of patterned social practice.

Drift vandalism

Whilst 'exploratory' vandalism may be committed by children in the spirit of innocence, what we label drift vandalism tends to be committed in groups during the transient phase of youth. We owe David Matza (1964) and his classic text *Delinquency and Drift* more than a degree of intellectual debt in applying this term in a vandalism context. drift vandals may be relatively law-abiding youths who may be in education or starting out in employment, but who sometimes commit acts of vandalism. drift vandals do not always come from marginalised or disempowered backgrounds, and in fact may come from 'respectable' or even middle-class families. Moreover, this relatively 'low-level' transgression very rarely results in a progression to long-term, career criminality.

Drift vandalism can often start with 'low-level' anti-social activities such as the destruction of 'For Sale' signs attached to residential properties. Yet, even such apparently innocuous activities have victims. The *Bristol Evening Post* (2008) reported under the headline 'Vandals Are Making Cul-de-sac a Misery' that the lives of Bradley Stoke residents were being made a misery by this sort of low-level anti-social behaviour. The residential cul-de-sac of Shepherds Walk and Manor Farm Crescent leads to a public access point to a supermarket with resident Tracey Angel reporting that she witnessed youths smashing up a 'For Sale' sign outside her home. The youths then proceeded to use the vandalised pole from the sign as a mock javelin. This sort of vandalism is common throughout the country, particularly in urban and residential areas. A resident of Burnham in Essex, John Scott, reported that he had been the victim of this kind of vandalism on no less than three occasions during the latter part of 2008 and early 2009. As well as the persistent uprooting of 'For Sale' signs in the neighbourhood, a plant pot had been thrown onto the bonnet of his wife's car, leaving a hefty repair bill. He nevertheless rather philosophically observed,

> I am hopeful the vandals are youngsters, perhaps living with their parents, and placing a time frame on these rampages may get parents wondering what they were doing in the early hours. At the moment we are all taking some bizarre satisfaction from the fact there are several of us, and that these attacks are not personal.
>
> (Maldon and Burnham Standard, 2009)

The above observation that these attacks are 'not personal' is a significant one and demonstrates exactly what separates drift vandalism from other forms such as 'hate' vandalism, which we will explore later in this book. Thus, there is no particular motive, and the acts are not committed in order to further any political cause. The vandalism is insufficiently targeted to constitute an act of direct hatred levelled against a particular individual or specific social group.

Stories shared with us by middle-aged men when reflecting on their tales of 'misspent youth' included the common theme of the joys of the sound of breaking glass. A second common theme was the ever-presence of alcohol as a factor in the commission of these offences:

> We were bored stiff with nowt to do. We'd end up chucking these stones at windows of houses and then we'd run off. You know, these plated glass windows in town. We'd break those for fun. Another

> thing we did was what we called 'garden skipping'. We'd pinch the clothes off people's washing lines and end up wearing them for a laugh. We'd be walking round in other people's clothes holding onto their garden gnomes that we'd nicked as well!

Essential to this account is the recognition that the stone throwing appears not to have been targeted against particular people as in the case of acts of hatred with a vindictive element. Again the theme of boredom was a common one in explaining why offences of vandalism were committed. Present additionally in the narratives was a sense of built-up aggression being unleashed:

> One time I put my fist through a dentist's window. I was bloody lucky as it nearly caught my main vein. I walked past where it had happened and my arm was absolutely covered in blood. The cops had pulled up and were right outside there but I never got done for it.
>
> Another time I put my fist through a shop window. I felt so bad about what I'd done I went straight up to a copper nearby and told him. He kept telling me to piss off and go away. He wouldn't believe me and kept telling me to just go home. Eventually he got pissed off with me pestering him and he arrested me and put me in the back of a police car.
>
> (Male: late 40s)

Another form of low-level vandalism associated with adolescence and the drift from childhood to adult status is that involving supermarket trolleys. The fact that specific cultural objects such as supermarket trolleys are selected for use by vandals is itself worthy of consideration. We can begin to see how even 'non-political' or 'non-hate' vandalism is targeted – not directly in terms of a conscious decision to attack certain individuals – but in the sense that specific cultural objects are selected so routinely that to argue that vandalism is merely 'random' becomes implausible. For instance, in 2002, it was reported that vandals had gone to the trouble of pushing a trolley over the edge of a cliff (BBC News Online, 2002a). The use of supermarket trolleys by vandals can be explained at least partly as they can be seen to constitute a kind of adapted vehicle with wheels that can (at least to some extent) be steered. Supermarket trolley riding or racing is very common when trolleys are left discarded in or near to the vicinity of supermarkets. This phenomenon is superbly captured in the YouTube clip posted under the title

'Ye Old Supermarket Trolley Jousting' (YouTube, 2008a), which involves a mock-up of two knights who fight for the honour of a woman by 'jousting' each other whilst they sit in trolleys in what appears to be a car park. An equally hilarious clip involves a song posted by Caroline Guirr entitled 'The Life and Death of a Supermarket Trolley', in which to the backdrop of a video of abandoned supermarket trolleys in muddy lakes and rivers, the singer barks out the lyrics 'the life and death of a supermarket trolley, short and not very jolly! (You Tube, 2007a).'

Much of what could be labelled as 'drift vandalism' in objective terms carried the subjective feeling of 'the prank' for those who embarked on such activities. Take the following example, which was recounted to us:

> We'd go round and lift the gates off people's houses. We'd swap the gates by people's gardens so the postman would end up getting the wrong address for the letters. I'd be about ten years old when that happened. We'd go knocking on doors as well and running through gardens.
>
> (Male: late 60s)

Towards a criminology of 'the prank'

The above would be characterised as a 'prank', which ordinarily implies a mischievous trick or practical joke. The above prank in terms of the swapping of the garden gates has a degree of light-heartedness about it, and any 'damage' done is largely non-permanent and reversible. Such antics have received popular cultural acclaim with the cult following of *Jackass: The Movie*, which was an American reality comedy film in 2002, directed by Jeff Tremaine and starring the leader of the cast, Johnny Knoxville. Some of these pranks, such as the infamous golf buggy scene, did involve the simulation if not commission of acts of vandalism, and evident in both this movie and in most pranks is the sheer delight of pulling off what Katz (1988) has described as the 'sneaky thrill'. According to the seminal work of Jock Young (2004), orthodox criminology would fail to account for the nature of the prank because it has little to offer in terms of understanding the emotional and experiential aspects of transgression. Orthodox criminology fails to understand why interference with other people's property in the spirit of 'high jinks' is often committed because those involved are committed to attempting to offset the sheer boredom and mundaneness of their lives (see Ferrell, 2004).

Drift vandalism: beyond the prank?

In highlighting the emotional and experiential attractions of the prank, one has to acknowledge, however, that 'drift vandalism' can be far more serious than playing with supermarket trolleys, uprooting 'For Sale' signs or swapping garden gates. Not only can it be distressing for victims and have an impact on the 'quality of life' in communities but it can have tragic human consequences as we explore below.

Railway vandalism

A very common example of what Cohen (1973) termed 'malicious' vandalism would include incidents directed against railway lines and even trains themselves. It is a form of targeted vandalism which has a long history. As far back as 1998, a Railtrack survey reported that 30 per cent of 11- to 16-year-olds admitted to railway vandalism, with some 20 per cent saying that they had taken shortcuts along or across the track (Times Education Supplement, 2000). The reality that approximately one in three children have admitted to engaging in anti-social acts or vandalism on railways is itself of significance. Railways are targeted because they involve high-speed transit vehicles, and when there is speed there is always danger. The prevalence of danger thus offers the railway as an attractive target of vandalism.

Back in 2001, for instance, vandals caused half a million pounds' worth of damage to seven trains in Glasgow's Shields West maintenance depot. The British Transport Police reported a total of 3,551 crimes in Scotland alone in a 12-month period between 2001 and 2002, with stone throwing and trespassing offences increasing by 17 per cent and 9 per cent respectively (BBC News, 2002b). Vandalism of trains is a very common social practice with there being, for example, a recorded 1,162 incidents of stone throwing in one single year between 2009 and 2010 (Travel UK, 2010).

Such incidents can be described as drift vandalism because the evidence suggests that it is children and teenagers who engage in this activity, very often in the school holidays. Indeed as reported by Mullin (2012), out of the 49 accidental deaths on railway lines between 1 April 2011 and last year and 31 March 2012, 88 per cent were male, with more than a third aged between 16 and 25 years. This is perhaps why it has been recorded that the common items left on rail tracks include dustbins, supermarket trolleys, bikes, traffic cones, discarded prams and even an inflatable bouncy castle!

According to Westcott (2014), the number of people killed by accessing rail tracks is at its highest since records began to be kept by the Rail Safety and Standards Board a decade or so ago. The problem has become such an issue that Network Rail has used former world 400m hurdles champion Dai Greene to star in a safety campaign which warns of the dangers of railway trespass. Not only are railway vandals a danger to themselves but their activities often involve putting the lives of others at risk. In March 2010, for instance, vandals put the lives of railway users and residents at risk as they struck on the Cross Country line between Tamworth and Birmingham (Tamworth Blog, 2010). A late night Cross Country train with some 50 passengers aboard was badly damaged as it hit concrete blocks and debris on a journey between Birmingham New Street and Nottingham. Miraculously, no passengers sustained injuries, but the driver was badly shaken after bringing the train to a standstill. Just 24 hours later, two trains collided with tyres strategically placed on the tracks outside Wilnecote station on the same line, with the driver needing medical treatment for shock. This type of vandalism significantly impacts on the quality of life of those using public transport and costs the economy thousands of pounds when commuters miss work due to delays. What can appear to be a small-scale localised incident can have a substantial impact on national rail services. The incidents in the Tamworth area caused massive delays to train users throughout the country. The latter incident, for example, was responsible for the whole or part cancellation of 55 trains, with some 176 journeys being delayed.

What can appear to be relatively 'low-level' vandalism such as stone throwing can cause injury and even catastrophic outcomes. In October 2009, for instance, a passenger was hit by a stone which passed through an open window on a train passing through Sundridge Park Rail Station, and he sustained cuts and bleeding to his face (The Missing List, 2009). On a more devastating scale, back in 1994, for example, vandalism was reported as the likely cause of a train crash in which driver Arthur McKee and 21-year-old student Alan Nicol were killed in Strathclyde, Scotland (The Independent, 1994). This problem has been acknowledged to be so endemic by Network Rail that it launched its 'No Messin' campaign, which is supported by local community groups and clubs across the country. World boxing champion Amir Khan from Bolton has thrown his weight behind the campaign (Entwistle, 2008) by observing that

> If you mess about on the railways, the best you can hope for is that you won't get injured, arrested or even killed.

It is sometimes the case that what appears to be drift vandalism at the outset can occasionally be more sinister and have politically motivated undertones. One such high-profile case was that of 48-year-old Allan Nicol of Yardley, Birmingham, who was jailed for ten years in 2007 for a campaign of destruction, which cost Network Rail more than £4 million in repairs and compensation for delays. Between the summer of 2004 and the end of 2005, former railway worker Nicol severed cables and set fire to equipment on at least a dozen occasions. Nevertheless, his actions were far more politically motivated than that of the 'drift vandal' because he carried a grudge after having to lay off many of his staff when Network Rail gave a contract to a rival company (The Daily Telegraph, 2007). He was also significantly older than the usual drift vandal.

Not all drift vandalism which tends to be committed in the transient and passing phase of youth involves endangering lives, and sometimes it encompasses a high level of human aspiration and creativity. Such is the case with a significant proportion of railway graffiti, some of which is legal because it is state endorsed. In 2008, for example, a so-called 'graffiti gang' from the Swindon-based Youth First Centre painted a mural surrounding a former railway museum as part of a £1 million regeneration package, including a brand new youth centre complete with cafe, recording and dance studio and advice centre (Golden Map, 2008).

More often than not, however, railway graffiti is simply censured as being an act of criminal damage. In October 2010, for instance, graffiti artist Robert Martin of Hockley, was jailed for a year after causing an estimated £45,000 worth of damage to trains. Martin reputedly went on a prolonged campaign spraying the word 'Wear' on trains across the county of Essex (Echo News, 2010). Eventually apprehended by the British Transport Police, Martin was discovered to have incriminated himself by having taken video footage on his mobile phone of him carrying out acts of graffiti. The capacity of mobile and cyberspace technology to facilitate, promote and publicise acts of vandalism will be explored more fully later in this book.

Acts of railway graffiti can, like other acts of railway vandalism, sometimes have devastating and tragic human consequences. In 2010, lovers Steven Longstaffe and Megan McAuley, both in their early 20s, were intent on spraying their 'tags' on railway warehouses next to Sprainger Street in Liverpool. During the process of the act, having climbed a 20-foot-high wall and overcome razor wire, Longstaffe tragically fell through a roof, sustaining fatal injuries. To compound the tragedy, a day later, overcome with guilt and grief, Megan McAuley committed suicide, leaving a poignant note which stated, 'I'm really sorry, but I'm in a better place and with the man I love. I've never been so happy since I met Ste'. Liverpool Coroner Andrew Rebello described the tragic sequence of events as 'the closest thing to Romeo and Juliet I have experienced in my court' (Liverpool Echo, 2010).

As well as vandalism on the railways, another very common form of drift vandalism is that of throwing stones at targeted vehicles. As we will see later in this book, the motor vehicle holds a grip on the collective cultural imagination to the extent that it becomes a routine target for the vandal.

Throwing stones at cars

The throwing of stones at cars is an inherently 'risky' form of criminal damage because it can endanger life. Following a number of incidents in the Washington area of Wearside in January 2014, acting neighbourhood inspector Dave Cole commented that 'these youngsters may see this as a prank but it's completely irresponsible and dangerous ... they are putting people at risk' (Northern Echo, 2014).

The stoning of cars is an act of vandalism often committed by youths which can have tragic consequences. In 2009, in Merthyr Tydfil, 28-year-old driver John Wells was killed as his Fiat Ibiza veered into the path of an oncoming car. This catastrophic crash involving 11 vehicles occurred as the outcome of Wells' vain attempt to swerve clear of a shower of rocks being hurled down from a bridge by a group of teenagers. Coroner Peter Maddox described the loss of life as the outcome of 'an act of breathtaking stupidity' with the teenagers admitting causing criminal damage and acting recklessly with regard to endangering life at Merthyr Crown Court and receiving custodial sentences (South Wales Evening Post, 2009).

The following year, a 10-year-old boy was arrested on suspicion of manslaughter after a recovery truck passenger, 47-year-old Michael Baker from West Sussex, died shortly after a lorry crash in Kent. Police officers reported that a group of young people had been witnessed standing on the grass bank at the wooded side of the A20 near the Swanley interchange. Shortly after passing the group, the lorry driver realised an object had struck his windscreen and pulled over into a lay-by. Upon arriving at the scene, the recovery truck tragically hit the lorry while it was stationary, causing the fatality (BBC News, 2010c). A boy aged ten was arrested on suspicion of manslaughter.

The question remains as to how to begin to make sense in theoretical terms about such a diverse range of social practices referred to above.

Reflections on drift vandalism

Reflecting on the early examples cited in this section on drift vandalism – the uprooting of 'For Sale' signs and the misuse and abuse of supermarket trolleys – it is possible to observe theoretical links with the rational actor model of crime and criminal behaviour (Hopkins Burke, 2013). At first sight the model might seem inappropriate for explaining expressive non-economically motivated acts of vandalism (Trasler, 1986), but as Clarke (1987) observes, while the motivation behind such crimes may be pathological, their actual planning and execution may be highly rational. Indeed, expressive crimes such as vandalism are actually well explained by the related concept of crime as a function of opportunity and routine activities (Cohen and Felson, 1979). Such offences are thus usually unplanned, and most likely to occur in places where the potential perpetrators are likely to find themselves in the normal course of their lives (see Hopkins Burke, 2009). Thus, the 'For Sale' signs and supermarket trolleys make 'suitable targets' which are readily available on routes home from public houses or other such places of the night-time economy, and does explain to an extent why these objects are targeted – that is, they happen to be conveniently 'there' and are unguarded at night when people tend to be asleep. The concepts of 'routine activities' or 'opportunity' are thus useful in helping to explain why drift vandalism occurs – the ready supply of available attractive and easily damaged targets – but they are limited to the extent that they do not help us explain why it is that some people offend and others do not (Akers, 1997).

It is David Matza's (1964) notion of 'delinquency and drift' that provides us with the seminal explanation of why it is that some young people seem to drift between delinquent and law-abiding behaviour. With close links to – albeit a non-determinist variant of subcultural theory – this work suggests why much drift vandalism is committed by groups of children or young people rather than individuals acting alone. The determinist subcultural account of Albert Cohen (1955) had proposed that young people on 'the street' can achieve status and 'respect' for involvement in all the things the official culture rejects: hedonism, aggression, dishonesty and vandalism, and thus in Matza's account,

> He (the deviant) hears and perhaps sees others in the group approving of or doing daring, but illegal, acts and assumes that, to be accepted, he must join in and show that he is just as good (or bad), if not better

> than, all the others. So he steals things, vandalises things, hits people not because he 'really' wants to but he feels he 'ought' to want to.
> (Hopkins Burke, 2013: 154)

This notion of drift proposes this form of vandalism tends to be committed by those going through a temporary and passing phase of youth before the significant social controls of adult life such as employment, family life and mortgages take over for most of us (see Hirschi, 1969; also Nye, 1958; Reckless, 1967), while Hagan et al. (1987), for example, usefully propose that dominance of patriarchal attitudes in many homes explains why it is that adolescent boys are far more likely than girls to drift into low-level vandalism and anti-social behaviour.

Much of drift vandalism is relatively 'low level' and does not result in the 'vandal's' developing a long-term criminal career. From a cultural criminological perspective, it was simply fun at the time and part of having a laugh with your mates, often fuelled by alcohol and sometimes when going through those developmental uncertainties posed by adolescence.

The sheer joy of drift vandalism is captured by Katz's (1988) notion of the 'sneaky thrill'. This type of vandalism is inherently linked to the drift phase of transgression of adolescence, in that 'vandals and pranksters often play with conventional appearances, for example, when driving down local streets, they may issue friendly greetings one moment and collectively drop their pants ("moon") to shock the citizenry the next' (Katz, 1988: 53–54), a form of vandalism often committed by subcultural youth in a 'playful spirit' (ibid.: 66), the essence being to proverbially 'get away with it'.

This testing of the boundaries is often an inherent part of 'growing up', and Katz (1988) utilises three graphic metaphors to highlight the seductiveness of this type of transgression. First, he likens property crimes, of which vandalism is, of course, one to 'scoring in a game', arguing that 'one dimension of the thrill is ludic: the process is a kind of game' (p. 67). Second, with reference to the notion of a 'black sacrament' (p. 69), he utilises a religious metaphor to articulate the kind of 'secret defilement' which characterises late night property destruction. Third, he acknowledges that the property criminal is likely to experience an increase in both heart rate and adrenalin 'buzz' during the act of transgression, which is music to the ears of contemporary cultural criminologists who encourage us to give primacy to the emotional and experiential aspects of crime. To this end, Katz (1988: 72) offers the sexual metaphor whereby, 'colloquially, the thief and the vandal fuck their victims'.

These three metaphors go some way towards accounting for the seductiveness of drift vandalism. Nonetheless, most young men desist from involvement in such activities when they simply grow up and such deeds no longer have the appeal they once did. In his review of the work of David Matza, Hopkins Burke (2013: 155–56) observes that from this perspective, genuine desistance tends to occur 'when two young men confess to each other that they do not like offending or when the particular individual is sufficiently old to stop feeling anxieties about masculinity and adult status'. Chu (2007) helpfully notes that 'desistance' is the observable and voluntary termination of criminal behaviour, while Maruna (2001: 17) had previously observed that 'that sustained desistance most likely requires a fundamental and intentional shift in a person's sense of self'. Thus, many drift vandals will go on to form relationships, and most will find steady employment and learn the value of private property by owning their own home and car. They grow up and acquire significant social bonds. A process that may well involve internalising the notions observed by left realists and the radical moral communitarianism (Hopkins Burke, 2013) – we will encounter at the conclusion of this book – that this 'low-level' vandalism can have a significant negative effect on the quality of life of the communities in which they live and they thus desist from low level criminality and anti-social behavior which was characteristic of their younger days.

Having explored vandalisms which are characterised by both exploration and drift, our next chapter asks the questions as to whether these conventional vandalisms of the young are merely 'sporadic' and 'random', or whether they are more patterned, thus making them to some extent predictable.

3
Target Vandalism

It is a central theme of this book that vandalism is rarely 'random' or even 'mindless', but invariably systematic and deeply meaningful to the perpetrators. This is very much the case with criminal damage to motor vehicles, which constitutes a very significant proportion of all episodes of vandalism recorded by the police with over 4 million incidents each year (TalkTalk, 2014). This routine target vandalism of the motor vehicle is clearly a criminological phenomenon, and in seeking an explanation of this actuality it will be useful to explore the centrality of the motor vehicle in wider discourses of youth offending.

The centrality of the car in youth offending

In the late 1990s, an estimation reported in *The Times* (17 February 1997) suggested that if legal, the proceeds from professional vehicle theft would rank fifth in the earnings of the world's top companies! In fact, car crime is so prevalent that it is thought to be the third most common offence type in the industrial world behind domestic burglary and violent crime (see Corbett, 2003). More recently, Mills et al. (2013) estimated the costs of organised vehicle crime were at £330 million per annum, and this figure spiralled to an estimation of £920 million when taking into account wider social and economic costs.

It was not until the Road Traffic Act 1930 that 'theft of vehicle' offences was formally recognised in law. Post-World War II and the transition towards a consumer society, Harold Macmillan's 'You've never had it so good' and the 'swinging sixties' saw the Theft Act 1968 making 'Taking without owners consent' (TWOC) a notifiable offence. This legislation was updated over two decades later following a huge moral panic about 'joyriding' in working-class urbanised areas in the North of

England in the early 1990s. Like 'vandalism', the notion of 'joyriding' is a social construct which actually has no legislative foundation at all. The Aggravated Vehicle-taking Act 1992 created the aggravated offence of TWOC(king), or 'taking without consent', which was designed to cover a car's being driven dangerously and/or with a person or property being damaged. The moral panic that followed this well-publicised spate of 'joyriding' had led to what some felt were draconian measures, with the introduction of a maximum sentence of five years' imprisonment and an unlimited fine where death results.

'Joyriding' – or 'TWOCK', taking [a car] without the owner's consent, can be explained by reference to the twin postmodern notions of 'spectacle' (Baudrillard, 1983) and 'performance' (Presdee, 2000). It is a classic synoptic (Mathiesen, 1997) social practice with the many appearing to watch, the deviant, risk-taking, daring few. Beatrix Campbell (1993) observed the essence of what was undoubtedly one of *the* moral panics of the 1990s. She interviewed one such 'joyrider' who appeared to endorse the idea of the 'joyride' as spectacle, and 'then it became pure display. That is the whole point, there's no use doing handbrake-turns down the A34 because there's no spectators' (1993: 257). She herself attributed the facilitation of this spectacle to public access to – and mass ownership of – the camcorder in the 1990s. This facilitation has been substantially increased since the mass ownership of mobile camera phones, and with readily available forums such as YouTube, the narcissist has access to an instant worldwide audience.

Whilst offering a degree of sympathy to the 'joyrider', Campbell's journalistic ethnography – albeit tempered by her Marxist feminist perspective – has to be compared to more of a left-realist perspective which would emphasise the physical, emotional and material damage done by car crime, which tends to be committed invariably by young men invariably from loosely termed working-class origins against people from other sections of the working class.

When one considers that cars are customarily treasured by their owners in Western culture, certainly not least because they are artefacts of some considerable value, their theft and destruction are profoundly anti-social and unambiguously criminal.

By late 2011, however, car crime, specifically the act of TWOCKING, had fallen from centre stage as a form of crime and anti-social behaviour, but this is not to say that the problem has simply disappeared. Undoubtedly, technological innovations – target hardening in criminological speak – have reduced instances of car theft for 'pleasure' because the latest models are much harder – indeed nigh impossible in some cases – for the gifted amateur to 'hotwire' and steal.

Following a study of 1,721 young people in England and Wales, Graham and Bowling (1995) found that males were six times more likely to steal a car than females, confirming earlier research by Spencer (1992), who suggests that car crime tended to be committed in groups but that females were less likely to be instigators, tending to be passengers. The inextricable link between masculinity and the motor vehicle is central to understanding not just vehicle theft but also vehicle damage. The association between manliness and virility somehow manifests itself in a desire to appropriate and dominate the motor vehicle either through its acquisition or through its destruction and defilement. If we can understand the desire to appropriate a motor vehicle through the desire to enact a 'performance', then it is entirely plausible to suggest that motor vehicle vandalism also has a performative aspect when located in a subcultural context.

The centrality of 'the car' in Western culture

The motor vehicle occupies a central place in Western culture, and correspondingly is central to much offending. Corbett (2003: 1) observes that 'the last century saw everyday lives, global economies and national infrastructures constructed around motor cars and the culture they have spawned'. Speed is of the essence in a world in which the instant, the 'here and now', are seen to be essential.

When we begin to see how cars are more than simply vehicles for transporting people from A to B, we begin to understand how their ownership takes on the symbolic value of distinction or the marking of difference. If cars differentiate and distinguish their owners from others, then surely their desecration and defilement are a way of 'levelling the playing field' of a very unequal market economy.

At the beginning of the new millennium, cars were rated the second most popular item on people's most wanted list of possessions. Almost 50 per cent of young people who do not have a car want one more than any other material possession (The Independent, 1997). Well beyond its practical utility, the cultural dynamic of the car cannot be underestimated. Thoms (1998: 45) suggests that, 'the motor car differentiates, it has a symbolic quality which takes many different forms'.

The fascination with the car is inextricably linked to the pursuit of speed. This was epitomised in the movie blockbuster *Days of Thunder* by Tom Cruise's character Cole Trickle, who exhorts, 'Speed. To be able to control it. To know that I can control something that's out of control'. This theme is also to the fore with *The Fast and the Furious* series of films, the 2001 original of which was a street racing action film featuring elite racer and ex-convict 'Dom' Toretto, played by Vin Diesel. As a society we have a voyeuristic preoccupation with speed, and this goes some way towards explaining how at the turn of the millennium it was estimated that Formula One (F1) races were regularly attracting in excess of 350 million global viewers (Hotten, 1999).

Many social commentators have observed that the car is a symbolic reflection of wider society. Jean Baudrillard (1988: 54) proposes that 'all you need to know about American society can be gleaned from an anthropology of its driving behaviour'. Lack of car ownership at the end of the twentieth century was equated with a negative kind of deviancy. With specific reference to Los Angeles, he noted that 'If you get out of your car in this centrifugal metropolis, you immediately become a delinquent; as soon as you start walking, you are a threat to public order, like a dog wandering in the road. Only immigrants from the Third World are allowed to walk' (1988: 58). This cultural phenomenon is captured brilliantly in the 1993 classic *Falling Down*, which stars Michael Douglas. Billed as 'An Ordinary Man Goes to War with the Everyday World', the film follows the central character, Bill Foster (played by Douglas), as he is stuck in his car during a typical traffic jam in downtown Los Angeles on a baking hot day. With his air conditioning failing, Foster promptly abandons his vehicle in the midst of the traffic. Much to the amazement of fellow irate motorists, he begins to walk, telling bemused onlookers that he is simply 'going home'. This opening scene of the movie leaves the viewer to contemplate just who is 'crazy' in this scenario. Do we laugh at the individual who chooses to walk over cars and rough ground to take a direct route home, or is the real joke on the capitalist system which produces cars for speed and ends up spawning massive irrationalities such as regular and predictable traffic jams (see Ritzer, 2004)?

Holden (1998: 29) observes that the car has come to embody the values of 'freedom' and 'individualism', which are the embodiment of rampant capitalism in the twenty-first century. The motor car has thus become an example of the classic Marxist 'commodity fetish'. Indeed Holden (1998) cites Aldous Huxley (1932) and his novel *Brave New World* in whose dystopian future, Fordism is raised to the status of a religion with subjects 'thanking Ford' rather than 'thanking God'.

Thus, in 1950s Britain, cars like the Vauxhall Velox, Cresta and Victor came to represent what Holden (1998: 30) refers to as 'grounded spaceships to the final frontier'. The epitome was the Rolls Royce, which represented 'the pinnacle of British social class and its very name has other connotations in keeping with its exclusivity, quality and quiet excellence' (Holden, 1998: 31). The Silver Cloud model cost £5,000, which at the time was the equivalent to buying a 12-bedroom house in the stockbroker belt.

In the 1970s, when the Cold War was still at its peak and before Mikhail Gorbachev launched perestroika in the Soviet Union, the binary opposite of car ownership in the United States was that of Eastern Europe. Holden (1998: 28) discusses the infamous Trabant, or 'Trabi', and how it came to symbolise the relative backwardness of East Germany as opposed to West Germany. This was evident also with Western jokes about the Czech-made Skoda, and these remain popular throughout many parts of Western Europe (Skoda Jokes, 2011):

Q. Why do Skodas have heated rear windscreens?
A. To keep your hands warm while you're pushing it!
Q. Have you got a wing mirror for a Skoda?
A. Okay seems like a fair swap!
Q. What do you call a Skoda with a sun roof?
A. A skip!
Q. What do you call a Skoda at the top of a hill?
A. A miracle.
Q. Why are a Skoda and a baby similar?
A. They both never go anywhere without a rattle.

In contrast to the 'backward' and economically doomed Eastern Europe, cars in Western Europe have certainly been portrayed in a far more positive light. For example, the famous 'Vorsprung durch Technik' adverts for the Audi vehicle have undertones of German 'efficiency', 'economy' and 'effectiveness'. The BMW has come to represent German quality and engineering. French chic and style are embodied in the Citroen DS 19, and Swedish safety and welfarism by the Volvo and Saab (Holden, 1998). Skoda is ironically now wholly owned by Volkswagen, and it is worth considering whether an estimated 15 per cent growth in sales in 2010 may at least be partially explained by a shift in the perceived status of the vehicle, not least because many of its components are now identical to the highly rated and popular VW Golf.

Not only does the possession and public display of the motor car represent material and social status in class terms but it is inextricably linked to the public display of virile masculinity. Heining (1998) argues that there is a clear link between the car, masculinity and pop music. What was probably the first rock and roll record of the genre, *Rockett 88*, by Jackie Brenston and his Kings of Rhythm, was evidently about this. Ry Cooder's 'Crazy 'bout an Automobile (Every Woman I Know)' was unashamedly about the male sex drive and cars. Sexual frustration is the key theme in Chuck Berry's 'No Particular Place To Go', with lyrics about a testosterone-fuelled man wanting to unlock the sexual door of the woman whom he is trying to woo in his car.

Heining (1998) also refers to Wilson Pickett's classic and much covered 'Mustang Sally', which is clearly a song about women being sexually unfaithful to men, as evidenced by the double meaning of the lyric 'All she wants to do is ride'. Heining (1998: 97) observes that 'the suggestion of a link between the car and sex in popular song hardly represents a major insight. We are all familiar with the facile notion that the car can be seen as a phallic symbol'. This is captured in satirical form in the classic Hale and Pace comedy sketch which parodies a male who claims he does not understand women, who think a car is an extension of a man's penis before the camera pans away to display him driving what appears to be a pink penis on wheels, which becomes erect as he drives past two attractive women who are walking in close proximity on a pavement. It is a notion that is inherent in popular culture and even features on a website for men considering penis enlargement:

> Sports car – phallic symbol of modernity
>
> Money means power, power makes sexy. This opinion's still going strong, but if you take a closer look at this, it may not seem completely right. It is true that most people are not free of a certain craving for recognition and they are trying to get this while showing off their belongings. This goes for real estate as well as for designer clothes, expensive high-tech supplies and for the German's favourite toy: His car. Especially if it is a beautiful, fast-driving, red-coloured sports car. Men are known for comparing their power in terms of horsepower. Who has the loudest, biggest, best? This does not only go for the motor, it can also be the exhaust pipe or cubic capacity: The man with the loudest, biggest, best one is the most masculine, most powerful man.
>
> (Internet Advert, 2014)

As well as the link between the car and sexual prowess, Campbell (1993: 263) observes other celebrated masculine virtues, car advertising during the 'Eighties unabashedly celebrated danger, irresponsibility and excitement', noting the Peugeot 405 advert This is where the vehicle is seen to fly across the country leaving a trail of blazing fields of fire behind it, while the evocative *Top Gun* theme music, 'Take My Breath Away' is played. Campbell (1993: 264) perceptively points out that this advert, designed to attract the custom of the middle and affluent working classes, is actually underpinned by the hidden desire to 'joyride', which is actually a far more universal fantasy than the myth that it is desired only by a criminal minority: 'The advertisement spoke right into the fantasy and the reality of the joyrider who became the escape artist of the motoring fraternity as well as of the criminal justice system'.

Car crime itself has become romanticised and aestheticised in our culture, and this is reflected in the popularity of computer games such as 'Carmaggedon' and 'Grand Theft Auto'. In the latter, players are allowed to assume the role of a criminal in a large city rising through the ranks of organised crime. The player as criminal is given numerous tasks by 'kingpins' in the criminal underworld which contribute to the storyline. As well as illegal driving and racing, other crimes, such as assassinations, are simulated. In 2009, a six-year-old boy boasted that he had 'learned' to drive from playing the game before taking his father's car on a ten-mile journey before crashing (Softpedia, 2009).

Car crime has also been romanticised on screen, perhaps most notably in George Miller's *Mad Max* films. Gelder (1998: 56) observes that '*Mad Max* itself presents a "road warrior", a rogue policeman who monitors the roads and cleans up gangs of criminals identified through their "feral" automobiles and motorbikes and "savage" attitude', with the film's exploring a dystopian future in Australia, where law and order have broken down. Crawford 'Nightrider' Montizano is a deranged biker and gang member who is fleeing from the police after breaking free from custody. He encounters the police's 'top pursuit man' in the form of the leather-clad Max Rockatansky (played by Mel Gibson) and, following a high-speed chase, is killed, although the surviving motorcycle gang continues to run riot, with the local population suffering vandalism and theft of fuel. One of the gang members kills Max's police colleague, 'The Goose', and at this point Max becomes disillusioned with the police force and decides to quit. While Max takes a vacation with his family, his wife and son fall afoul of the gang, and Max arrives to find their crushed bodies in the middle of the road. Fuelled with rage, Max decides to systematically hunt down and kill the gang members, and he eventually succeeds, as the film ends with him riding off into the Outback on his bike.

There is clearly a link between depictions of car crime in a variety of media and their manifestation in 'real' life. The motor vehicle has had a central place in youth offending, and by understanding this one can begin to comprehend the vandalism of the motor vehicle.

Car vandalism

Statistics have revealed that the majority of car owners – approximately three-quarters – are victims of car vandalism at some point in their car-owning lives. (Insurance Daily, 2008). The most common form of car vandalism (43 per cent) was scratched paintwork or cars being 'keyed'. This was followed by damaged wing mirrors (23 per cent) and smashed windows (21 per cent) (TalkTalk, 2014). Perhaps not surprisingly, it appears that the majority of car vandals strike after dark, with some 63 per cent of victims reporting that damage to their cars had occurred during this period.

As is the case with vandalism in general, there is thought to be a huge hidden figure of unrecorded and unreported offences of criminal damage against cars. It has been estimated that 8.5 million – or 58 per cent – of victims over the past 20 years have not reported the most recent incident of victimisation. Almost half of these (49 per cent) felt that reporting the crime would be pointless as it was highly unlikely that the offender(s) would be apprehended; 35 per cent considered the incident too trivial to report; 77 per cent did not claim on their insurance; thus, 59 per cent felt that the cost of repairs did not warrant making a claim. Much of this failure to claim on their insurance policy is clearly explained by a perceived loss of the 'no claims' discount, which was admitted by 23 per cent (TalkTalk, 2014). Motor vehicle insurers are well aware of the high levels of criminal damages and give situational crime prevention advice to drivers, including making sure cars are parked either on driveways or, better still, in garages; parking in police-approved 'safer parking scheme' car parks, and tucking in wing mirrors and putting down aerials, all of which can have an impact on the size of already very high insurance premiums paid (Direct line, 2014). The very high cost of car vandalism impacts very clearly on all legally insured motorists. There are, moreover, different types of criminal damage inflicted on motor vehicles which have different motivations and meanings for the perpetrators of these offences.

Collateral vandalism

Cohen (1973: 42) considered acquisitive vandalism to be 'damage done in the course of or in order to acquire money or property'. We have used the term 'collateral vandalism' to refer to (a) trying to steal something from the car, or (b) trying to steal the car itself, and feel this term more appropriate because the intention is to steal and possess rather than to defile, and so by definition the damage is collateral.

According to the Office for National Statistics (2013), the latest estimate shows approximately 1.1 million vehicle-related thefts against the household population in England and Wales for the year ending June 2013. Thefts of or from vehicles has shown a significant decrease of 21 per cent compared with the previous year, with these estimates being 28 per cent lower than those reported in the 2007/2008 survey, and 55 per cent lower than in 2002/2003.

Tales of the 'acquisition' of motor vehicles have been recounted to us, and a male in his late 40s told the story of a caravan being stolen not for material gain but for the sheer 'fun' of doing so:

> I once pinched a caravan while people were actually asleep in it! We pinched it from this lay by and ended up driving it about 10 miles from the caravan park. We parked up near a field. We'd seen a similar sort of thing done on an Episode of 'The Likely Lads' and thought we'd try it!

The same person recounted the following story, which again appears at face value to be motivated by the desire for acquisition, but the explanation offered is far more complicated:

> There were two of us, I remember it must have been going back to 1979. We broke into a car but we couldn't drive it. Some Jamaicans chased after us and my mate got stabbed in his side. I ran down the road but the two Jamaicans caught up with me. I got arrested and spent the night in the cells. I had to go to court on a Saturday and got a £150 fine plus a 2 year suspended sentence. It was just fun. We didn't even really want the car we broke into.

The above recollections present a problem with any 'objective' typology of vandalism. What may appear to be a crime of acquisition is, from the subjective point of view of the transgressor, merely a 'prank', and in the above instance certainly not an attempt to permanently deprive another person of a material possession.

Another form of acquisitive theft which involves collateral vandalism involves the breaking into cars in order to steal satellite navigation systems, and the number of these offences has soared in recent years as ownership of these accessories has become increasingly popular in the United Kingdom. The inevitable outcome of this upsurge in criminal offences has been an increase in motor insurance claims and premiums.

The phenomenon of satellite navigation thefts has itself spawned an industry around the crime control and prevention of such crimes. Two such companies are Stoplock and Pacsafe. The former has created the Strongbox, which is in effect a small metal safe which can be attached to a suitable fixed point inside the vehicle itself, inside the vehicle itself and retails at £40. The Travelsafe device designed by Pacsafe consists of laminated stainless steel wire mesh construction in the form of a drawstring bag, with its brass padlock offering a high level of security, and which costs £25 (Motoring Bible, 2010) although it might be easier and cheaper to carry such small mobile accessories with you when not in the car. It is also likely that the theft of satellite navigation systems will decrease as the retail price of the systems itself continues to reduce, making the theft less of a rational activity.

Other common targets of acquisitive vandalism include bank cards, number plates and mobile phones left on display. Direct Gov (2010) advises us that stolen number plates are an act of acquisitive vandalism which is often committed by those intending to commit further offences, such as speeding, illegal parking, non-payment of congestion charges, driving away from a petrol forecourt without paying, not paying for parking tickets or speeding fines and attempting to 'disguise' a stolen vehicle.

Another common form of acquisitive vandalism is that involving the targeting of laptops which are left on display in motor cars. One such high-profile case which occurred back in January 2008, involved the theft of a laptop from a vehicle which had been parked in the Edgbaston area of Birmingham. The car belonged to a Royal Navy officer, and the computer was thought to be holding the personal details of 600,000 people who had made enquiries and begun the application process for either the Navy, the Royal Marines or the RAF. The personal information was sensitive and included bank details, and passport and national insurance numbers (BBC News, 2008).

Another classic offence connected with the motor vehicle which is deserving of cultural criminological attention is the theft of hubcaps. Whilst not strictly an offence of criminal damage, because the removal of hub caps does not provoke permanent or lasting damage to a vehicle, and whilst the offence is likely to be classified as 'theft from a vehicle', from the point of view of the car owner, their removal certainly does deface and desecrate (albeit temporarily) the image and appearance of the vehicle. During a routine enquiry about the theft of four hubcaps from a Vauxhall Vivaro, for example, Thames Valley police in Milton Keynes remarkably retrieved over 200 wheel trims and hubcaps with an estimated value of £3,000 from the conservatory of a house in Stacey Bushes (Thames Valley Police, 2009).

Whilst collections as large as these may suggest offenders are perhaps planning to sell the alloy metal on for material gain, often this 'acquisitive' crime is committed by those who simply want a 'trophy' from a drunken night out rather than any attempt at organised criminality for material gain. From a cultural criminology perspective we can learn much from the collective humour concerning car criminality, of which the hubcap occupies a unique place worthy of attention:

> Heard the one about the hubcap?
>
> This guy goes into a restaurant for a Christmas breakfast while in his home town for the holidays. After looking over the menu he says, 'I'll just have the eggs Benedict'. His order comes a while later and it's served on a big, shiny hubcap. He asks the waiter, 'What's with the hubcap?'
>
> The waiter sings, 'Oh, there's no plate like chrome for the hollandaise!' (Joke Buddha, 2014)

Jokes about hubcaps are often underpinned by caricatures of the type of people who are assumed to be responsible for stealing them. Nowhere has this myth been more targeted than on the people of Liverpool. Jokes about the acquisitive vandalism and the hubcap are inextricably bound up with perceptions of the working classes on Merseyside. Fans of Manchester United have periodically chanted the following:

> Sung to the tune of 'You Are My Sunshine':
>
> You are a scouser
> A dirty scouser
> You're only happy on Giro Day
> Your mum's out thieving
> Your Dad's drug dealing
> Please don't take my hubcaps away…

This appears to be a classic case of Baudrillard's (1983) notion of 'hyperreality' or the 'death of the real'. According to Home Office figures for 2007–2008, in contrast to the popular stereotype, Greater Manchester actually has a marginally higher percentage of people victimised by personal crime (6 per cent) compared to Merseyside (5 per cent). In fact, the single area of crime in which the figures indicated that Merseyside had a worse problem than Greater Manchester was in the number of recorded drug offences (12,627 in Merseyside compared to 11,790 in Greater Manchester in 2007–2008) (World Soccer Talk, 2009). Arguments about this cultural stereotype hit the news back in 2002 in an uproar involving popular Liverpool comedian Stan Boardman. Leeds United FC threatened to withhold the Liverpool-born comic's £4,000 fee and barred him from subsequent appearances at the club after complaints he offended guests with 'racist' remarks at a Player of the Year dinner, during his stand-up comedy routine. In defending himself, Boardman stated he was not a racist and had been involved in an exchange of 'banter' with an Asian solicitor who apparently made the comment, 'Go back to Liverpool, you have stolen our hubcaps!' Whilst there was some dispute about which party initiated the verbal exchange, at some point Boardman told the heckler to 'go back to your curry house in Bradford – your elephant is waiting!' The comedian best remembered for his one-liner about Germans bombing his Liverpool chip shop – the Fokkers – was adamant that 'If someone stands up and heckles me and says Scousers are thieves then I am going to give it back. It was banter' (BBC News, 2002c). It should be noted that this occurred two months after two Leeds players had been charged with assaulting an Asian student.

Whether it be hubcaps, car stereos, satellite navigation systems, or laptops, whilst there is a clear material motive to acquisitive motor vehicle vandalism, sometimes the motor vehicle is targeted for political reasons.

Political vandalism and the car

As we will see in greater detail in Chapter 8, what Cohen (1973) referred to as 'ideological' vandalism, we have labelled 'political' vandalism. In this specific context, vandalism to motor vehicles has been committed by people seeking to publicise an issue of principle or conscience. For these people, the use of the motor vehicle itself is perceived to be fundamentally anti-social. Such an occurrence took place in July 1995 in London, and involved the radical environmental group Reclaim the Streets. In attempting to voice dissent against the so-called 'cult of the motor vehicle', the group of around 1,000 people emerged from Angel tube station in the lunch hour and congregated on one of London's busiest junctions. Bizarrely, an armoured personnel carrier then drove into the street whilst booming out the Jimi Hendrix version of 'All Along the Watchtower' (see Penman, 1995).

As a result of the on-foot occupation, massive tailbacks on the roads in the surrounding areas quickly built up, and the police had to be proactive in diverting the traffic through alternative routes. Meanwhile the occupied street was decorated with a carpet. A miniature paddling pool and sandpit designed to entertain children was installed, and stalls were built to sell food. In an attempt to pacify stranded motorists and to spread their political message, some protesters were seen to be offering drinks to the motorists. Lamp posts along the street were scaled by protesters imploring the state to wake up and take notice of the 'tyranny of the motor car'. A spokesman for the campaign group commented:

> We're here to show that life is a lot pleasanter without cars. We want to see car access to cities restricted and more pedestrianized areas within them. We also want a coordinated transport policy with the emphasis on cycling, walking, trains and buses.... They (cars) also lead to out-of-town developments, such as superstores that kill local businesses and destroy more countryside.
>
> (Penman, 1995)

With the numbers of protesters thinning out by the evening, the police attempted to clear the road, but scuffles broke out as the environmentalists and their supporters were moved from Upper Street in Islington, which resulted in riot police driving the protesters back towards Kings Cross station. It was at this stage that much of the vandalism is thought to have taken place, with bottles and cans being thrown by protesters, and that is when arrests were made (Penman, 1995).

It could be argued that the vandalism of motor vehicles by campaign groups in the above scenario is incidental or collateral rather than being deliberate or targeted. The campaign may have been planned to be disruptive but peaceful, and the damage which occurred tended to be a by-product of attempts to resist being moved on or displaced and ultimately arrested by police officers. It is not surprising that political protests against the motor vehicle have continued around the globe because of the perception by some of the devastating effect that cars have had on the environment and ultimately on people. Compared to the damage caused by adolescent 'joy riders', campaigners would argue that their transgressions pale into insignificance in comparison with the far more profoundly and routinised anti-social effects of the motor vehicle. Thoms (1998: 41) notes that in the United States, more land has been appropriated by the car than by houses:

> The motor car has been responsible for traffic accidents resulting in millions of deaths and serious injuries, pollution of the atmosphere, extreme examples of aggressive behaviour and rapid depletion of some of the world's most precious natural resources.

A high-profile case of politically motivated vandalism against the car occurred in Los Angeles in 2003. Twenty Hummer H2 cars were 'torched' by so-called 'eco-arsonists' representing the Earth Liberation Front at an estimated cost of $3 million. It is believed that the Hummer H2 was specifically targeted because of the perception of it as an environmentally unfriendly and therefore fundamentally anti-social 'gas guzzler'. In addition, numerous vehicles were spray-painted graffiti style with abusive messages pertaining to 'Fat, Lazy Americans' (Hybrid Cars, 2009). Events took another twist when Barak Obama's Democratic administration announced in 2009 stricter rules for automobile fuel efficiency standards and plans for the encouragement of the use of more environmentally friendly 'hybrid' motor cars such as the Toyota Prius. It is believed by some that this policy led to a subsequent spate of attacks on such vehicles in Seattle from people from the political Right keen to defend the interests of the established motor vehicle industry. Priuses were first attacked systematically in 2004 when a number of them were 'keyed' in Las Vegas. Bricks and rocks were used in seven reported incidents of what appeared to be politically motivated vandalism against these cars in Petaluma, California, in 2008, and the police investigated one disturbing case of a Prius being deliberately rammed off the road by another vehicle (Hybrid Cars, 2009).

Politically motivated car vandalism has also occurred at the party political level, notably in recent times in Canada. In October 2008, the Liberal Party in Toronto reported that 25 party supporters had suffered vandalism to their cars in the form of brakes being tampered with. Those targeted were residents of the St. Paul's area of Toronto who had been displaying Liberal campaign signs outside their homes prior to elections. The damage was confirmed as being politically motivated because anti-Liberal party graffiti was also found daubed on some homes. One such victim, Jennifer Lithgow, had a lucky escape after realising, just moments after strapping her six-year-old daughter into her seat, that her brakes had been cut:

> I can't believe that somebody would do that, it's dangerous, I could have hurt myself, or my daughter who was in the car at the time, I could've hurt somebody else if I hadn't been able to stop.... If they slashed my tires or something to make a point that is one thing but to actually sabotage my car and potentially put me and other people in danger because of that is just mind boggling. (The Globe and Mail, 2008)

Once again this incident of motor vehicle vandalism was far from random because other Liberal Party supporters had been targeted in similar incidents reported in the Toronto area of Willowdale and in Guelph, Ontario, earlier in that year, both in the lead-up to crucial by-elections (The Globe and Mail, 2008). As well as politically motivated vandalism, some offences directed against the motor vehicle could be classified as being driven by the politically regressive practice of 'hate'.

Hate vandalism and the car

This chapter has emphasised the centrality of the motor vehicle in Western culture, and this can account for why the car can often be the target of hate vandalism, which we explore more in Chapter 6. Thoms (1998: 47) observes that:

> Cars are more than simply a means of transport since for many people they represent an extension of personality... manufacturers and their advertising agencies seek to draw a relationship between the product and the personal characteristics, real or imagined, of the customer. Cars are rarely portrayed as merely useful load carriers but as objects of desire, which reflect on the good taste and even technical knowledge of the owner.

To understand hate car vandalism is to understand one of the central themes of this chapter, which is that the car is not simply an inanimate object but rather it has enormous symbolic value. Thoms (1998: 46–47) considers that:

> the motor car differentiates on a personal basis; through their particular characteristics cars interact with the individual, perhaps in terms of a status (or inverted status) relationship with the external world, or merely through internalised self-identification. How else does one explain the purchase of high-powered cars with the capacity to far exceed the maximum legal speed? Similarly, why are 4x4 vehicles in such demand when so many of them hardly ever forsake the tarmac?

Thus, to deliberately single out and target such a vehicle can often be due to a deeply held prejudice against the type of person who drives such a car. Unlike 'politically' motivated car vandalism, however, 'hate' car vandalism tends to be more personalised and is not part of a concerted attempt to bring about a make a better social order.

An example of hate vandalism is that of a disabled housewife who had tyres on both of her family cars slashed three times in four months. In the summer of 2010, Susan Lee of Bicester, who was left disabled after sustaining spinal damage, had sets of tyres on her black Audi Estate continually slashed. Worryingly, Mrs Lee's husband had failed to realise the act of vandalism on one specific occasion, having lost control of the car near Tesco's supermarket. As well as tyre slashing, the family had encountered incidences of glued hubcaps and broken wing mirrors. The incidents were thought by the victim to be motivated by hate because there were no other victims of such vandalism in the same street (Oxford Mail, 2010).

Incidents of vehicle-related hate vandalism can often be underpinned by homophobic prejudice. In November 2010, for example, in Boston in the United States, a homophobic slur was daubed on the car of an openly gay student at University of Massachusetts Dartmouth (Boston News Channel, 2010). In another such case in the United Kingdom, a Nuneaton man had his car vandalised after arranging to meet another man through an online gay dating agency. When arriving at a local car park in Burbage to meet whom he assumed was his prospective date, the 50-year-old victim was attacked by a gang of four men who both robbed and beat him before going on to vandalise his car (Edge News, 2010).

Remarkably, even gay police officers have suffered car vandalism as a result of the prejudice of other officers. One such victim was the former chair of the Gay Police Association, Paul Cahill, who as a probationary constable in the early 1990s had his locker superglued shut with the words 'poof' and 'faggot' written on it. His pigeonhole at work was regularly filled with leaflets from the AIDS-based charity the Terence Higgins trust, with the insinuation being that he was a carrier of the disease because of his sexual status. His motor car was also singled out, targeted and vandalised (Johann Hari Gay Issues, 2010).

As well as hate vandalism of a kind driven by deep-seated prejudices, our new typology of vandalism allows for 'hate' to be an individual expression of a 'grudge' or a 'spat' or 'tiff', which is what Cohen (1973) originally labelled as 'vindictive' vandalism. One such example of this kind of hate vandalism is that of 'tit for tat' vandalism which centres around damaged inflicted on vehicles by spurned lovers or ex-lovers. In September 2010, the so-called Small-World News Service reported how a 'spurned mistress' had been given a restraining order after she poured paint stripper over her married lover's car when he ended their two-and-half-year affair. 20-year-old Corinna White attacked Michael Blower's Citroen Picasso after being jilted by the so-called 41-year-old 'love rat' who had seduced her as a virginal 17-year-old. Sales assistant

Corinna met coach driver Michael in 2008 as he was teaching one of her best friends to drive. The pair started texting, and embarked on a two-and-a-half-year relationship, during which they frequently went on the proverbial 'dirty weekends' away to Blackpool, Bournemouth and London. The proverbial 'wheels fell off' the relationship in April 2010, however, after an anonymous caller rang the 'love rat's' wife at work to inform her that her husband had been having a long-term affair. North Somerset Courthouse heard how White remained 'obsessed' with the much older man even after he had confessed to his long-suffering wife and committed to working through his marital difficulties. Disturbingly, White was once spotted travelling past the married couple's home 14 times in just one day on a bus! Things came to a head when White poured paint stripper over the car outside the couple's home in Weston-super-Mare, Somerset, causing an estimated £2,600 of damage. White admitted one charge of criminal damage, and was given a two-year restraining order and told to pay £150 compensation (SWNS, 2010).

The caricature of mentally disturbed women 'stalking' ex-lovers occupies a special place in working-class male culture, and is worthy of cultural criminological attention. Surely most males have engaged in bar room banter about such a phenomenon when joking about the proverbial 'ex-missus'? The pejorative notion of the 'bunny boiler' is heavily gendered in that it carries the implication of an obsessive, dangerous and psychotic woman. The term derives its origins at least in popular culture from the 1987 classic film *Fatal Attraction*, in which a jilted lover, Alex Forrest, (played by Glenn Close) stalks an increasingly petrified lawyer and family man, Dan Gallagher (Michael Douglas). In the relevant scene, the scorned lover places his daughter's rabbit in a pot of boiling water while the family are away from the house. When the family return, the child vainly searches for her beloved pet in the garden before her mother makes the horrific discovery of its being dead in the boiling pot in the kitchen.

Whilst it is indeed the infamous 'bunny boiling' scene which has fuelled the barroom banter of a thousand pubs and a generation of men, it should be noted that the film portrays an escalation of 'stalking' behaviour. After Gallagher decides to move his family from Manhattan to the New York Village of Bedford in an attempt to escape the unwanted attentions of the increasingly delusional and obsessive Forrest, he alarmingly finds that she remains undeterred and stalks him to a parking garage, pouring acid over his beloved and prestigious status symbol – his motor vehicle. So once again, in popular culture and depictions of popular culture, we find that the desecration of the motor vehicle is a constant narrative.

As well as the motor vehicle's being a target of vandalism as a result of hatred, it can also be the object of desecration perhaps at a more innocent and less personalised level.

Drift vandalism and the car

Drift vandalism has often deliberately been targeted at cars because of their status as possessions of symbolic value. This is something which emerged as a result of our conversations with two senior police officers in Nottinghamshire. Cars were felt to be a big cultural target, especially incidences of tyre slashing, which did not appear to be committed for 'political' or 'hate' reasons. Much drift vandalism was thought to be the result of frustrated and displaced anger. It was felt by these two senior officers that there was a clear association between vandalism of motor vehicles and proximity to licensed premises in terms of routes home from the pub. Whilst in terms of the policing of this kind of vandalism, they reported that forensics were being called to 'extraordinary events' such as multiple wing mirror attacks and tyre slashings, they admitted that forensic involvement was yet to yield a positive result.

The above was something which was alluded to by an Asian female in her 20s who lived in Nottingham. She spoke about her perception of how rife car vandalism was in the area and how the police had tended to 'normalise' it by their lack of responsiveness:

> There was a kid on a car roof, jumping up and down. Our neighbour phoned the police. We could all see it had been stamped on – there were big black footprints all over it. When the police came out, they didn't even bother to look at the footprints. They just basically said, 'Well this happens, it's what kids do sometimes, what else can you expect?' The neighbours got a visit from Victim Support a few days later, but that was about it as far as police involvement was concerned.

This person went on to describe the incidence of burnt-out cars and had reported one herself, but she remained convinced that no one, including the authorities seemed bothered. Recounted stories of car vandalism are often interspersed with recollections of drink-fuelled alcoholic binges. Consider the following:

> I had mates that kicked car doors and dented them when we'd come out of the pubs at closing time.
>
> (Male: early 50s)

Similarly, another of our cohort spoke of vandalising cars under similar circumstances:

> We used to like run up and down the whole street, up the bonnet over the roof, off the boot, whole road, then we used to call this one bonnet fighting, we just used to throw each other onto the bonnet of a stationary car, however, I took it too far and started trying to do it with cars in slow moving traffic, which put an end to that game, at least mates playing it with me anyway.
>
> (Male: mid-30s)

The above are scenarios which appear to be repeated across the country. On 27 March 2010, 'The News' in Portsmouth reported the case of the 'laughing and jeering' vandals, Harry Taylor and Andrew Cook. Even when apparently caught 'red-handed' by police trying to rip off a car wing mirror, the two miscreants both denied involvement in the damage spree and found the situation 'funny'. A night of 'mayhem' found that residents of Widley in Park Road, Lone Valley, London Road and Serpentine Road:

> woke up to discover a trail of damage with car windscreens smashed, wing mirrors ripped off, fences damaged and mud thrown at windows. Two expensive Mercedes cars were wrecked. At 5 a.m. on 15 November 2008, Sheila Barker of London road looked out of her window to see the pair causing havoc in her garden and throwing boulders at her windows. Her neighbour, Scott Murray decided to confront the pair in his dressing gown but were threatened by Taylor and Cook who shouted 'If you keep coming over I am going to smash you up like we are smashing up the car'. When the case came to court, Murray recounted that 'They seemed intent on damaging the vehicle. They were laughing a lot and appeared to be enjoying what they were doing'.
>
> (The News, 2010)

PC Neal Skinner, who arrived on the scene, told the court that Taylor, who had drunk ten bottles of Stella Artois and a measure of vodka was 'loud and aggressive', and he had to pin him to the floor. Magistrates convicted Cook and Taylor on no less than 11 counts of criminal damage. Seventy-nine-year-old resident Gordon Webster significantly passed comment that 'They smashed the windscreen, the wing mirrors and had a good go at the bonnet. I am glad they have been caught. *To them it's just a bit of fun'*. This last sentence captures the spirit and the essence of the type of drift vandalism directed against motor vehicles.

The sound of a broken wing mirror snapping or being kicked off is indeed joyful and humour provoking for those involved. Take the following:

> Looking back I can hear the laughter as wing mirrors were knocked off and car aerials snapped. I can hear the giggles disappearing off into the night air. These things are funny when you've got ten pints inside you.
>
> (Male: early 40s)

More often than not with drift vandalism, it is not a specific vehicle which has been targeted, but it can be partly explained by routine-activities theory in the sense that rows of vehicles may be vandalised sporadically in the course of the way home from the pub or nightclub. They are there in the same time and space as a motivated offender. One former car vandal continues:

> It wasn't driven by malice. It wasn't a vindictive act driven by hatred of a particular person. There was no sense of revenge. We never thought about the victims. It wasn't personal against them – the cars just happen to have been there at the time and were there on a plate for us.

This form of vandalism is profoundly anti-social when one considers the distress caused to victims whose pride and joy has been defiled or desecrated. Take the following example from someone who was a victim of such an offence himself:

> I got out to my car after an evening in the pub and somebody has put a spanner through my window. It left a slot in the window – there was this spanner shaped hole in the window! A few months earlier the neighbour woke me up one morning to tell me someone had stuck a 'For Sale' sign through the rear windscreen while my car was on the drive.
>
> (Male: early 60s)

The above again throws into question the difficulties of developing objective typologies of vandalism. Whilst the second act of vandalism alluded to above is likely to have been that of drift due to the 'weapon' used – namely a 'For Sale' sign – it may be that the first act of vandalism could have been an attempt to acquire either the vehicle or an object of desire within the vehicle. This is because drift vandals are unlikely to routinely carry a spanner on their way to and from a pub, suggesting this attack may have been more premeditated than a drift attack.

Whilst the criminal justice system convicts the individual of such acts, drift vandalism is an overwhelmingly subcultural phenomenon involving groups of usually young men. The vandalism appears to be 'mindless' because it serves no purpose in terms of acquisition, but it is in fact highly *meaningful* to those who engage in this social practice. It is the group dynamic – the attempt to prove one's daring, bravado and subconsciously one's masculinity – that makes it a meaningful crime. One former car vandal adds:

> I was never very confident with women. I wasn't much of a street fighter either. Along with drinking, vandalising stuff kind of gave me an image, a status amongst the lads who I hung out with. It gave me a bit of credibility.
>
> (Male: early 40s)

What is also significant about drift vandalism is that there tends to be an escalation or 'ramping up' effect. Hopkins Burke (2005: 114) observes that 'In a state of desperation the young person needs to do more than simply repeat an old offence; after all, as his or her peers would say, "anyone can do that"; in the state of desperation, they need to do something that they have not tried before'. So rather than their sticking to knocking off car wing mirrors we may find more diverse and 'daring' acts of car vandalism superseding previous ones. In 2009, for example, it was reported in the Kilmarnock Standard (2009) that a 'Kilmarnock man damaged a car roof by running over it'. Christopher Bell, age 21, admitted jumping onto both the bonnet and the roof of the vehicle in the town's Archibald Craig Place before attempting to run away but being apprehended by police, having caused some £500 to the vehicle. Significantly, in remanding Bell into custody, Sheriff Iona McDonald told him, 'You have previous for vandalism and this time you have done £500 worth of damage. Vandalism is something we are plagued with'. The point about Bell's having previous convictions for vandalism offers support for the proposition that there is indeed a 'ramping up' effect. Whilst subject to speculation, it may well be that his previous history of vandalism has involved a career progression from knocking wing mirrors off and snapping car aerials to the more daring and risky activity of running over cars. This is something which is confirmed by one former car vandal:

> I think it started off with pretty harmless things like wooden 'For Sale' signs and then it progressed on to car aerials and then wing mirrors. Looking back, there was always this 'ramping up' effect. I think we ended up trying to break into our old school, not to steal anything but just for the hell of it. I guess to keep proving yourself to the group you had to look for something bigger and better to vandalise.
>
> (Male: early 40s)

This 'ramping up' effect was further reinforced by the comments of others:

> We'd start off by letting down the tyres of these cars which were parked on drives. We did it by putting match sticks in the valves and the tyres would deflate. It was a one off thing we did for the crack really. We'd move on to other stuff – it was always wash wipes that me and mates did. We'd pinch them plus car aerials and then throw them away down the streets. I must have been 20 going on 21 at the time. It was always done in a group, never on my own. We even slashed a couple of car tyres one time just for the fun of it. It even made the local paper. When you are young you have no sense of fear. I remember once being outside the ****** pub. I was pissed out of my head and was stood on top of this car roof, jumping about. I had dented the roof and the bonnet. I just did it because a mate had dared me to do it. I must have caused about two and a half grand's worth of damage.
>
> (Male: late 40s)

Inherent in this description of car vandalism is the sense of 'ramping up' or moving on to different and more 'risky' types of vandalism. The idea that to stick with letting tyres down is boring and there must be some form of career progression and this indeed led eventually to the attempted theft of a motor vehicle.

Heavily associated with car vandalism are the acts of car keying and tyre slashing. Car keying is an interesting one in the sense that there may be numerous motivations for this act. It could be an act of fun-related drift vandalism if it involves rows of cars or alternatively it could be an act of hate vandalism if it appears that just one car owner has been singled out. Moreover, it could even be an act of acquisitive vandalism whereby the thief uses something like a key to try and force the lock open in an attempt to steal the vehicle, but ends up inadvertently scratching the vehicle itself.

Car tyre slashing is another relatively common form which can be associated with drift vandalism, particularly when it involves slashing en masse rather than seeking out single vehicles. In October 2009, the *Daily Record* reported that vandals had apparently gone on 'Britain's worst-ever tyre-slashing spree' in Kirkcaldy, Fife. It was thought that there were some 65 victims in the space of a few streets, with a staggered RAC Foundation commenting on the incident in which more than 100 tyres were hit as the worst car vandalism they had ever heard of in the United Kingdom (Bayer, 2009).

One of the points for discussion here is that on the one hand it could be argued that there may be a progression from knocking car wing mirrors off to keying cars and ultimately to tyre slashing. First of all, we have no clear and decisive evidence of such a linear vandalistic career progression, and secondly, tyre slashing involves the use of a flick or pen knife. This latter point is significant in that it implies the potential for a different kind of offender – namely the type of person who routinely carries a weapon for self-defence or as a status symbol or both. This is materially different to the more instinctive wing-mirror kicker or the aerial snapper or even the teenager who carries his car or house keys routinely in his pocket and uses them to deface a car. One former car vandal suggests that – certainly in his case – there is no automatic progression from one act of car vandalism to the next:

> I wasn't the sort of bloke who ever carried a knife. I guess knives are far more prevalent these days than they were in the late 80s and early 90s. I remember one of my mates once telling me he'd keyed a car. I was pretty disgusted. It's not something I would have done yet it's strange somehow car aerials and wing mirrors just seemed like a bit of fun.
>
> (Male: early 40s)

Hayward (2002: 1) observes that this kind of transgression often involves the 'controlled loss of control'. Thus, the vandal is never so 'out of control' that he or she does not know where the moral and practical boundaries lie. There is always a point at which they can say to their peers or even just to themselves, 'this has gone far enough'.

From a cultural criminological perspective one has ask to whether it is at all surprising that drift vandalism of the motor vehicle takes place.

We live in a culture which actively embraces and celebrates the routine destruction of cars in a sporting context. Nowhere is this better exemplified than in the cultural phenomenon of stock car racing, which is performed on oval tracks predominantly in the United States and Canada, as well as New Zealand, Great Britain and Brazil. There are several classes of stock car racing, each with slightly different rules; however, some varieties involve attempts by drivers to routinely bump each other in the course of races, causing extensive collateral damage, much to the joy of paying spectators. Take the following enticement from the UK wing of the organisation of the sport:

> From the pure adrenaline and Unlimited Power of the F1 Stock Cars to the destruction and crazy antics of the Bangers – you can see it all at the Norfolk Arena! With up to fifty cars in every race, action is guaranteed and here at the Norfolk Arena we encourage 'full contact' where spinning and hitting other cars is all part of the racing! You will see more overtaking, smashes, crashes and action in one lap of a Stock Car Race than any other type of Motor Racing! Many Banger events end with a famous 'Destruction Derby' where the object of winning a race is to go out and destroy the opposition and the winner is the last car running!
>
> (Trackstar Racing, 2014)

Hopkins Burke (2008) observes the 'schizophrenia of crime' – and how we are quick to condemn and censure criminality on the one hand, yet how we secretly crave a 'piece of the action' ourselves on the other. As the 'respectable' classes in society, we may have an overwhelming if not universal intolerance of car damage, yet at the same time a significant proportion of our population is thrilled by the prospect of organised car carnage, whether it be stock car racing or tuning in to Formula One on a Sunday lunchtime with the sneaky hope that a good old-fashioned 'pile up' might occur at some point.

This chapter has demonstrated that much of car vandalism is profoundly anti-social in nature, particularly when motivated by the desire for acquisition or when it is driven by hatred or the desire to affirm one's status in the adolescent crowd. When one considers the actions of the 'political' car vandal, one is forced nevertheless to question whether the motor vehicle with its propensity to wreak havoc on the environment and to maim and kill other human beings, is itself fundamentally anti-social. This point is alluded to by the work of the transportation think tank EMBARQ, which recently found that global advertising and marketing amongst the automobile sector totalled a staggering $21 billion. The report pointed out that attempts to attract more global customers inevitably had unintended negative and profoundly 'anti-social' effects, such as increasing congestion, expanding carbon dioxide emissions and undermining attempts to reconfigure more sustainable public transportation policies (Green, 2011).

Having considered in this chapter the fact that vandalism is far from mindless and sporadic, and indeed is targeted against certain culturally recognisable and desirable objects, particularly the motor vehicle, in the following chapter we consider the proposition that vandalism is not just object specific but also context specific.

4
Context Vandalism

Introduction

In the previous chapter we explored how vandalism is very much targeted and directed towards certain cultural objects, such as motor vehicles. It is a theme of this chapter that in certain social contexts, criminal damage is not only targeted but almost expected, if not encouraged. To explore the so-called 'normalisation' of vandalism in certain contexts, the specific cultural phenomenon of the 'house party' will be explored. This is precisely because behaviour which is censured in other social contexts is thought to be 'the norm' in this particular context.

Colin Sumner (1994) advocated the abandonment of the concept of 'deviancy' because he considered it a concept rendered meaningless when one paid particular attention to a multiplicity of diverse social practices. Thus, what is considered 'deviant' in certain social contexts is turned on its head by the carnival of the house party. Indeed we will see through the course of this chapter that to *not* pursue hedonistic desires, including the routine damage and destruction of property at house parties, is widely deemed 'deviant' by participants. At the house party, it is considered 'criminal' not to have fun, with abstention from such vandalistic practices running the risk of the censure of being called a 'nerd' or 'square'.

The centrality of the house party in youth culture

The enduring appeal of the house party is captured on YouTube with the classic 'Yellow Pages' advert from the early 1990s. A teenager wakes up in his house the morning after the night before and sticks his head out of the window to grab a whiff of fresh air in the vain attempt that it will sober him up. He then goes into a bedroom to see someone just awakening in a bed. 'Wake up, my parents fly back today' he exhorts. Upon realising that this person is probably a gate-crasher, he asks, 'Who are you?', only to be met with the same response from the young man who has just awoken in his house. Their attention quickly switches to an attractive young lady who appears to be wrapped in a towel after apparently taking a morning shower. The three of them then embark on a massive clean-up operation, most of which is focussed on the living room area. As they near the end of their epic battle against time to make the living room look habitable, a record is lifted from a wooden antique table to reveal a deep and probably deliberate scratch made on the otherwise shiny, brown surface. The big yellow book, the Yellow Pages, is frantically poured through until the young man grabs the phone to deliver the now immortalised line, 'Hello, French Polishers, it's just possible you could save my life!' When the French Polishers arrive, the antique table is treated and duly restored to its former glory, just as the house phone rings. 'Mum, just landed?...Oh quiet, I'm on my way'. Just as he puts down the receiver on the phone, the young man's attention shifts to a portrait on the wall which has been defaced by graffiti, in what appears to be a black marker pen, drawn on the portrait in the form of glasses and a fake moustache. The advert ends with a shocked and bemused look on the face of the young man, who has to face picking his parents up from the airport in the awareness that he has literally and metaphorically 'run out of time' in terms of being able to repair any damage! (You Tube, 2011).

The narrative of the house party

This classic advert from the early 1990s offers a fascinating insight in terms of the narrative of the house party. Firstly, there is the theme of the overuse of alcohol, with the teenager waking up and apparently needing to sober up by taking a few gulps of fresh air outside. The use of alcohol is inextricably linked to the house party. The ability to consume alcohol in relatively large quantities at such gatherings is a 'rite of passage'. It is a vehicle by which teenagers attempt to publicly demonstrate that they can 'take their drink', thus conferring a kind of adult status upon themselves. Of course, the expectation that alcohol will be readily available and its prevalence at house parties serve to fuel the kind of vandalism which again is expected to take place.

What is interesting, secondly, is that house parties may involve different kinds of vandalism. If one thinks again of Cohen's (1973) typology, we can see that much of what goes on at house parties in terms of music and dancing is done in the spirit of play or what we have termed 'exploration'. Paradoxically, at the same time that teenagers are trying to prove their adulthood through the public consumption of alcohol, they are also reaffirming their youth, if not childishness, through party games such as 'spin the bottle' or 'Twister', the latter of which was popular in the 1990s. The spirit of 'mischief' and 'devilment' of the house party is captured in the following recollection:

> We went to this house party which was being thrown by some student, years back. She lived in this block of flats – basically a 3-storey flat. We were on the 1st floor, and when we got there we could see that the door had been kicked in. The girl was upset – stood there looking at this smashed door and telling us that she'd had some gate-crashers who'd done the damage. We took a look at the damage, and my mate says to me, 'Come on, follow me out to my car'. We went to his car outside, and he had this tool box inside. He grabs his tool box, and we headed back inside. The door that had been smashed in was green, so we wanted to replace it with an identical one. We went upstairs to the 3rd floor and saw this door and thought, 'That one will do'. We managed to prise the door open and used the tools to unscrew this door completely off its hinges. We took this undamaged door downstairs and basically then unscrewed the damaged door. We then replaced her smashed-in door with the new door from upstairs. To try and cover our tracks, we changed the locks and then screwed the damaged door back onto some hinges upstairs where we'd nicked the door from. We then even went to the trouble of swapping our door numbers, and we wiped down the damaged door to make sure we hadn't left any prints on it in case the police came to dust for them. So we'd basically swapped two doors over – we'd swapped the damaged one for a good one – so some poor girl came home to found her door had been kicked in, and she was none the wiser!
>
> (Male: 50s)

As well as spur-of-the-moment pranks, much house-party vandalism is unintentional and tends to occur in a spirit of play or exploration, and when large crowds congregate in relatively confined spaces damage is almost bound to occur. On the other hand, the defilement of the antique table and the graffiti on the photograph in the Yellow Pages advert probably represent what Cohen (1973) would have referred to as 'malicious vandalism'. It may well have been committed by someone who knew the party thrower, who resented them in some way. These two acts may have been committed by a more anonymous 'gate-crasher' out of spite.

Thirdly, the Yellow Pages ad carries the ever-present theme of 'the gate-crasher'. The house party as a spectacle would not be complete without the presence of such people. To gate-crash a party is something which young men and women are socialised into aspiring to. It involves risk, sometimes deception and a great deal of cunning. It is a sought-after achievement to 'gate-crash' a party, and those who do so are invariably thought to be responsible for the criminal damage which occurs in such settings. This is the case because there tends to be more of a social distance between 'the gate-crasher' and the party thrower. Of course, with the proliferation of the Internet and social networking sites such as Myspace and Facebook, the gate-crasher is presented with an increased opportunity to gain illegitimate access to parties precisely because they are advertised in the most publicly accessible of places online. The exchange between party thrower and gate-crasher in the Yellow Pages ad is a classic – 'Who are you?' they both ask each other. Whilst the party thrower may fear the 'gate-crashing' element, he or she also knows that 'the gate-crashers' provide him or her with the cultural capital to be able to say, 'It was a cracking party'. Without the presence of the gate-crashing element, the party may come to be seen as 'boring' or 'dull', and thus this status may also be conferred on the party thrower him- or herself. Someone we spoke to during the course of this research recounted the following anecdote:

> Our old postman was a bit of a sad bastard really. He decided to throw a house party while his mother was abroad in the Canary Islands on her honeymoon. He threw this party, but he didn't really have many friends. The problem was that the friends that he'd got weren't really his friends, if you know what I mean. The evening of the party, he calls my mum up all hysterical, saying, 'They've smashed my house up'. We rushed round there armed with a crowbar expecting trouble, but everything had quietened down. But the place was absolutely covered in flour in both the kitchen and the living room. They'd pissed in all the plant pots, and his two Yorkshire terriers had also been pissed on – they were soaked in piss. All the baking contents had been thrown round the house, and the dogs were soaked in piss. His so-called mates had been throwing stones at the house and ended up breaking a window by the back door. They'd totally trashed the place.
>
> (Male: early 30s)

The presence of the opposite sex is the fourth narrative contained in the Yellow Pages advert. 'Who's she?' exclaim the party thrower and the gate-crasher as a scantily clad, attractive young female appears as they look on in lust, by the stairs. For many males at house parties, attractive young women at the party may represent the 'unobtainable other'. They can be sought after by the majority, but in reality the occurrence of people becoming sexually involved with each other at house parties tends usually to be something achieved by a small minority. Indeed, the idea that house parties are places where sex is readily available 'on tap' for everyone is a myth. It is part and parcel of the mythological narrative of the house party. Recounted stories of sexual conquests at house parties will tend to involve gross embellishments if not complete fabrications. Yet still they serve an important purpose. The perceived opportunity for sexual encounters is an important myth in order to sustain the idea of the party as a suitably exciting carnival. It makes both the legitimate attendee and the 'gate-crasher' feel that the party is worth going to, just in case they 'get lucky'. The following anecdote highlights that where there is a lack of opportunity for sexual encounters, the conquest of property can supersede the conquest of the opposite sex:

> It was all very booze fuelled, we nicked half a case of out-of-date lager we got cheap from **** (name of off license), all strong stuff, cheap imports, went to this party, carried on drinking, and soon *got bored, no loose women,* (our emphasis) so grabbed the kid whose party its was' guitar and smashed up his extensive collection of airfix models, taken years to make and minutes to smash up. Then we moved into the next room, picked up the Hoover and smashed it against the mirror of the wardrobe and then everything else, this kid was crying by now and saying if we didn't stop he'd call the police, we didn't and he did but we'd fucked off by then.
>
> (Male: late 30s)

The fifth narrative of the house party contained in the Yellow Pages ad is that of the 'clean-up' operation. Whilst the routine destruction and displacement of property is commonplace on the night of the party, and ordinarily continues long into the early hours of the morning, when those left on the premises awake in the morning, there is almost a sense of common duty to assist with and take responsibility for the 'clean-up' operation. Whilst the gate-crasher and the attractive young woman in the ad only have a fleeting awareness of the identity of the party thrower, they are now bounded by a sense of responsibility to each other. They have abandoned their 'second lives' (see Bakhtin, 1984), which may have involved drug taking and or vandalism the night before, and have returned to what may be termed their routine selves. They have abandoned the hedonism of the night before and once again become responsible and responsibilised young adults who must respect the value of other people's property.

The sixth narrative of the house party contained in the Yellow Pages advert is that of the attempted 'cover-up'. Whilst public displays of drunkenness and vandalism may have been actively encouraged the night before, now that the morning after has arrived, there is a desperate attempt by the party thrower to conceal the carnival which occurred in the hours before. Paradoxically, the better the party in terms of its hedonistic abandon, the more difficult this concealment becomes. Whilst the scratched coffee table can be repaired, the party thrower has to live with the fear and uncertainty that there is actually far more damage that has occurred than was originally realised. Concealment is therefore a futile exercise, as damage may be discovered (as in the case of the graffiti on the portrait) days or even weeks after the event.

An analysis of depictions of house parties via popular cultural representations adds insight into their social practice in the 'real' world.

Depictions of house parties in popular culture

The so-called 'skins party' has entered the common vocabulary after a party shown on the British E4 drama *Skins*, which is set in the South West of England and follows a group of teenage six formers in Bristol. The show, which premiered on E4 on 25 January 2007, was created by father and son television writers Bryan Elsley and Jamie Brittain for Company Pictures. The controversial plot line exposed issues including family breakups, eating disorders, drug and alcohol abuse, mental illness and teenage pregnancy.

According to one entry on the *Urban Dictionary* (2014) website, 'A skins party is a huge party in someone's house where nearly everything is broke, lots of people are having sex and almost everyone is either drunk or drugged up'. By 27 July 2014 there were no less than about 15,200 YouTube entries related to the throwing of skins-type house parties. This is clearly an instance of real life imitating art. One such entry was that of 'Jake's House Party' (Real Life Skins)' which, lasting some 7minutes, 3 seconds, had by the same date achieved 19,384 viewings. As well as the number of hits this posting received, what was of equal interest were the comments posted on the viewing page. 'Jabberwocky 700', for instance, commented, 'Looks below average party. Hah. I've been to far better'. 'Lucasadams2005' simply stated, 'the worst party I've ever seen'. What is interesting about this is that YouTube provides the opportunity for parties to be benchmarked in performance terms. Viewers can sit in judgement like a panel on *The Voice* or *X Factor* talent shows and pass comment on the 'entertainment' value of what they have seen. 'ImEuanAndIGotSkeelz' posted the following comment:

> Lol 16 year olds trying to make out they are 'hardcore' by drinking shitty beers and acting pretentious, sure, you might have a bunch of people shuffling around half arsedly to some crap music, a few beers and that, but nobody is having fun, can tell by watching they are all trying to look cool, want to actually have fun you got to calm down, relax and put some decent music on, get some weed and some nice beer, till you figure that out go back to drinking md 20/20 in the park like everyone else.

What is interesting about the above comment is that it is perceptive enough to realise that what is posted on YouTube is a 'performance' rather than 'reality'. Seven minutes and three seconds of edited highlights represent a kind of 'Match of the Day' format in house-party terms. In 'reality', the party may well have lasted hours, but what the YouTube viewer is treated to is a series of strung-together edited highlights. These 'highlights' are designed to act as a witness and testimony to the fact that 'fun' and joy' were had on the night concerned. The party goers had living proof posted on YouTube that they had consumed the pleasure and the carnival of the party (see Presdee, 2000).

One house party which made the national news several years ago and which has provoked discussion on the website Skinsparty.com, was that thrown by Rachael Bell in County Durham. In April 2007, the £230,000 family home was apparently trashed after an estimated 200 revellers arrived at the house following the so-called skins party being advertised on 17-year-old Rachael's Myspace website under the heading 'Easter Monday Bash Skins Unofficial Party'. Tellingly, the subtitle read 'Let's trash the average family-sized house disco party'. After seven police cars and a dog unit were called to her Woodstone village address, Rachael attempted to defend herself by claiming that someone must have accessed her Internet account to alter the party invitation so that a much larger audience of teenagers across the country was reached. Rachael told the *Sunderland Echo* (2007) the following:

> It was just supposed to be a small gathering with about 60 people – my friends are DJ's and said they'd play. The party wasn't supposed to start until 10 o'clock, but at half nine we saw people pulling up in cars. We didn't recognise them and didn't know what was going on, so we bolted the door – but they just started climbing through the window. We heard people at school talking about gate-crashing a party, but we didn't think it would be ours – we didn't think anyone would want to come. There were even eleven-year-olds trying to get in. I just had a panic attack because of everything that was going on, just because I was so powerless to stop it.

The damage at the party included bedding, clothes and furniture being destroyed with Rachael's mother's wedding dress being pulled out of a wardrobe and urinated upon. Light fittings were destroyed in addition to cigarette burns piercing mattresses. Lager cans were strewn across the entire house, and plastic buckets of vomit contributed to the after-party stench.

Rachael's 48-year-old mother returned from vacation to discover that her home had been trashed, and her daughter was effectively in hiding. The teacher told the Press Association the following:

> It's worse than a burglary, I can't believe it. Whoever has come in here are worse than animals, it's like house rape. They've been sick everywhere, urinated and trashed the house. It will take a month for it to be professionally cleaned, and we are having to stay in temporary accommodation.

Ironically it was Rachael who was arrested by Durham police on the grounds of criminal damage, but interestingly, the following comment was posted by 'JD' on a 'Skins party' related website in a specific 'discussion' about the party: 'I went to that house party, and there wasn't £20,000 worth of broken stuff, it was the media trying to make it sound more worse than it was. Hardly anything was broken at all'. This is deserving of discussion because a central tenet of the house party is the 'myth making' which occurs after the event. Teenagers and young people who are trying to impress their peers may routinely exaggerate the extent and the amount of 'damage' done, and ironically make a story more 'newsworthy' (Chibnall, 1977). It is thus easy to see how newspapers may spin particular stories like the Rachael Bell house party to make it 'newsworthy'.

Another discourse which may be detected in the above blog posting may be that of the fantasist, and it may also be commonplace for teenagers to claim that they were 'there' in the thick of the 'action' at such events when in actual fact they were not, again in order to gain some 'status' among their peers. This is of course a cultural phenomenon not restricted to the house party. For example, it is well known that whilst Wembley Stadium had a 100,000-spectator capacity at the time, considerably more people claim to have watched the historic 1966 World Cup Final between England and West Germany than could possibly or logistically have been present on that summer day.

'JD's' posting on Skins Party related website did not pass without comment, with one critical retort eloquently posting 'shut up you gay skins party r the best partys u can get'. There is clearly something apt about the use of 'text speak' in terms of its cultural fit with house parties. It is both 'lazy' and 'cool' at the same time, and its directness and linguistic incorrectness sit well with the so-called 'deviancy' of the house party. What is particularly pertinent about the quoted response is the anger which seems to be directed at the poster of the original message. It is almost as if to shatter the myth or the illusion of the 'trashed' house party is a cardinal sin.

The commodification of the party

Some sites have encouraged the potential party thrower to publicise their party and maximise attendance thus, 'You can now also post your upcoming skins parties in our Upcoming Skins Parties section – just email us with the details'. Sites have openly promoted those parties whose aim is to 'trash the host's house' with the expectation that those who enjoy alcohol, drugs, sex and going 'on the rampage' will be most attracted to its contents. One website contained space for users to post 'real-life' footage of their own imitation skins parties either in the form of videos or photographs. The user is moreover encouraged to 'Post your Upcoming Skins Parties for Free'. The inextricable link between the masculinity of criminal damage and the assertion of male sexual prowess is nowhere better displayed than in a website link to the online shop. A proliferation of pornographic magazine advertisements greets the web surfer with titles to the effect of 'Girls Gone Wild: Platinum Extreme Orgy 2' and 'Girls Gone Wild: Wildest Sex'.

The late 1990s saw 'gate-crasher' clubbing events develop as an international brand label following the notorious gate-crasher (later crasher) dance music events held at the Gate-Crasher One nightclub in Sheffield. This venue staged all night 'techno' and 'house' music party events, with famous DJs such as Judge Jules, performing at the events.

Significantly the use of the term 'gate-crasher' to brand the events was inextricably linked to the operation of a restrictive access door policy which served to increase the cultural capital of the events, and rather than deterring people from making the effort to attend, this policy seemingly made the event more desirable and seductive. People were enticed by the cultural capital of being able to say they had in effect 'gate-crashed' an event. Successfully getting admitted to the club only added to the sense of excitement. The door policy also ensured that only dedicated and committed clubbers gained access. Late 1990s fashion codes coupled with a rigorous door policy encouraged people to dress in a loud and flamboyant style in an attempt to be accepted at the events. Notoriously the self-professed 'crasher kids' developed their own subcultural style, based on dummies, fluorescent clothes and spiky hair (Gatecrasher, 2014).

The above two examples, skins parties and gate-crasher events provide firm evidence that so-called deviance in the form of house-party vandalism can be commodified and thus turned into productive capital.

The enduring legacy of the house party

There does, however, seem to be something permanent and enduring about the house party – something which has been passed on from generation to generation. Thus, the notion has been inextricably linked with pleasure and enjoyment historically. *House Party* (also known as *Art Linkletter's House Party* and *The Linkletter Show*) was a US radio and television daytime variety and talk show that appeared on the radio from 1945 till 1967. As well as guest speakers and celebrity interviews and music, the shows tended to involve audience participation quizzes with prizes. In the 1990s, *House Party* was released as a comedy film by New Line Cinema, starring the hip-hop duo of Kid n' Play. The film was a cultural celebration of the kind of sexual promiscuity, fighting and impending threat of police action for which house parties have been notoriously famous before and since.

The comedy film *Old School* was directed by Todd Phillips and released in 2003 with the subtitle *All the Fun of College. None of the Education.*

The film starred Luke Wilson, Vince Vaughn and Will Ferrell as men fast approaching middle age who decide to set up a fraternity in a bid to rekindle the partygoing spirit of the college days of their youth. The film centres on a party thrown by central character Bernard (played by Vaughn), and involves 'Frank the Tank' Ricard (played by Ferrell) being found drunk by his wife during a streaking escapade around the neighbourhood. Meanwhile Mitch 'The Godfather' Martin had stayed at the party and awoken the next morning to realise he had engaged in casual sex with the woman lying next to him. So once again we have the themes of nakedness and the availability of sexual experience culturally entwined with the house party. The 2002 film *Van Wilder: Party Liaison*, starring Ryan Reynolds, is about a student who has spent seven years at college without graduating due to his hard-partying lifestyle. When his father decides that it's time to put an end to this, Van Wilder digs his heels in and becomes a professional party thrower at the same time as trying to woo student journalist Gwen Pearson (played by Tara Reid), who is intent on writing an article about his exploits in the college magazine. Routine damage and destruction are again part and parcel of this caricature of student life.

In the fragmented contemporary world, it is impossible to overestimate the impact of modern technology in terms of facilitating the house party to be gate-crashed by those who are geographically and socially distanced from those throwing the party.

The house party in the culture of social networking

Writing for *The Sun* newspaper, Guy Patrick (2010), under the headline 'Facebook Party House Trashed' reported how a 'devastated couple' came home to find that their house had been 'trashed' by a 'gate-crashing' gang after their daughter had advertised her house party on the social networking site Facebook. Michael Ross and his wife, Nicola, returned home to the Wirral to discover that their £300,000 valued house had been looted and vandalised by an estimated 50 drunken revellers. Gate-crashers were allegedly heard by neighbours screaming, 'let's trash the house' as they ran wild at the Wallasey property in front of a devastated 15-year-old Rachel Ross. Amongst the damage, reputedly, were Rachel's father's ornamental samurai swords, which were reported to have been 'thrown around the house like spears' with some even becoming embedded in walls. The carpets and laundry were allegedly soiled by red paint, and bedding had been urinated on. Additionally, a decommissioned rifle was wrenched off a wall and used as a weapon to smash the light fittings in the house. The television remote control was 'cooked' in the microwave, and the television was saturated by bubble bath. The Wendy House belonging to the children was destroyed in the garden. As well as the damage, two laptops, phones, an Xbox and Wii games consoles, in addition to jewellery were all stolen during the 'riot'. It is believed that Rachel was so intoxicated that she passed out during the party, with her drink possibly being spiked by a gate-crasher. According to a Merseyside Police spokesman:

> We were called at 12.15am on Saturday morning following reports of a party getting out of hand, people turning up, drink cans left, people messing around on the front lawn and loud music playing.... Patrols went to the address and reported nothing untoward. The next day at 10.50am officers were called by the owners of the house, who reported a significant amount of damage and some items taken from the property, including a small quantity of cash.

It is cases such as this that makes producing a typology of vandalism problematic. What may be what Cohen (1973) referred to as 'malicious' vandalism driven by hate merges here with the collateral vandalism of the desire to acquire by means of theft and burglary of property. Rachel's father, Michael, 34, alluded to the ability of modern technologies such as Facebook to contribute to situations getting 'out of hand'. Ironically, because of the creation of cyberspace, he managed to track down some of the vandals online, and discovered that they had been boasting online about the carnage and destruction that they had left behind. He observed:

> Rachel is gutted about what has happened, she's so upset, she never intended any of this.... We were out at a wedding and she was supposed to be staying with a friend and her mum and dad, but unknown to us she'd organised a party on Facebook and sneaked back... Suddenly from being a small party for her and her mates from school it turned into a riot, with men in their late twenties turning up in cabs.... They ran riot, smashing up anything they saw and now they're bragging about it on Facebook.... I tried to track down some of the people responsible and found one thug bragging about stealing my coat. I'll be handing all the names over to the police.... They acted like wild animals and showed no respect for the fact they were in someone else's house. When we saw it, we felt sick to our stomachs. My wife was hysterical; we feel our home has been violated. (Patrick, 2010)

The vandals went on to steal Mr Ross's collection of antique weapons, which included a valuable Second World War bayonet and a Napoleonic broadsword. In total, the damage was estimated at around £10,000, with the couple's insurers offering to lodge them and their children in a hotel whilst repairs were carried out. This combination of 'drift' and 'acquisitive' vandalism was something which was recounted to us in the following recollection:

> I went to this house party once and I was absolutely wrecked. I went outside for some fresh air and ended up jumping in this guy's car and taking it for a quick spin around the block. The person whose party it was came out the house and chased me. He was fuming and telling me he was going to report me to the cops, but he didn't and I got away with it... I remember being about 23 years old and turning up at this house party. Four of us went in and ended up pinching the video and the TV, record player and the microwave! The people who owned the house were on holiday. Apparently when they came home half the house was missing!
>
> (Male: late 40s)

In writing for the *Evening Standard*, in an article entitled 'Gatecrashers invade £1m Kingston House for Boy's Facebook Party', Benedict Moore-Bridger reported in February 2010, how a schoolboy who advertised a house party on Facebook was left facing a massive repair bill after his parents' £1 million home was smashed up by drunken revellers (London Evening Standard, 2010). Sixteen-year-old Aneesh Shukla was a sixth form pupil at the exclusive Westminster School who hit the headlines when more than 100 revellers descended upon his parents' gated property in Kingston-upon-Thames. Cars were vandalised, chandeliers smashed and people urinated out of windows. Neighbours twice called the police, with two revellers being arrested on suspicion of theft, although charges were subsequently dropped. Neighbour Sally Manton, aged 47, observed:

> There were teenagers all over the road, shouting and screaming, making a huge amount of noise. You could not see the grass for bottles and cans. Lights were smashed, decking in the back garden ripped up, the table tennis table thrown in the hedge, plant posts broken. More and more people were just piling in. They were keying cars – a BMW and a Mercedes. There were CDs thrown on our roof, bottles, cans all in our garden. It started at about 9pm. Kids were drinking, vomiting, things were being thrown out from windows – an indoor fan – and

> even people weeing out of a first-floor window. I don't know if the people coming were just Westminster boys, because there were an awful lot of people wearing hoodies and I couldn't identify them. We are on a bus route, so what's to say people didn't just see this party going on and pile in? (London Evening Standard, 2010)

Aneesh's father, Ra Shuklaj, who owns an information technology (IT) supply company, and his mother, Nishi, arrived home on Sunday afternoon. By Monday morning, contract gardeners and cleaners were brought in to clear up the devastation in the vicinity of the house.

Once again, house-party vandalism is likely to be simulated because of the culture of celebrity which surrounds it. In May 2009, Paris Hilton was forced to deny claims that she was involved in a spate of vandalism involving motor vehicles at her Hollywood Hills home. Hilton allegedly had a party at her new home at which revellers both 'egged' and keyed expensive cars outside. A Los Angeles Police Department spokesperson commented that 'as the party let out, some of the partygoers did some vandalizing' (Access Hollywood, 2009).

Having acknowledged that the house party has a central place in youth culture; having identified the underlying narratives of house parties; and having appreciated the impact of social networking sites such as YouTube, Facebook and Twitter on this cultural phenomenon, we will now consider explanations of the vandalism which seems a routine event on these occasions.

Theorising house-party vandalism

It was Auguste Comte (1976) who argued that the development of industrialised society tended to erode the moral authority of that society. Thus, Émile Durkheim (1933) observed an increasing breakdown in social solidarity, and the previous intense and rigid collective conscience in which members had held very precise shared ideas of what is right and wrong. The breakdown in this community solidarity in a period of rapid social change invariably led to a state of 'normlessness' or 'anomie' in which attitude and values are diverse and very different. Thus, the context of the house party seems to invite an environment of normlessness whereby the conventional moral order is expected to be deliberately subverted and actively turned upside down all in the name of 'trashing the place'. This is particularly the case in which modern technologies such as Facebook and Twitter encourage people to feel part of a transient cyber-community rather than of a firmly rooted and morally ordered geographically located community. Why should people who read about a party via Facebook, for instance, have any loyalty or show any respect to someone throwing a party hundreds of miles away whom they have never met before and are unlikely to ever meet again? They certainly seem to lack some well-developed moral code that deters them from such obviously criminal victimisation of fellow human beings, or does the fact that these activities clearly occur in a group context in which the individual can clearly submerge their individual self within the herd help us better understand this clearly anti-social worldview?

Albert Cohen (1955) long ago proposed that 'the gang' – or a collective group – offers the potential for status when more legitimate avenues seem to be in short supply. David Matza (1964) later observed that deviancy is a 'status', with those who committed these acts being 'role players' who 'drift' between conventional law-abiding behaviour, on the one hand, and 'delinquency', on the other. Thus, from this perspective, it is suggested that middle-class, predominantly law-abiding teenagers can turn up at house parties and routinely break and loot property, yet return to a 'normal life' of work or study after the weekend. It is nevertheless clear that not all young people who attend these parties are actually involved in the wanton destruction, with many being simply hangers-on. As Matza observed all those years ago, young males can remain within the 'subculture of delinquency' *without* actually taking part in offending behaviour, and there is no reason why we cannot assume that young women can also behave in the same way nowadays. In other words, the destruction of property at the house party may be orchestrated by the few and witnessed by the many. In this sense it is very much a 'performance'. People also get 'sucked into' behaving in a way at a house party in which they would not dream of behaving if on their own, and can clearly call upon an extensive range of 'techniques of neutralisation' (cf. Sykes and Matza, 1957) in order to minimise and neutralise their sense of guilt and even justify the commission of vandalistic acts. Classic neutralisation techniques of house-party vandalism involve excuses such as the party thrower deserved it for not inviting 'me' or 'us' and that the bill for damages incurred would be picked up by the parents rather than the party thrower him or herself or indeed the insurers.

It is significant that the posting of house-party footage on YouTube is now commonplace and extremely widespread. Mathiesen (1997: 219) observes that 'in a two-way and significant double sense of the word we thus live in a *viewer* society' focusing on the acceleration of the mass media (especially newspaper, radio and television) between

1800 and 2000. His concept of 'delocalization' has a massive application when trying to understand the posting of house-party activities on YouTube. Thus, Mathiesen (1997: 222) observes that 'the older institutions of spectacle differed in several respects from the modern ones. In the older context, people were gathered together; in the modern media context, the "audience" has increasingly been delocalized so that people have become isolated from each other'. In simple terms, the ancient theatre, festivals and the coliseum have given way to Internet-mediated communication forms.

Katz (1988) offers great insights into how we might explain house-party vandalism while writing about 'magical environments', of which the house party is clearly one. It is because of the promise of readily flowing alcohol, the absence of parental constraints and the possibility of sexual encounters that the house party offers the partygoer or gate-crasher an 'enchanted land' (ibid.: 54), or 'an environment which is sensually endowed' (ibid.: 56). Potential objects to be vandalised seem almost to entice and seduce those present because house-party vandalism is a distinctively emotional experience with inevitably an element of 'play' or 'exploration' involved. It is an environment in which, paradoxically, teenagers or twenty-somethings can prove their independence and status as 'adults', yet at the same time in the absence of parental control or adult supervision can return to 'childish' and 'childlike' ways. Katz (1988: 66) observes that 'an essential attraction of these (vandalistic) practices is that although they are risks taken in the real world and home not just play, they are accomplished in a playful spirit'.

In Chapter 2, reference was made to the work of Katz (1988: 67) in terms of his offering of a number of metaphors which account for the seductive appeal of vandalistic practices. You will recall that what he termed 'the ludic metaphor' was likened to 'scoring in a game'. '"One dimension of the thrill is ludic; the process is a kind of game; and it can be tried and tried again", "with no more justification than that it seems to be fun"'. House-party vandals are on the proverbial 'same side' as each other, and they know who the 'opposition' are in terms of 'party poopers' who can spoil the fun. House-party vandalism takes the form of 'ambulatory sports contests' and 'the sense of a getaway implies at least an amorphous goal line' (ibid.: 67). There are 'winners' and 'losers' in house-party vandalism, and the fact that there can be 'an infinite variety of plays' (ibid.: 68) explains why despite frantic attempts to cover up vandalism in the aftermath of the event are often futile, because there is always something else which has been defiled and not spotted, as in the parting shot of the graffitied photograph in the Yellow Pages advert.

People of course do go to parties, and try and gate-crash them in an attempt to 'score' with members of the opposite sex in a sexual sense, which links to the 'sexual metaphor' proposed by Katz. Cultural criminologists have been at pains to point to the emotional and experiential aspects experienced by the subject particularly in the commission of non-acquisitive crimes, and this is evident in house-party vandalism. Increased heart rates and adrenaline are the body's natural responses to the gaining of the 'sneaky thrill' of vandalism. In Chapter 2, you may recall our coverage of how Katz (1988: 72) likened this to the act of sex in the sense that 'the sneaky property criminal is not participating in a consensual act; the pleasure is distinctively asymmetrical' with victims being metaphorically if not literally 'fucked'.

At this stage it is worth a passing thought for the work of Sigmund Freud (1905), who had much to say about repressed sexual desires. Whilst house parties offer the possibility of sexual encounters, this possibility remains out of reach for the many – the desirable is unattainable as in the Yellow Pages advert, in which the two young men gaze adoringly at the towel-clad young woman who appears just to have taken a shower before exclaiming, 'Who's she?!' Whilst no causal link between sexually frustrated desires and vandalism can be established, it is plausible to suggest that house-party vandalism may occur because of high levels of adrenaline, endorphins and testosterone, and that failure to 'score' in a sexual sense may mean some displacement in terms of aggression against property which can be proverbially 'fucked', especially when lubricated with a steady supply of alcohol and probably recreational drugs (You Tube, 2011).

We can thus note that the 'context vandalism' of the house party is both anti-social and pro-social at the same time. On the one hand, the routinised destruction of other people's property costs money and has an emotional impact, ordinarily on the parents or guardians of the teenager who has thrown the party, often without their knowledge or consent. On the other hand, through recourse to subcultural theory we can see how property destruction is pro-social in that it binds members of the offending group together so that they can reaffirm their status as friends who collectively carried out their acts of desecration.

Having explored the conventional vandalisms of 'exploration' and 'drift', and having looked at how these conventional vandalisms are both targeted against certain cultural objects and are context specific, we now move on to explore other manifestations of vandalism. Our next chapter explores the fact that some 'anti-social' acts are driven by the pursuit of material acquisition.

Part III

Cultural Criminology and Vandalism

5
Collateral Vandalism

This chapter focuses on what we have chosen to call 'collateral vandalism', a notion which can be further subdivided into 'junking', 'collecting' and 'looting' (cf. Cohen, 1973). The term 'collateral' is derived from the medieval Latin word *collateralis*, which means 'parallel' or 'additional'. At the heart of the notion of 'collateral damage' is the issue of intentionality. Collateral damage is unintentional in the sense that it is *incidental* to the commission of another act. The term has been controversially used in military contexts as a euphemism for civilian casualties and has been defined by US Air Force documentation as 'unintentional damage or incidental damage affecting facilities, equipment, or personnel, occurring as a result of military actions directed against targeted enemy forces or facilities. Such damage can occur to friendly, neutral, and even enemy forces' (USAF Intelligence Targeting Guide, 1998).

The notion of collateral criminal damage or vandalism is an appropriate term precisely because of the prevalence of the term in Western culture and in the context of the ongoing war on terror. The US administration led by George W. Bush, wrote to the United Nations (UN) in October 2001 informing them of their decision to retaliate in response to the 11 September attacks, under Article 51 of the UN Charter, which defines the right to self-defence in such circumstances (Beard, 2002). The subsequent wars in Iraq and Afghanistan ensured that the term collateral damage was to feature frequently in news reporting of these controversial invasions.

In cultural terms, the preoccupation with this notion was reflected in the release of the 2002 American action movie *Collateral Damage*, which starred the iconic Arnold Schwarzenegger (in real life, governor of California between 2003 and 2011), who plays Los Angeles firefighter

Gordon Brewer. The storyline follows a bereaved and enraged Brewer, who is intent on avenging the death of both his wife and son, who were killed by a Columbian terrorist attack. Their deaths are actually a result of the unfortunate unforeseen consequences of US military operations, but the motivation for vengeance is driven by a perceived lack of justice, which is a consequence of government policymaking, with the innocent son and wife of the film's main protagonist considered to be 'second order collateral damage' (Weber, 2004).

The Columbian terrorist El Lobo (The Wolf) bombed the Columbian consulate building in Los Angeles as apparent retaliation for US oppression of Columbia. Ironically, the release of the film was delayed by several months because of its coincidental timing with the 11 September attacks in New York and Washington. Indeed, the original trailer was dropped due to fear of offending sensibilities as it showed a major bomb attack in the United States, and a pivotal scene in which an airliner was hijacked simply had to be scrapped because of the outrage which would have been caused in the immediate aftermath of 9/11. There nevertheless appears to be no concern about upsetting the sensibilities of the Columbians.

The ambiguous relationship between the US government and morality has been demonstrated time and time again by Hollywood through the medium of film, in which unjust attacks on US citizens or territory have to be met with the correct degree of retaliation. This tension and ambiguity are particularly apparent in US film production post-Vietnam, a war characterised by blurred political and moral justifications. Films such as the *Rambo* series, however bereft of sophisticated dialogue, adequately illustrate these mixed and blurred rationalities and explanations for military interventions abroad.

Having touched upon depictions of collateral damage in popular culture, we now focus on the type of collateral damage which would be labelled as 'vandalism'. We do this by revisiting the acquisitive practices of 'junking', 'collecting' and 'looting', originally cited by Cohen in 1973. Cohen noted that the explicit aim of these three social practices was to acquire material artefacts rather than to damage or destroy them.

Junking

A contemporary example of collateral vandalism in the form of junking would be the commonplace crime of stealing or attempting to steal lead from the roofs of churches. Lead has been used on church roofs because it is both malleable and resistant to corrosion, and the high prices it can command when sold as scrap make its acquisition very attractive to thieves.

In 2013, it was reported that the Cornish village church of St Stythians in Sithians had lead stolen from its towers just a matter of hours after it had been installed (BBC News, 2013a). The Diocese of Truro reported that stolen lead had cost churches across Cornwall some £70,000 in 2011, and a spokesman added that:

> It is not just the cost of replacing the stolen lead, but also the consequent weather damage to precious interior fabric and irreplaceable items that cripples small community churches, which are already struggling to make ends meet. (BBC News, 2013a)

In 2012, it was reported that Britain's most prolific church lead thieves had received custodial sentences totalling in excess of 20 years, after their activities across the three counties of Lincolnshire, Leicestershire and Nottinghamshire had left the Church of England facing an estimated £1 million repair bill (Marsden, 2012). The gang of six Lithuanian men struck at 20 churches, with their crimes of acquisition causing considerable collateral damage when the ripped-off lead was thrown to the ground, destroying monuments and gravestones. The Lincoln-based gang made around £70,000 from selling the stolen metal. Nationally it has been estimated that between 2000 and 2004 there were just 20 thefts of lead a year from churches across the country, but that this figure rocketed between 2007 and 2011 when the scrap metal price of lead soared, with there being more than 14,000 reported cases at an approximate cost of £32 million.

As we previously observed in our Chapter 2 discussion of drift vandalism, there is evidence of the 'cranking-up' of the act, effectively meaning that those who engage in such practices are willing to take increasingly more chances. According to the London Metal Exchange, the price of copper, which increased from $1,500 per tonne in 2002 to $8,500 in 2012, seems to have encouraged thieves to take bigger risks than ever before. Mason (2010) reported that acquisitive vandals were stealing power lines, which dangerously carry thousands of volts of electricity. Vandals, armed with chainsaws, had cut down some 14 odd wooden poles which carried copper wires, leaving thousands of Midlanders without power. This stolen copper is ordinarily sold on to scrap yards, which were now offering higher prices for the metal in line with the current market, and according to the managing director of E.ON's distribution business, John Crackett:

> Like everyone else, we've seen metal thefts increasing for a number of years but what we hadn't seen before was thieves going to such lengths.... Even ignoring the danger of cutting down a pole that has wires carrying 11,000 volts at the top of it and leaving those wires, which could still be live, hanging near to the ground, this costs us money and causes a massive amount of inconvenience to customers.

According to British Telecom, there had been a 9 per cent surge in the theft of copper wire in the recent past, and scrap prices had hit a high of £5,000 per tonne in April 2010. It was a trend that seems to have been being repeated across the country, and is undoubtedly linked to the current economic climate of recession and austerity.

At a national level, the theft of scrap metal was being taken so seriously that the Association of Chief Police Officers (ACPO) set up a national task force to deal with the problem. Estimates by the ACPO Metal Theft Working Group put the annual cost of scrap metal theft at £770 million per annum, which is not that surprising considering that Britain is the world's fifth-biggest exporter of scrap metal (Daily Record, 2010). Between 2006 and the end of 2009, there were an estimated 2,500 thefts from Network Rail property alone, with an estimated cost of £22 million. As a significant cause of train delays, it is estimated that these thefts have caused around a million minutes of delay. Ecclesiastical, the insurer which provides cover for churches, has reported that since 2007 it has received 30,000 claims for metal theft, and it emphasises that often the value of the collateral damage caused to the churches far surpasses the value of the scrap metal stolen (Post Online, 2014).

Following the Scrap Metal Dealers Act of 2013, all scrap dealers and motor salvage operators in England and Wales were statutorily obliged to both apply for a license from their local authority and to keep records of purchases made, with non-compliance leading to possible prosecution and fines of up to £1,000 being imposed (BBC News, 2013b).

Having considered the social practice of 'junking', we now consider that of 'collecting'.

Collecting

A contemporary example of vandalism involving collecting would be the stereotype of students stealing traffic cones, objects which for generations have 'appeared' mysteriously in their rooms overnight. Both the theft and the misuse of traffic cones and similar items such as street signs and mobile barriers have achieved such notoriety that a number of higher education establishments have devoted pages of rules and advice for students outlining the consequences of their stealing such artefacts. The student blog site Student Direct (Student Room, 2010) says that the theft of traffic cones in the Greater Manchester area is at an all-time high and remains an extremely popular activity, while *The Rundown* (2005) has carried a feature on how the Welsh town of Llanddewi-Brefi – popularised in the television series *Little Britain* has seen a rise in the theft of street signs, presumably for the purposes of collecting 'memorabilia' from the show.

Such activities can clearly be seen in the context of the postmodern notion of the commodification of crime (see Ferrell et al., 2008), and it is not uncommon for students to attempt to sell such items on the Internet site eBay. As local authorities continue the process of replacing aluminium with plastic signage (BBC News, 2011a), it will be interesting to see the impact on the theft of traffic signs, for although the scrap value will be nil, they will presumably retain their student trophy value.

Another example of collateral vandalism involving 'collecting' is the phenomenon of the theft of badges from cars. Whilst the intention here is not to damage the vehicle necessarily out of spite or malice, in reality this form of theft often defaces the vehicle. In the Drayton area of Oxford, for example, it was reported that there was a mini three-hour 'crime wave' in March 1999, with more than 40 badges being recovered by the police from cars as diverse as Nissans, Volkswagens, Fords and BMWs (Oxford Mail, 1999). Investigating officer PC Alan Robinson commented that 'Swapping and selling car badges is a craze that is going on in schools at the moment, rather like the time when teenagers were stealing Volkswagen badges to be like the Beastie Boys a few years back'.

This is interesting from a cultural criminological perspective because it shows that what appears to be a purely acquisitive crime actually needs to be understood at a more complex cultural level. These thefts and the subsequent damage they cause to vehicles may be fuelled as much by fashion and by making a 'statement' as they are by money. The Beastie Boys are a rap-punk crossover band from New York who burst onto the charts back in 1986 with their debut album, *Licensed to Ill*. Their lyrics, including the infamous 'fight for your right to party', were always controversial, leading to some of their songs receiving a broadcast ban. In creating a fashion for wearing car badges on chains, particularly the VW badge, they also inadvertently contributed to fans' stealing car badges in an attempt to simulate their idols. While once thought of as a crime from another generation, car badge thefts clearly remain a problem (Swindon Advertiser, 2011). This type of collateral vandalism would appear to have a cyclical nature in terms of its appearance, disappearance and then re-emergence as a cultural phenomenon. McEwen (2012), for example, reported the theft of some 13 car badges in Edinburgh from a diverse range of vehicles including a BMW, an Audi and a Renault Megane as a 'comeback' crime, last witnessed significantly back in the 1980s.

More recently, 49-year-old Maxine-Ann Sokil was found guilty by Coventry Magistrates Court of stealing car insignias from vehicles, plus handling stolen badges taken from the Transport Museum in the city. A police search of her flat yielded the discovery of more than 700 car badges. Sokil's crimes were uncovered only when a potential buyer recognised one of the badges on the eBay auction website and rang Coventry Transport Museum to alert them. Whilst the cars whose badges had been stolen by Sokil would have been vandalised due to their appearance being defaced, significantly she was charged with offences relating to theft and the handling of stolen goods (Dimmer, 2013).

In taking account of the above, one needs to be careful, therefore, to make the distinction between acts of acquisition which are about a genuine desire to 'collect' for personal ownership, on the one hand, and acts of acquisition which are for material gain in terms of objects being sold on at a later date, on the other.

Having explored both 'junking' and 'collecting', we now turn our attention to the acquisitive crime of 'looting', which once again has ramifications for the occurrence of collateral vandalism.

Looting

Collateral vandalism, in the form of what Cohen (1973) refers to as looting, can be evidenced by reference to the relatively common occurrence of theft of cash from telephone boxes. This offence may not be as common as it was decades ago due the relative decline of public pay phones and their replacement by the ownership of private mobile phones, and this is a key societal difference between the present day and when Cohen produced his original typology.

Nevertheless, in 2013 a gang of Romanian men targeted telephone kiosks across the United Kingdom, stealing some £44,000 and causing an estimated £26,000 of damage in the process, through their modus operandi of drilling into the side of cash boxes. Incredibly, phone boxes in Newcastle, Durham, Sunderland, Carlisle, Wetherby, Exeter, Bury St.

Edmonds, Glasgow, Derby, Oxford, Croydon, Bradford and Plymouth were all targeted (Kennedy, 2013).

Looting can take many different forms, and there are different motives for doing this, at least at first sight. Thus, looting phone boxes for money is an act of theft motivated, at least in part, by financial gain. The looting that nonetheless occurred on a much larger scale in the United Kingdom during the Toxteth riots of 1981, for example, was initially sparked by racial tensions between the Afro-Caribbean residents and the police, and thus was far more politically motivated (see Chapter 8). Heavy-handed policing and the overuse of the 'sus' (suspicion) laws had caused unrest and tension leading up to the events of that July. The 'spark' to the 'powder keg' came after the arrest of 20-year-old Leroy Cooper by police for assault. The following riots took the police nine days to quell, and at least one man was killed after being run over by a police van. Looting occurred on a large scale as shops and electrical goods stores had their merchandise plundered. Other sites targeted included the Galleon Wine Lodge. The resulting damage to the buildings of Liverpool clearly illustrates the class tensions underpinned by the poor living and employment conditions found in Liverpool's poorer communities, particularly the Black and ethnic communities. As Larry Neild poignantly noted in the *Liverpool Daily Post* (2007), 'the old Racquet Club, seen virtually as a colonial outpost for Liverpool's upper classes, was burned to the ground'.

Thus, as the above two examples given clearly illustrate, 'looting' can take different forms and occur as an individual act driven by financial gain or as the outcome of group conflict, with the police using strategies that are perceived to be unfair. This is a problem with *any* typology in the sense that rationalities are often not mutually exclusive and indeed they may well overlap – in this sense, the riots of the early and mid-'80s may have resulted in looting which was both financially *and* politically motivated.

This is interesting in that it is difficult to see how individual acts of junking, collecting or looting can in any way be seen as 'pro-social'. When carried out by individuals, they would appear to be profoundly anti-social in the sense that they are a direct contravention of capitalist economic and moral principles which advocate the sanctity of property ownership. When one adds a subcultural dimension to the social practice of looting, the waters are muddied further. Resistance to the 'establishment' resulting in large-scale rioting is a relatively rare occurrence in the United Kingdom since the onset of modernity. Civil unrest en masse occurs as a result of negative sets of constellations, such as low socio-economic position driven by high levels of unemployment. In the case of the Toxteth riots, these conditions were further exacerbated by racially biased policing strategies that affected disadvantaged minority communities disproportionately. These constellations of tension have a 'touch paper' moment, whether it is the arrest of a member of the oppressed community, as with the Toxteth riots, or some other equally pivotal moment (see Waddington, 1996). In this sense the collateral vandalism caused by looting can, at least from a critical criminology perspective, be seen to potentially offer something far more 'pro-social' than individual acts motivated by private greed. Under certain social conditions, collateral vandalism has the potential to offer a critique of a perceived unjust social order and points a way towards one which is less 'anti-social' in terms of the economic, political and cultural marginalisation of certain 'excluded' groups.

Thirty years later, these riots were to be replicated in somewhat similar circumstances. Between 6 and 10 August 2011, thousands of people took to the streets to riot across numerous London boroughs as diverse as Hackney, Brixton and Barking. Their anger and protest soon spread across cities and towns throughout the nation, including Birmingham in the Midlands and Manchester in the North, to name just two locations, as reported by Phillips et al. (2013) in their geographical assessment of the events of that summer. The disturbances led to widespread vandalism, arson and in some cases acquisitive vandalism in the form of the looting of property often from high street stores.

The riots were triggered in London and led to clashes between the public and police due to a feeling that the death of a local man, Mark Duggan, had been unjust as he had been shot dead by the police several days previously (BBC News, 2011b). Many in the black and minority ethnic communities in London felt that a show of strength was needed in order to protest what was perceived as a gross injustice. Over the next few days, violent clashes with the police would result in both public and private property being attacked and destroyed by those motivated to take to the streets, and in terms of vandalism, damage to police cars, homes and businesses would all occur.

The riots generated significant ongoing debate amongst the academic and political communities, with the former keen to talk about causation, and the latter just as eager to apportion some sense of blame for the breakdown of the social order (see Gainsbury and Culzac, 2011). The Home Secretary, Theresa May, was forced to wade into a House of Commons debate on the causes and consequences of the riots, and a moral debate about social responsibility and individual choice to commit crime ensued between those who blamed the individual on the one hand and those who pointed the finger at society on the other (BBC News, 2011d). At one point the former prime minister, Tony Blair, was drawn into adding his perspective on what was reportedly a 'broken society' which seemed to be increasingly occupied by both alienated and disgruntled youth who did not live in the kind of society of 'rights' coupled with 'responsibilities' which he had espoused when he was occupying No. 10 Downing street (Blair, 2011).

The media of course had the proverbial field day, with the right-wing journalist Max Hastings (2011) of the *Daily Mail* choosing to conveniently blame a culture of welfare dependency which was presumably the result of policies, which would by some standards be deemed to be far too 'liberal'. The left-wing press disagreed vehemently, with many journalists blaming both material deprivation and the apparent increasing gulf between the wealthy and the poor in society, and others begging to differ (see for instance Batmanghelidjh, 2011; Democracy Now, 2011; Topping, 2011; Ross, 2011; Easton, 2011). In some quarters, tentative links were made to the Arab Spring revolutions of 2011, with a range of causal factors being discussed to do with the disempowerment and disenfranchisement of youth (see Ryan, 2011). In expressing his concerns about how the debate was potentially being framed in the aftermath of the damage of the previous days, David Lammy, Member of Parliament for Tottenham, was vocal in his concerns that the riots had the potential to be exploited by far right groups, such as the English Defence League, which would seek to blame minority ethnics who resided in Britain (The Independent, 2011).

The most extensive academic study conducted on the riots was led by the esteemed London School of Economics, which together with *The Guardian* newspaper produced a significant report titled 'Reading the Riots', which extensively covered the events (see The Guardian, 2011c). Whilst acknowledging a multiplicity of causes, the report reached the conclusion that many of those who took to the streets to riot believed they were participating in explicitly 'anti-police' demonstrations, triggered by the sheer outrage over the police shooting of the aforementioned Mark Duggan. This conclusion was perhaps unsurprising in light of the longstanding awareness of the historical tensions between the police and members of the black and minority ethnic community not just in London but once again across the United Kingdom, including the perceived overly aggressive use of stop and search tactics by the police which had a long history, of course, dating back to the Brixton riots of 1981 (see BBC News, 2011c).

Sometimes collateral vandalism in the form of looting occurs as an outcome of a natural disaster or as a response to the failure of the state to effectively respond to a given crisis. To use an international example, it was reported in March 2010 that the Chilean military was trying to restore order in the country's second city, Concepcion, after an outbreak of looting following a massive earthquake (BBC News, 2010d). It was reported that one person had been shot dead and a further 160 people arrested following intervention by troops to try and prevent the looting of food during the imposition of an overnight curfew. A high proportion of the city's half a million residents was thought to have been short of food and having to deal with the cutting off of their electricity and water supplies. The military was called upon to assist the civil police force, with looting believed to be getting out of control. People were reportedly seen filling shopping trolleys with groceries, with others going way beyond 'necessity' in taking the opportunity to vandalise shops in order to steal 'non-essentials' such as plasma televisions (BBC News, 2010d).

A similar event occurred in Haiti in January of 2010 following the devastating earthquake, when it was reported that 'bands of machete-wielding earthquake survivors' were roaming through the ruins of Port-au-Prince (Daily Telegraph, 2010b). In the city cemetery, one looter was seen dragging a corpse from a coffin so that the latter could be stolen. The situation was reported to be even worse in the most deprived areas, with teenage gangs trampling through the concrete debris and piles of dead bodies to try and find food.

Whilst looting appears to be overwhelmingly a crime of acquisition which may incidentally cause collateral vandalism, things are never this simple. In July 2010, in Oakland, California, a white former transit police officer was found guilty of involuntary manslaughter rather than murder following the shooting of an unarmed black man in 2009, which was captured on videotape and passed to the authorities. Video footage of victim Oscar Grant lying face down on a train station platform was shown both on television and the Internet (Reuters, 2010). This racially charged trial saw the defendant, Johannes Mehserle, testify that he mistakenly drew his gun instead of an electric taser and subsequently inadvertently shot Grant during an attempt to arrest him on New Year's Day 2009. Whilst prosecutors demanded a conviction for second-degree murder, arguing that the shooting was not accidental but intentional, the jury passed a charge of involuntary manslaughter, arguing that the former transit cop exhibited 'gross negligence' rather than a deliberate intent to kill.

The verdict triggered outrage among the minority ethnic groups of the city, and was believed to be a major contributory factor in fuelling a wave of destruction and subsequent looting. What started out as a peaceful protest during the day gave way to stores being vandalised and looted. This included shoes being stolen from a vandalised Foot Locker store in downtown Oakland. The slogan 'Riot for Oscar' was spray-painted on the wall of a bank, with fires being lit in trash cans, car windows being smashed and fireworks being thrown at the police.

History looked likely to repeat itself in a similar case three years later, but the widely expected outcome did not materialise. On 26 February 2012, George Zimmerman, a white man, fatally shot 17-year-old African American high school student Trayvon Martin in The Retreat at Twin Lakes community in Sanford, Florida. Zimmerman was the neighbourhood watch coordinator for the gated community in which Martin was temporarily staying and in which the shooting occurred (New York Times, 2012). The Twin Lakes Neighbourhood Watch program was not registered with the National Neighbourhood Watch Program, but was administered by the local police department. Following a previous call from Zimmerman, police arrived within two minutes of a gunshot during an exchange in which Zimmerman fatally shot Martin, who did not possess any weapons. Zimmerman was subsequently taken into custody, treated for head injuries and further questioned for five hours. The police chief said that Zimmerman was released because there was no evidence which doubted his claim of having acted in self-defence, and that under Florida's Stand Your Ground statute, the police were prohibited by law from effecting an arrest. The police chief added comment that Zimmerman had a right to defend himself with lethal force (Huffington Post, 2012a). As news of the case spread, thousands of protesters across the country demanded Zimmerman's arrest plus a comprehensive investigation. Six weeks after the shooting, amid widespread, intensive and sometimes conflicting media coverage, Zimmerman was charged with murder by a special prosecutor appointed by Governor Rick Scott (NBC News, 2013). The trial commenced on 10 June 2013, in Sanford, and one month later, a jury acquitted Zimmerman of the charges of second-degree murder and manslaughter (DJVESTV, 2014; The Wall Street Journal, 2013). Nevertheless, while much of the United States held its collective breath, and protests did occur throughout the country, riots – widely predicted by conservative commentators – did not occur after calls for restraint and dignified protest by the parents of Trayvon Martin were heeded.

When considering the notion of looting, we must proceed with caution. In Stan Cohen's (1972) earlier work, *Folk Devils and Moral Panics*, he draws particular attention to the role the media plays in distorting or exaggerating events. Returning to looting and specifically that which occurred following Hurricane Katrina, Barksy et al. (2006) observes that what the average citizen and public official expect and learn about natural disasters is shaped, although not exclusively, by media reporting. In their qualitative study of Hurricane Katrina survivors, the researchers make the distinction between two types of theft which occurred during those circumstances. First, there is looting in the sense of a person's taking goods that are considered luxury items and superfluous to basic needs dictated by the disaster, and second, 'appropriating behaviour', which is the taking of goods necessary for survival, food and water, for example. Ironically, it appears that the instances of crime fall in the aftermath of a disaster. Whilst this may be true, the mechanism by which crime is officially recorded, is also disrupted.

In Goltz's (1984) analysis of media reporting, it appears that the media tends to focus on social breakdown and efforts to control and restore law and order. Stories depicting altruistic responses, such as the stealing of water trucks from the water company premises, went underreported in the media, which suggests that there is another dimension to 'appropriating behaviour' – pro-social responses by a few for the good of the many. It would seem therefore that the media has a vested interest in presenting acts of looting as being inherently and categorically 'anti-social', whereas 'pro-social' discourses are somewhat neglected. What emerged from Barksy et al.'s (2006) study was that there was no unified agreement amongst either the public or the authorities as to what exactly constitutes looting or its more morally acceptable counterpart, 'appropriating behaviour'. It appears that once again the act – or the deviancy – is so defined in the eye of the beholder, to paraphrase Becker (1963).

Having considered examples of junking, collecting and looting across a number of contexts and across different countries, the task remains to attempt to make some sense of this phenomenon.

Theorising collateral vandalism

The central tenet of rational actor model theories is the assumption that potential offenders logically calculate whether there is more to be 'gained' than 'lost' when deciding to commit in particular a property offence (see Hopkins Burke, 2013). Thus, such theories have usually been associated with economic 'cost-benefit'-style calculus at the heart of their analysis (see Nobel Prize winner Gary Becker, 1968), in which those contemplating offending consider the potential material gains to be made by engaging in the illegitimate activity and weight them up against the likely punishment that they will incur if they are apprehended. There is a multitude of factors that potential offenders can take into account when making such decisions, and these can significantly include whether or not they have anything to lose (for example, employment, home, family) or little or nothing to lose (no job, no home, no family). There is nonetheless no simple motivational dichotomy between offenders on a fairly wide spectrum, ranging from near-complete 'rationality' on the one hand to near-complete 'irrationality' on the other (the complete extremes tend not to exist). In their research on alcohol and offending, for example, Keane et al. (1993) made the point that rational, logical calculation is often replaced by the overwhelming desire for immediate gratification in the here and now, in which human beings are concerned not least where alcohol and other drugs are involved.

Situational crime prevention – usually meaning some form of target hardening or removal – is the practical application of rational actor theories simply removing or significantly reducing the opportunity to get at the desired target. This is clearly where collateral damage or vandalism enters the equation. Many potential motivated offenders will be deterred by security measures, but others will not be, for whatever reason, and it is at that stage the collateral damage will be done. Rational actor theories thus make a lot of sense in explaining collateral vandalism, although of course they do not explain why it is that some individuals are motivated to take advantage of opportunities presented to them and others do not.

There is a multitude of explanations of individual criminal motivation within the extensive criminological canon, and the reader is referred to Hopkins Burke (2013) for a full review of the biological, psychological and social variants of the predestined actor model and the more radical victimised actor model tradition, which in an overly simplified summary here of a complex tradition argues that involvement in criminality is actually a very rational activity for many people excluded from the good things in life and invariably alienated from a society that spawns such inequality. Indeed, this is a radical reworking of the rational actor tradition, in which, for example, disadvantaged and dispossessed young people feel that there is (a) no real disadvantage in their becoming involved in social disorder or rioting in the context of their lives, and (b) a real material advantage to be gained from participation in such events or even in cultural criminological terms some excitement and fun to be had. It is little wonder that in such circumstances, a highly concerned and worried society responded with such punitive measures against those involved, as evidenced by the reaction to the

English Riots of August 2011. It was a clearly a logical rational actor model response, which sought to deter others considering involvement in future social disorder.

This being said, there is some question as to whether a blind adherence to rational choice is wise even when considering crimes of acquisition. To articulate why, let us return to the phenomenon of junking, which was explored earlier in this chapter. One such company that is keen to cash in on the prevention of lead theft is SelectaDNA, whose website (SelectaDNA, 2014) proclaimed that 'Lead theft is currently spiralling out of control', with the 'problem' showing 'no sign of going away soon'. The website promotes fear by having announced that 'nobody is immune' to being a victim of lead theft. There was the bold declaration that property marking through the company's product will ensure that 'nobody wants to go near it'. The website has made equally strong claims about the efficiency and effectiveness of the police in terms of their being able to identify stolen metal and prosecute offenders. Apparently, the 'police have immediate evidence that the lead thief has been up to no good'. One has to remember that companies like Smartwater that proudly proclaim a 100 per cent conviction rate have a vested economic interest in promoting the idea that their products are infallible. The reality may be that offenders still vandalise in order to steal property with so-called 'DNA'-style marking such as Smartwater, or indeed that operational police are unaware of how to check apprehended offenders for traces of the substance by which the property has been marked.

It is also worthwhile considering the notion of 'strain' as a potential explanation of collateral vandalism. Robert Merton's paper 'Social Structure and Anomie' (1938) and subsequent book, *Social Theory and Social Structure* (1957), revived and reformulated some of Émile Durkheim's ideas concerning 'anomie', or normlessness, and developed a theory of the middle range, more popularly referred to as strain theory. Merton wrote about (a) cultural goals in society – such as material or status possessions and (b) institutionalised means – these being the distribution of opportunities across society, by which people could legitimately achieve these cultural goals. The basic tenet of strain theory was that when the acquisition of cultural goals cannot be met through institutionalised means, the resultant frustration creates a sense of 'strain' in society, with some 'innovators' choosing to adapt their social practices to deviant or even criminal means. While strain theory has significant limitations as a grand all-inclusive theory of criminal behaviour, it nonetheless does shed some important light on a number of important issues, of which acts of collateral vandalism such as stealing lead off church roofs is clearly one. The lead is not stolen from church roofs for reasons of achieving status, but tends to be committed by organised groups which know exactly what they want to materially gain from the theft. In these contemporary recessionary times, a link between the economic downturn and acquisitive crimes, some of which involve vandalism, has been proposed. At the beginning of 2009, for instance, the director of the Centre for Crime and Justice Studies at King's College London, Richard Garside (2009), commented that 'It has long been recognised that trends in economic growth and recession have a tendency to impact on crime. These figures add to the sense that the economic downturn is having a real effect on the crime level'.

Having explored this notion of 'collateral vandalism', the following chapter continues the discussion of strain theory as we explore how a rise in profoundly 'anti-social' hate vandalism can partly be explained by the material conditions generated by a double-dip economic recession before considering alternative explanations.

6
Hate Vandalism

Cohen (1973: 44) originally used the term 'vindictive vandalism' to refer to 'the use of property destruction as a form of revenge', observing that those who commit such acts often consider that they have been unjustly treated and their actions can be seen, 'as a form of spite, in order to get one's own back or to settle a long term grudge'. Moreover, targets of vindictive vandalism often have a symbolic value which in many ways confirms our previous observations in Chapter 3. Times have nevertheless changed in the four decades since Cohen wrote and, whilst acknowledging that certain acts of vandalism do have a vindictive element, we have opted for the term 'hate vandalism'. We feel that this latter notion rightly encapsulates the political nature (albeit regressive) of acts which are nowadays referred to as 'hate crimes'.

Gerstenfeld (2004: 9) proposed that a hate crime is simply, 'a criminal act which is motivated, at least in part, by the group affiliation of the victim'. So effectively it is the fact that the *impact* of the crime is felt not just by the individual victim but by the wider group of which the victim in some way belongs, which makes it a hate crime, such as the 'gay' community or 'Jewish' community. Perry (2001: 10) elaborates on this point and observes that:

> Such crimes of hate are usually directed toward already stigmatised and marginalised groups. As such it is a mechanism of power and oppression...It attempts to re-create simultaneously the threatened (real or imagined) hegemony of the perpetrator's group and the 'appropriate' subordinate identity of the victim's group.

In view of this definition, it is well worth reflecting on the reality that many people who commit acts of hate vandalism do so because they consider they are furthering a particular political or ideological cause. Nevertheless, while this kind of vandalism is inherently political, it has attracted the label 'hate vandalism' because of its invariably regressive nature, and the authors of this book have thus chosen to take a moral stance against what we consider to be the misguided social practices articulated in this chapter.

Hall (2013) pertinently observes that hate crime does not technically exist in legislative terms, but legislation such as the Crime and Disorder Act 1998, the Anti-Terrorism, Crime and Security Act 2001 and the Criminal Justice Act 2003 recognise existing offences which are 'motivated' or 'aggravated' by hate, typically of the racial or religious kind.

Hate vandalism is born of prejudice and, according to the Chambers English Dictionary, prejudice is 'a judgement or opinion formed beforehand or without due examination' (Schwarz, 1988). In his classic, *The Nature of Prejudice,* Allport (1954: 10) commented that prejudice is 'an antipathy based upon a faulty and inflexible generalization. It may be felt or expressed. It may be directed toward a group as a whole or toward an individual because he is a member of that group'. In *Prejudice and Racism,* Jones (1972: 61) went further by arguing that prejudice is 'the prior negative judgement of the members of a race or religion or the occupants of any other significant role, held in disregard of the facts that contradict it' (see Brown, 1995: 6). As we shall see later in this chapter, hate vandalism can be directed against other diverse groups, and it is not something which is restricted just to race or religion. Hate crime, as it has become popularly known, involves any criminal offence committed against a person or property that is underpinned by the offender's hatred of people, typically because of their sex, race, religion, disability or sexual orientation or other aspect of diversity.

Recorded hate crime figures

Hate crime figures for England, Wales and Northern Ireland were published for the first time in 2010, with some 52,028 crimes recorded in 2009 for which it was decided that the offence was motivated by prejudice. Typically victims were targeted because of race (43,426), religious belief (2,083), sexual orientation (4,805), disability (1,402) or transgender issues (312). Although data was not collated nationally before 2009, the Association of Chief Police Officers (ACPO) were of the belief that there had been an increase in types of hate crime over the previous years (BBC News, 2010f), or it may well be the case that they had started to take the issue more seriously and had thus become more aware of the issue. By 2011, the overall aggregated figure had dropped slightly with police recording 48,127 hate crimes, of which 39, 311 were racially motivated; 2,007 religiously motivated; 4,883 were related to sexual orientation; 1,569 were related to disability; and 357 were related to transgender issues (ACPO, 2011). By 2013, the figure had risen slightly, with an aggregated total of 41,204 offences being recorded, of which 33,434 were related to race; 1,543 to religion; 3,964 to sexual orientation; 1,853 to disability; and 410 to transgender issues. Significantly, 385 cases of specifically anti-Semitic hate crime were recorded (ACPO, 2013a).

As symbolic interactionists and phenomenologists have consistently reminded us, however, these figures are not social facts, but are dependent upon (a) the level of reporting of offences to the police and (b) the way in which these reports of offences are recorded by the police themselves.

Racially motivated vandalism

ACPO (2013b) defines a racist incident as 'any incident in which it appears to the reporting or investigating officer that the complaint involves an element of racial motivation; or any incident which includes an allegation of racial motivation made by any person'. More specifically, therefore, racially motivated vandalism is thus any incident of criminal damage that can be categorised in this way. Implicit in the notion of hate crime is an essential acknowledgement that these offences have a profound psychological effect on their victims because of a fundamental attack on their identity and status as a human being.

The Racial and Religious Hatred Act of 2006 strengthened existing criminal legislation by introducing the offence of 'inciting' racial hatred against the person on the grounds of religion, creating new offences around the use of words and behaviour which are considered threatening, abusive or insulting and likely to increase either racial or religious hatred.

The British Crime Survey (2004–2005) indicated that 20 per cent of all vandalism incidents involving Black and Minority Ethnic (BME) groups were thought to have been racially motivated. In comparison, less than 1 per cent of white vandalism victims thought that the incident had been racially motivated (Home Office, 2006b).

There are numerous examples of hate vandalism. Thus, in February 2006, for example, it was reported that a Muslim student at Anglia Ruskin University entered a Muslim prayer room on campus to find it decorated with US and Israeli flags, as well as anti-Islamic racist graffiti (Varsity, 2006). The words 'Go away Muslims' and 'We will not forget Sept 11' were found in the prayer room. A piece of paper with the controversial Danish cartoon image of the Prophet Mohammed wearing a bomb-shaped turban was discovered on the floor.

Similar hate crime vandalism incidents have been reported from overseas, although these are clearly dealt with in terms of different legislation. In September 2009, in Fountain Hills, Arizona, United States, Mike and Michele Jaber and their black friends were the subject of racist vandalism, with the windows of two family cars being daubed with the slogan of the overtly racist Ku Klux Klan (Arizona Republic, 2009). Deputy Lindsey Smith of the County Sheriff's office confirmed that in a separate incident a vandal had daubed 'Jew' on another car in Fountain Hills.

In March 2012, a significant incident of racially motivated vandalism occurred at a burial site sacred to members of the Aboriginal community at Fingal Head, New South Wales, Australia. Graffiti with the racial slogan 'white power' and swastika symbols were spray-painted onto a wall in the site, and several memorial stones were damaged, with photos destroyed. The cemetery is the resting place of many indigenous families from the area, and was a burial site for Aboriginal people from 1864 to 1964, with many families still living in the area. Kevin Slabb's family was buried at the site, and he was very shaken by the vandalism. 'This is the roots of our people', Mr Slabb said, 'we have never seen violence here before' (The Queensland Times, 2012).

In 2013, an act of racially motivated vandalism occurred to a plaque in Guernsey. The Holocaust plaque was laid in memory of three Jewish women who were deported to France in 1942 and who were believed to have later died in Auschwitz. Anglican Dean of Guernsey, Canon Paul Mellor, reportedly said:

> It does smack of a racially motivated, particularly nasty hate crime. Of all memorials to target this one is particularly poignant and significant one; it commemorates people who suffered because of the worst excesses of human behaviour. For this to happen is another example of just how awful we can be. People in general have just been totally stunned by the action.
>
> (BBC News, 2013c)

Closely linked to the notion of racially motivated vandalism is the phenomenon of religiously motivated property damage.

Religiously motivated vandalism

The social practice of religion has historically fuelled conflicts among a plethora of religious groups. There are, for instance, the well documented clashes between Protestant and Catholics in Northern Ireland (and indeed Scotland); the atrocities committed amongst Serbs, Muslims and Croats in Bosnia; and the Arab-Israeli conflicts in the Middle-East, to name but a few. Allport (1954: 444) observed that the social practice of religion 'makes and unmakes prejudice...some people say the only cure for prejudice is more religion, for others it is too abolish religion'. There is indeed abundant evidence that the social practice of religion is linked to the fostering of prejudice. Batson and Burris (1994), for example, reported that over a 50-year period between 1940 and 1990, some 37 out of 47 research studies they reviewed showed a positive relationship between 'religiousness' and prejudice, observing that 'religion is not associated with increased love, but with increased prejudice and bigotry' (1994: 152).

The Forum Against Islamaphobia and Racism (FAIR) was established as an independent charitable association in 2001. In the two-week period immediately following the terrorist attacks on the World Trade Center in New York City and the Pentagon in Washington on the 11 September in that year, there were a staggering 600 or more cases of Islamaphobic harassment, violence or criminal damage reported by the organisation. The anti-racist Runnymede Trust argues that those who exhibit 'Islamaphobia' tend to see the religion as a monolithic block which is unchanging and resistant to change. Islamic culture is seen to be 'inferior' to that of the Western world, being considered 'irrational', 'primitive' and 'barbaric'. As a religion it is seen as aggressive, confrontational and violent and as encouraging terrorism.

Between January 2002 and March 2003, the Metropolitan Police in London recorded some 394 faith hate incidents, with approximately half related to Islamaphobia, with around one-third related to anti-Semitism. The Home Office (2001) study, *Religious Discrimination in England and Wales,* found that Muslims were more likely to express a perception that they were the victims of religiously motivated prejudice. Indeed an overwhelming 93 per cent of all survey respondents stated that Muslims were likely to be the victims of racial prejudice. Muslims (13 per cent) were additionally more likely than Christians (2 per cent) to say that they had been discriminated against on religious grounds, particularly in a workplace context.

There are many examples of religiously motivated hate vandalism which are worthy of consideration. In February 2012, for instance, a Sikh Temple being built in the Sterling Heights area of Michigan was daubed with graffiti in what many considered to be a hate crime. The graffiti on the outside wall of the building depicted both a gun and a Christian cross. The words 'Mohmed', 'Don't Builed' and 'fcuk you' were also legible. The Sikh American Legal Defense and Education Fund (SALDEF) contacted both local and state officials, requesting them to investigate the incident as a hate crime. The apparent reference to Mohammed, the Islamic Prophet, who is obviously not a figure in the Sikh religion, led some to argue that the vandalism was in fact directed at Muslims rather than Sikhs (Huffington Post, 2012b). This is an interesting observation, and may well be indicative of the fact that those who commit acts of hate vandalism may often display ignorance in terms of the intended target. It may be quite common, for example, for racial and religious identities of intended victims to become blurred or wrongly confused. This is all reminiscent of an analogous story during a paedophile scare during the summer of 2000 when self-styled vigilantes attacked the home of a hospital paediatrician in Wales after apparently confusing her professional title with the word 'paedophile' (Allison, 2000). It seems perfectly reasonable to suppose that such people are more than capable of confusion over religious leaders and artefacts.

Homophobic vandalism

Neil Chakraborti and Jon Garland (2009) observe that the term 'homophobia' is a controversial and contested one. Some people feel that it is an inappropriate term that depoliticises a serious issue by reducing it to a matter of individual pathology in terms of a 'phobia'. The Crown Prosecution Service (2014) has stated that 'Homophobia (is a) term used to describe a dislike of lesbian, gay, bisexual and transgender people or aspects of their perceived lifestyles…the dislike can be based on any sexual act or characteristic that the person associates with a LGBT person…'. This definition importantly allows for the existence of 'institutional' as well as individual homophobia, with the former evidenced by the exclusionary or discriminatory policies, procedures and practices of organisations. Thus, there are clear links between the definitions of homophobia and that of 'racism' in terms of Recommendation 12 of the Stephen Lawrence Inquiry Report. The Metropolitan Police Service's *The Investigation of Racist, Domestic Violence and Homophobic Incidents: A Guide to Minimum Standards* (2000) advises that the previously orthodox 'objective' definition of a homophobic incident has more recently been replaced by a subjective definition which places the views of the victim(s) at the centre of dealing with the particular incident. Overall, police forces saw a slight rise in anti-gay crimes, from 4,805 offences to 4,883 between 2009 and 2010 (Pink News, 2011).

In order to understand acts of homophobic vandalism, we must go back to the thirteenth century to understand how the legal censure of homosexuality in England supports and even encourages abhorrence of such practices. Thus, the first mention in English common law of a punishment for homosexuality is in 1290, with the following Treatise of 1300 prescribing that sodomites should be burned alive. The Buggery Act of 1533 introduced by Henry VIII brought sodomy within the scope of statute law for the first time and made it punishable by hanging. The Offences Against the Person Act 1869 formally abolished the death penalty for buggery in England and Wales.

Fifteen years later saw the first published use of the term 'homosexuality' (*Homosexualitat*) by Karoly Maria Kertbeny, a German-Hungarian campaigner. The Labouchere Amendment to Section 11 of the Criminal Law Amendment Act, which was passed on 7 August 1895, created the offence of 'gross indecency' in England and Wales, and thus became the first specifically anti-homosexual act. It became known as the 'blackmailer's charter'. The trials of Oscar Wilde followed two years later, and the famous author and poet was sentenced to two years imprisonment with hard labour under the 1885 Act, interestingly only sixteen years after he could have been technically hanged for the same offence. Two years later, the English edition of the book *Sexual Inversion* by Havelock Ellis and John Addington Symonds was published, and this was the first text in the English language to treat homosexuality as neither a disease nor a crime, instead proposing it to be an inborn and unchangeable condition (Stonewall, 2014).

It was not until 1967 in England (1980 in Scotland and 1982 in Northern Ireland) that homosexual acts in private between consenting males above the age of 21 years were decriminalised. In 2000, the government lifted the ban on gays and lesbians serving in the armed forces, and the following year the general age of sexual consent for gay couples was lowered to 16. The Employment Equality (Sexual Orientation) Regulations, in 2003, made discrimination against homosexuals illegal in the workplace, and in 2004, the Civil Partnership Act gave same-sex couples the same rights as married heterosexual couples in terms of inheritance tax, pensions and property. The year 2005 saw the registration of civil partnerships for same-sex couples, and in 2006, the Commission for Equality and Human Rights was instrumental in work which led to new sexual orientation regulations in the following year which protected the rights of gays and lesbians (Stonewall, 2014).

David Copeland's bombing of the Admiral Duncan pub in the old Compton area of London in April 1999 is thought to have been one of the crucial stimuli for the empowering of courts to impose tougher sentences for offences thought to be motivated or aggravated by the sexual orientation of the victim. This was stipulated specifically by Section 146 of the Criminal Justice Act of 2003, which came into effect in April 2005, and was further strengthened by the Criminal Justice and Immigration Act of 2008. Anti-gay violence is nevertheless still a major issue.

At the turn of the millennium, research undertaken by the National Advisory Group/Policing Lesbian and Gay Communities (Wake et al., 1999), *Breaking the Chains of Hate,* found that 6 per cent of 2,500 respondents had been the victims of a homophobic incident of criminal damage. In 2008, the gay rights organisation Stonewall found that fewer than 1 in 5 homophobic incidents are reported to the police for the following reasons: (1) a fear that they will not be believed; (2) a perception that the incident is not serious enough; and (3) a perception that the police will not act appropriately, or a worry that their sexuality will be made public (Stonewall, 2008).

In October 2009, it was reported that homophobic crime in London had increased by almost one-fifth, according to the Metropolitan police (BBC News, 2009), although we could really be observing a greater willingness on the part of victims to report these offences. During that summer, gay bars had been targeted by gangs in east London, and on one occasion a 21-year-old man was paralysed after he was repeatedly stabbed outside a bar in Hackney Road. This followed the homophobic attack on 62-year-old Ian Baynham in Trafalgar Square, who died from injuries sustained in the attack two weeks later. In Tower Hamlets alone, reported incidents had risen by more than 20 per cent between 2008 and 2009. The manager of the George and Dragon Pub, which openly welcomes gays and lesbians, stated that 'homophobic crime is definitely increasing.... A group of kids with bottles and sticks have threatened and attacked customers a number of times' (BBC News, 2009). Clearly the increase in attacks can be at least partially explained by the changing nature of London's East End, which until very recently did not openly encourage gay and lesbians, and certainly did not provide bars and pubs specially targeting such a clientele.

In 2008, a billboard aimed at tackling homophobia in schools in Blackburn was vandalised with abusive graffiti. It was one of six hundred billboard panels across the country displaying the message 'Some people are gay. Get over it!' and was being used by the charity to highlight their

Education for All campaign to tackle homophobic bullying in schools (Pye, 2008). Chris Gibbons, senior education officer at Stonewall, said

> Sadly, the vandalism of a small number of the new Stonewall billboards is a reminder that homophobia still exists in our society and highlights the need to address the issue in schools and in our communities. However, we are encouraged by the overwhelmingly positive response we have received to this campaign. It's clear that people think anti-gay discrimination is unacceptable and want schools to tackle homophobic bullying.

PC Kevin Little from the Gay Police Association said that the abuse written on the poster was classified as a hate crime by the police, and advised that 'The police would appeal for information on who has done the graffiti and anybody can report it'. George Haworth, secretary of the 4 Health Group, which supports lesbians, gay men and bisexuals in Blackburn, said:

> The defacing of the billboard makes us really angry. It's 2008 now, and people are still obviously not happy with a poster saying get real and get with the reality of today. We have done a lot of work in schools with Stonewall in the past and it's obvious that a lot more education needs to be done. Adults too need educating, not just children. There are a variety of reasons why people write such offensive things: sometimes it's hate, sometimes it's religiously orientated, but it's all ignorant.

The homophobic graffiti consisted of one word 'NO', and it is impossible from this to discern a motive. While clearly upsetting to gays and lesbians, it is impossible to establish that the person did this because they were part of a homophobic campaign, either as an individual or part of a group, or whether is something altogether more innocent, a misplaced sense of humour or a prank. We cannot tell.

Taking a cross-cultural perspective, in October 2010, in the United States, the homophobic vandalism of a homecoming float at the University of Missouri with images and graffiti prompted the November rally of Queers and Allies to let people know that diversity and inclusiveness were valued by the university. According to their spokesperson, Jay Hicks, 'One little word can make someone tear themselves down inside, and as we saw in the news lately with all the teens who die by suicide, it takes one little act of violence or hatred that turn the tables in their minds' (Fox News, 2010). Jenn Rieskamp, the rally organiser, spoke about the cohesive effect that the rally had had. 'We like to pride ourselves in our community creed, and we like to say we have an open and just community where everybody is welcomed'. This does seem indicative of a willingness to collectively protest against homophobic hate vandalism. A similar case occurred, for example, in 2011 at North Carolina State University, with several hundred students and staff united in their protest against an act of vandalism targeted toward the university's Gay, Lesbian, Bisexual and Transgender (GLBT) society after the words 'burn' and die' were daubed on the walls of the centre (Wral.com, 2011).

More recently in the United Kingdom, in the latter part of 2013, hate vandals repeatedly targeted the home of a Wigan woman on the grounds of her perceived sexuality (Hyde, 2013). The attack apparently saw offenders covering the glass panels on the front door of the victim's home and using a paintbrush to smear homophobic words on the living room windows. The fact that it was reported that the victim had suffered a similar attack in the summer of that same year is indicative of the trend that repeat victimisation is a common characteristic of these types of hate offences.

Vandalism against the disabled

The Disability Rights Commission conducted an attitudes and awareness survey back in 2003 which found that 22 per cent of respondents with disabilities felt they had experienced some kind of public harassment because of their physical impairment (Disability Rights Commission, 2003). In addition to this, the Greater London Action on Disability forum had reported during the previous year that 8 per cent of disabled people in London alone had suffered a violent attack compared with just 4 per cent of able-bodied people. In 2007, the Crown Prosecution Service launched its *Policy for Prosecuting Cases of Disability Hate Crime* (CPS, 2007), which acknowledged that hate crime has a 'significant negative impact on disabled people's sense of security and wellbeing. It also impacts significantly on their ability to participate both socially and economically in their communities' (p. 1). Whilst controversially not creating a new offence, Section 146 of the Criminal Justice Act 2003 imposed a duty on courts to increase the sentence of any offence, including criminal damage, thought to be aggravated by hostility based on the victim's disability or assumed disability. Section 2.5.2 of the legislation, however, introduced some limitations to the classification of offences against the disabled because of the difficulty of proving that the offence was motivated by the disability of the victim. This section states the following:

> However, not all crimes committed against disabled people are disability hate crimes – some crimes are committed because the offender regards the disabled person as being vulnerable and not because the offender dislikes or hates disabled people. For example, the theft of a wallet from a blind person; if the offender was preying on the victim's perceived vulnerability this will not be a disability hate crime within the definition of Section 146. (see Crown Prosecution Service, 2007)

Recorded incidents of disability hate crimes rose from 800 to 1,402 between 2008 and 2009, and this figure reportedly caused alarm amongst disability charities, which remain convinced there is still massive under-reporting and recording of such offences (see Community Care, 2010). David Congdon, Mencap's head of policy, commented:

> People with a learning disability do not always go to the police. When they do, the police do not always record or investigate the crime as a hate crime, instead choosing to investigate it as anti-social behaviour. Hate crime against people with a learning disability needs to be taken as seriously as race-related and homophobic hate crimes. (Community Care, 2010)

The police responded through their ACPO lead on equality and diversity, who spoke about the determination of the police to both encourage reporting of these incidents as well as a commitment to reducing them in the future. Chief Constable Stephen Otter commented:

> Whilst we want to reduce the incidence of these crimes, it is vital that we close the gap of under-reporting. We are making real progress in this critical area through standardized reporting and better recording and we continue to work to improve our support to victims of hate crime. (Community Care, 2010)

There are numerous of examples of vandalistic attacks committed against disabled people. For example, in November 2010 a house being built for disabled people in Kirkton in Scotland was tagged with graffiti and vandalised, causing thousands of pounds worth of damage. Roof slates were smashed along with an external heating unit and fencing before the vandals systematically destroyed the inside of the newly refurbished property. Councillor Ian Borthwick commented:

> I think it's absolutely deplorable that this has happened, particularly because it's a new-build property that will cater for disabled residents once finished.... This is not just an isolated case, but an example of a problem that has been going on for some time... It's the sort of thing that causes the community to lose heart – and our people deserve better than this.
>
> (The Courier, 2010)

One high profile case of vandalism against a disabled family was that which occurred in October 2007 in Leicestershire. Fiona Pilkington (38) took her own life and that of her daughter, Frankie (18), who had learning difficulties (Sturcke, 2010). Despite a sustained campaign of hate by local youths spanning several years, Leicestershire police recorded Fiona Pilkington's systematic and regular complaints as evidence of low-level anti-social behaviour rather than as an ongoing hate crime. As far back as October 2000, Fiona Pilkington had called the police to report that youths were throwing eggs at the house. No officers were available to follow up the call and to make a home visit. In January 2004, Fiona's mother, Pam Cassell, rang the police to report youths throwing bottles and stones into the family garden and setting fire to both fences and gates. Once again, no action was taken by the police. In February 2007, it was reported that snowballs and bottles were being thrown at the house, followed by the vandalism of a 'For Sale' sign outside their home just a month later. In September and October 2007, windows were smashed at the family home as a result of stone throwing by the persistent vandals (Hopkins Burke and Hodgson, 2013).

Pilkington's car, a blue Austin Maestro, was found in flames on a layby by the side of the A47, not far from the family's home on the evening of 23 October 2007. The car had been set alight with petrol, and upon arrival at the scene, the emergency services made the grim discovery of the badly burned bodies of Fiona and Frankie. Disturbingly, the inquest heard evidence that the family's pet rabbit was taken in the car, probably as an attempt to calm Frankie, who was reported to have had a mental age of four years old.

Vandalism against the mentally ill

As well as vandalism committed against physically disabled people, those with mental health difficulties are often targeted. It is estimated that some 630,000 people use dedicated mental health services in the United Kingdom every year. Suicide is the biggest killer of young men under the age of 35 years, and the total costs of mental illness to society runs at an estimated £32 billion per annum (Daily Mail, 2006a), while a National Statistics report in 2007 noted that positive attitudes towards mentally ill people had decreased over the 13-year period since 1994 (National Statistics Office, 2007). Research by Crisp et al. (2000) found that approximately one in five people thought that those with 'severe depression' and who were suffering from 'panic attacks' should effectively 'pull themselves together'. According to a government-endorsed study, as many as 60 per cent of young people admitted verbally abusing the mentally ill. Amongst the most common terms of abuse were 'psycho', 'schizo', 'nutter' and 'loony'. Whilst the majority of people studied felt that racist language was not acceptable, only one-third felt that prejudice against the mentally ill was wholly unacceptable (BBC News, 2001).

A survey conducted by mental health charity MIND (2007), found that 71 per cent of those with mental health problems had reported some kind of victimisation in the local community in the two years prior to 2007. It was discovered that people with mental health problems were 11 times more likely to be victimised than those without such conditions. Just over a quarter (26 per cent) had their homes vandalised. Sixty-four per cent of victims of crime and harassment were dissatisfied with the response of the authorities to the reporting of the incident, with some 60 per cent of victims saying that the appropriate authorities did not take them seriously. Additionally, 36 per cent of those who did not report a crime felt police would not believe them if they did. The report discussed the case of a family targeted through vandalism and anti-social behaviour because of the mental illness of one of its members:

> It all started when my Mum had a nervous breakdown. People used to tease my Mum [...] I thought they were good neighbours, but then they found out my personal business. My son's been strangled, frog-marched, dragged by his ear. We've had our door spat upon, rubbish left outside our door. I'm so worried about my son growing up in that hostile atmosphere. The flat upstairs have purposefully flooded us. How much longer will it go on? The police come, but they don't take it seriously [...]. At the police station, if they hear 'mental health problems' then they are against you. (MIND, 2007)

In May 2012, a disabled woman was left stranded and home bound in Uxbridge after her disability scooter had been repeatedly vandalised over a number of years. Once again, this repeat victimisation suggests that this was an act of hate vandalism. Susan Heffernan, who suffers with spina bifida, commented that:

> They've taken the engine, the exhaust, a wheel and a window, and I'm sure they would have driven off with it if I hadn't had an alarm fitted after the last time it happened. I was shocked and upset. My bike is my life and without it I can't leave the house on my own.
>
> (Uxbridge Gazette, 2012)

Sometimes hate vandalism is most clearly targeted against the disabled, but there are other acts of vandalism which are slightly more ambiguous in terms of an assessment of their motivation. One such instance occurred in March 2014 in North Devon with screwdriver-wielding vandals causing an estimated £1,000 worth of damage to a disabled toilet at Bideford Football Club. Specific damage to the water pipe led to massive flooding of the Torridge District Council-owned building. The investigating officer, PC Adam Sinclair, was quoted as referring to the damage as both 'deliberate and malicious' (Keeble, 2014). What is less clear cut, however, is whether the toilet was targeted because it was a lavatory specifically for the disabled or whether the vandals actually would have directed their intent to damage against any such toilet, whether it was designed for able bodied persons or those with a disability.

Explaining hate vandalism

In his classic and highly influential social control theory, Travis Hirschi (1969) argued that delinquency results when the bond of the individual to society is weakened. Ben Bowling (1999) actually turns this notion on its head and argues that in the case of hate vandalism, it may in fact be the actual presence of social norms amongst certain groups which encourage discriminatory and ultimately destructive action. Many would argue that we do indeed live in an inherently racist, sexist and homophobic society and that what hate vandalism in fact represents is the way in which some individuals replicate the kind of prejudice shown by the dominant institutions in society. Indeed, Hopkins Burke and Pollock (2004) observe that hate crime motivation is simply normal and unremarkable in society as currently constituted. The powerful macro, mezzo and micro mechanical solidarities that exist in even the most complex contemporary organic societies – absorbed and internalised during a socialisation process that may well have prioritised notions of hard work, law-abiding behaviour and indeed conformity to the group – legitimate hate motivation as normal:

> Given the opportunity in the right venue among 'our own kind' where such views are very much the norm it is possible that latent hate motivation might well be actualised, where the at least tacit approval of the (perhaps) silent majority of conformists might provide succour, support and legitimisation for those prepared to act upon their hate motivation.
>
> (Hopkins Burke and Pollock, 2004: 15)

Agnew (1992), in an adaptation of classic strain theory (cf. Merton, 1949), argues that economic strain could understandably lead to anger by the disadvantaged and dispossessed. The notion that 'immigrants are taking our jobs' is a long-established tradition expressed about a succession of immigrants, from the Irish in the nineteenth century to the Polish and the Rumanians in contemporary society, but this all begins to sound somewhat absurd if comments such as 'gays are taking our jobs' or 'the disabled are taking our jobs' are substituted for particular ethnic groups. Clearly not all hate crime is economically motivated, because it has existed in times of boom and prosperity as well as times of depression, while acts of hate vandalism have not always been committed by the most economically marginalised groups in society. More sophisticated explanations are clearly required, although we should note at this juncture that economic boom and prosperity is not equally distributed and that hate crimes against immigrants are often rife in the more economically deprived areas of society (Hopkins Burke and Pollock, 2004).

McDevitt et al. (2002) have responded to the demand for more sophisticated explanations by developing a typology of hate crime offenders which includes 'defensive', 'retaliatory', 'mission' and 'thrill' types. An estimated 25 per cent of offenders were found to be motivated by 'defensive' factors where the perpetrators maintain that they're defending 'their territory' against the infiltration of 'outsiders' from 'other' cultures. 'Retaliatory' offences, on the other hand, tend to be committed by perpetrators acting alone in response to a perceived 'wrongdoing' committed against them personally or their reference point in terms of 'community', and about 8 per cent of hate crimes offenders fall within this category. This sort of offence may be committed because of perceived injustice or grievance with someone, which becomes, as Cohen (1973) mentioned in his original typology, of a vindictive nature.

A contemporary example of vindictive vandalism which would not be classified as a hate crime would be the case of the former disc jockey Anthony King, who in 1996 was jailed for two years at the Old Bailey for launching a campaign of obsessive terror against his former girlfriend as well as her family. After being jilted at the end of a two-year relationship, King had bombarded Gemma Jones, a magazine sales executive, with telephone calls. King was arrested and convicted after vandalising her father's BMW as well as spraying graffiti over their porch and garage in an inherently vindictive act because he felt it was the fact that he was black and not approved of that had caused the breakdown in the relationship between himself and the entire Jones family (The Free Library, 1996).

Whilst retaliatory or vindictive vandalism may not always be a hate crime, 'mission' vandalism certainly is. So-called 'mission' offenders were thought by McDevitt et al. (2002) to constitute a minority of just 1 per cent of the total of hate crime offenders, and these offenders were characterised as being fully committed to far-right political groups such as Combat 18. The researchers found that 66 per cent of offenders were in some way motivated by the 'thrill' of offending, which suggests that the vandalism committed against minority groups such as gays, ethnic minorities and the disabled may sometimes be carried out for reasons other than overwhelming prejudice against these groups.

To fully understand and contextualise hate vandalism, it is argued that one has to look beyond conventional criminological explanations to the influence of social psychology. Hall (2013) reminds us that hate crime is born of prejudice, but that prejudice itself is just one form of hate. Prejudice is cognitive and attitudinal and may or may not lead to discrimination, the latter of which involves acting on one's prejudices.

Early attempts to theorise the type of prejudice which one would associate with hate vandalism tended to focus on the characteristics of individuals rather than on group dynamics or social norms and conventions. Attempts to link prejudice with a particular personality type were first put forward by Theodor Adorno et al. (1950), through the notion of 'the authoritarian personality'. This idea was endorsed by Rokeach (1960), who argued that prejudice was linked to those of a fascist disposition. Prejudice was connected with those displaying over rigidity in their thought processes, and was said to be reinforced by socialisation patterns driven by harsh discipline. Based on the ideas of Sigmund Freud, hate crimes including vandalism, could be considered to be 'displaced' rather than intended targets of resentment, caused by unresolved conflicts locked deep in the psyche. Research in the 1950s by Campbell and McCandless (1951) and Pettigrew (1958) discovered a correlation between 'authoritarian' attitudes and prejudice against ethnic minorities, and this was endorsed far more recently in the eighties by Meloen et al. (1988).

Social psychologists have, however, criticised the tendency to reduce the roots of hate crime, including vandalism, to that of individual pathology. For these theorists, individual cognitive processes are influenced by social factors. Experiments conducted as far back as the 1960s by Sherif et al. (1961) and Campbell (1965) attributed prejudice to 'realistic conflict' between groups. This belief was supported in the eighties by Bobo (1983), who found that prejudice stemmed from competition between social groups for scarce resources. There is thus a clear link between the propositions of these 'realistic conflict' theorists and the strain theorists working in the traditions of Merton, as mentioned earlier. This economically deterministic view of the roots of prejudice resulting in crimes like hate vandalism has nevertheless been questioned and refuted by Green et al. (2001).

The notion that hate crimes, including vandalism, are caused by 'relative deprivation' was articulated by Festinger (1954), who talked about how people were socialised into making inevitable comparisons between themselves as 'insiders' and others as 'outsiders'. This contributed to the development of social identity theory by Tajfel and Turner (1979), which received empirical support from Cialdini et al. (1976), who found that hatred and property damage caused by football fans against rival clubs and fan bases was concerned with reinforcing a positive sense of social identity. For a fuller consideration of matters related to prejudice and discrimination see, for instance, Duckitt (1994); Brown (1995); Jones (2002) and Nelson (2006).

Having explored the notion of hate vandalism, the following chapter rejects the orthodox, taken-for-granted criminological view that the private individual should be the focus of blame for anti-social vandalism. We begin with an assertion that the state has the capacity to act in a malevolent and profoundly anti-social way in its vandalism of the environment, and discuss how and why this is very rarely subject to the censure of vandalism.

Part IV

Cultural Criminology, the Anti-Social State and the Pro-Social Vandal

7
The Anti-Social and Vandalistic State

So much of orthodox criminology is built upon an uncritical acceptance of the black letter law notion that 'crime' is simply what the statute book says. Critical criminologists have reminded us that because of this there is an unhealthy focus on the activities of 'blue-collar' criminals rather than paying due attention to the crimes of the powerful. In this context the term 'vandal' is associated with the adolescent standing by a shop window armed with a brick in hand or the youth armed with a knife ready to slash car tyres. This chapter asks the question whether these sort of vandalistic practices pale into insignificance when compared to the abominations committed by the state in terms, for example, of environmental destruction and damage caused through warfare.

State crime and vandalism

The type of targeted and large-scale vandalistic practices which are referred to in this chapter are examples of what critical criminologists would refer to as crimes of the state. This vandalism is not random or sporadic; rather, it is often highly systematised and targeted, and conducted to achieve some political end. Whilst not being accidental, some of it, for example in warfare, may be 'collateral' in the sense that property destruction may be affected in order to achieve an ulterior goal such as the killing of human beings or the immobilisation of military bases.

State vandalism has to be contextualised with reference to the wider notion of a 'state crime', which according to Friedrichs (2000: 74), 'refers only to one major class of crimes that can be committed by those acting within a government.' As well as government, the notion of 'the state' is used by social scientists to talk about the executive and a range of public agencies. Increasingly since the 1980s, private sector agencies that support the government through funded contracts are subsumed under the notion of the state (see Doig, 2011). In articulating what he refers to as a 'traditionalist' state crime approach, Doig (2011) argued that much of 'state crime' may not actually be considered to be a crime because it is not contravening laws contained within the statute book. As Hillyard and Tombs (2007: 12) suggest that many of the kinds of social practices which will be articulated in this chapter 'are either not covered by criminal law or, if they could be or are encompassed within its ambit, are either ignored or handled without resort to it'. In discussing environmental vandalism and warfare, a far more helpful contribution to the debate on state crime would be the notion of 'state harm' which is offered by a variety of commentators. According to Matthews and Kauzlarich (2007: 51) this more inclusive definition of state crime, 'would include all behaviours for which no legal definition of criminality exists'.

This chapter specifically looks at a number of social practices which could be subsumed under the label of 'state vandalism'. Firstly, there is the kind of environmental vandalism and destruction which organisations such as Greenpeace do so much to protest about. The reason that this example has been selected for analysis is because, as environmental campaign groups themselves argue, this sort of destruction is routine, commonplace and occurs daily through the activities of the government, the military and big business. It is a common, taken-for-granted and often uncritically accepted side effect of capitalism. It is only when matters are brought to the public attention through the campaigning issues of certain groups like Greenpeace and Plane Stupid that it becomes an issue to be debated. Even then, very rarely is what occurs presented as a 'crime'.

Secondly, the issue of state vandalism during times of warfare is discussed in this chapter. The reasons for including examples which are subsumed under this label is because, firstly, unlike routine and daily environmental destruction, warfare is still perceived (at least by those of us in large parts of the Western world) to be an extraordinary event. Warfare is not presented as being or perceived as being by the majority of the population to be a 'normal' occurrence. There is the perception that we as a nation try to exist relatively harmoniously with our international counterparts and that times of conflict are relatively rare and to be avoided if possible unless the 'national security' is threatened in some way.

The chapter then moves on to consider state vandalism which is committed or justified in the name of sport. Having researched this book in the run-up to the 2012 Olympics, we feel that this is a pertinent issue to discuss at this particular time. The chapter takes a look at other global sporting events, most notably international football tournaments, to explore how property has been systematically destroyed and populations routinely displaced in order that a nation can present itself and its sporting festival in the best possible light to the watching world.

The chapter then progresses on to consider an issue which may on paper seem far less important than issues of environmental destruction, damage through warfare and even property and population displacements in the name of sporting festivities. This example is built on a case study of an issue which has had a local relevance over the past few years in the brewery town of Burton-on-Trent, which is home to the lead author of this text. What many see as the mildly amusing if not comical issue of cars being impaled on bollards in the town centre is considered as a potential case of state vandalism. The reason that this relatively innocuous example has been selected is that Chapter 3 clearly locates the motor vehicle as perhaps *the* most culturally significant target of vandalism today. Much of the vandalism of the motor vehicle described in that earlier chapter was attributed to the kind of 'drift delinquency' (Matza, 1964) which one associates with the passing phase of adolescence. In considering the example of 'illegally driven' cars being impaled by rising bollards, this example raises questions about the legitimacy of state agencies to engage in such social practices in order to prevent motoring offences.

So let us begin with an exploration of the routine, environmental vandalism caused by the state along with big business, and attempt to assess the harm committed in comparison with the 'blue-collar' vandal of the street.

Environmental vandalism

As an independent protest group, Greenpeace asserts that it is 'passionate about protecting the Earth'. A small group of activists founded Greenpeace in 1971, and over the last forty years has developed a global network of over 40 countries in order to attempt to realise a 'vision of a green and peaceful world'. They do this by investigating, documenting and exposing the causes of environmental destruction. By recourse to 'political lobbying, citizen action and consumer pressure' Greenpeace aims to take 'peaceful direct action' to promote sustainable solutions to environmental problems (Greenpeace, 2014a).

When the lead author spoke with two members of Greenpeace, this prompted the question as to whether tactics which periodically involve property destruction should be even be labelled as 'vandalism'. This produced the following response:

> The less it's seen as reckless behaviour the better. Whilst members of Greenpeace occasionally deliberately damage properly, we would reject the label of 'vandalism'.

Inherent in this answer is the distinction between the perception of certain acts of vandalism as being 'reckless', with other acts being more 'Careful, precise and justifiable'. The example of Kingsnorth was cited in terms of the painting of a slogan on the chimney and the shutting down of a plant so that it became non-operational. The example of the Edmonton incinerator was used to explain how a banner had been bolted onto the side of the façade. When being prosecuted in court, an expert witness described the damage done by Greenpeace as tantamount to 'fleas on a dog's back' and this contributed to the result in the return of a verdict of 'not guilty'. The notion of 'proportionality' was used by both respondents to explain the justification in 'disabling something causing damage' as was the case with heatproof sheeting used to shut an incinerator.

This issue was raised with another protester who had been involved with campaigns as diverse as Trident, Earth First and Plane Stupid, as well as Greenpeace. When asked whether he thought his actions should be labelled as 'vandalism', he responded that 'It depends on who is doing the labelling. It's normally people in power that want to hang onto it'. He moved on to suggest that the label was 'Similar to that label of being a "terrorist"'. The respondent raised the rhetorical question of 'How many artists have been labelled as vandals?' before revealing that at the East Midlands airport protest he was almost given a so-called 'CRASBO' or Criminal ASBO.

The two people from Greenpeace with whom we spoke were keen to explore the notion that the state is a 'vandal' in our conversations. They spoke about being at a protest at which they saw that operational police officers had illegally let down their car tyres. They spoke of their disappointment in 'trust being broken' despite an off-the-record apology from a police manager about the incident. Incidents of assault by police officers were recounted from abroad, with the statement being made that sometimes Greenpeace members dropped complaints against the police in the interests of the wider campaign. The example of Kingsnorth in Kent was cited, whereby the police used an angle grinder to help remove a protester. This was unreservedly felt to be 'criminal damage by the police'. It was recounted that 'sparks were flying everywhere onto high pressure hoses and storage pumps machines', with the respondent saying this could have endangered his own life. He asked the police where the risk assessment was for this, and could not believe a thorough risk assessment had been carried out. In the Kingsnorth case, the verdict returned was one of 'not guilty' to the charges of criminal damage on the grounds that the actions of Greenpeace protesters actually prevented more damage than they caused in terms of emissions from the plant giving rise to climate change through flooding, crop failures and drought. According to one Greenpeace member:

> This is a good example of the law determining that we were not vandals but the energy utility company Eon and the government licensing their operations were.

Evidence of state terrorism was alluded to by those whom we spoke with in Greenpeace, in terms of the French sinking of a Greenpeace vessel and the murder of a photographer.

Case study: state-sponsored vandalism

In 1985, the Greenpeace ship *Rainbow Warrior* was sunk in the South Pacific, off the coast of New Zealand. As well as the physical destruction of the boat, this led to the death of one person. Evidence began to emerge that the Greenpeace office in New Zealand had been infiltrated by the French secret service. Despite overwhelming evidence that this was a state-sponsored crime, the French government refused to apologise. Whilst being sentenced to ten years imprisonment, the two French agents served their sentences on a French military base in the Pacific (see Doig, 2011: 54–55).

The state was seen to be a 'vandal' to some extent, as highlighted by the Ecoside movement to highlight alleged crimes against the natural environment. The potential of the state to vandalise was additionally highlighted by the acid rain campaign of the early to mid-1980s, and reference was also made to the case of the so-called Fairford 3 in terms of the notion of committing a crime in an attempt to prevent the commission of an even greater crime. There were in fact six Fairford protesters (three independent groups of people) who had illegally entered an RAF base at Fairford in an attempt to 'immobilize' B52 bombers intended for use in the so-called war on terror in Iraq (see Greenpeace, 2014b). One of the people from Greenpeace to whom we spoke continued:

> In terms of damage, everyone we target is causing a lot more than we are. Sometimes this isn't understood because of temporal and geographic dislocation. For example, Kingsnorth power station emissions caused the tundra to melt and Bangladesh to flood years afterwards. Sometimes it isn't understood because the damage being caused doesn't have legal protection as private property or isn't able to be visualised like the atmosphere or deep oceans.

A constant theme of this book has been the challenging of the uncritically held assumption that all acts of vandalism are automatically 'anti-social'. This has permeated political discourse to the extent now that people often understand vandalism and anti-social behaviour to mean one and the same thing. Our two Greenpeace activists rejected the idea that the vandalism committed by members of their organisation was automatically 'anti-social'. A firm belief was expressed that the activities of Greenpeace involving 'vandalism' were done to achieve political progression for a more peaceful and sustainable world. This was borne of a conviction that one 'shouldn't exploit natural resources without limitations'. For those to whom we spoke this led to a firmly held belief that one had 'the moral right to act outside the law', and reference was made to historical figures like Mahatma Ghandi and Martin Luther King Jr. The following of the moral example set by these two individuals was accompanied by the statement that:

> As the behaviour we're objecting to is normally on a large scale and economically productive, and in some sense aberrant or a deviation from 'business as usual', the courts tend to look for a way to use the law to criminalise us. Whilst there is usually a law which seems to provide us with a strong defence on a common-sense reading, the courts will be looking for a technicality which makes the defence invalid.

With reference to the above, a 'blatantly illegal' war in Iraq was cited in the context whereby the court ruled that the legality of the war could not be considered by that very court, but that the individual actions of Greenpeace protesters could.

In trying to articulate how and why in certain contexts vandalism could be 'pro' rather than 'anti-social', the legal notion of 'proportionality' was invoked to highlight this point. It was felt that Greenpeace's 'non-violent and non-threatening approach' was distinct from the tactics used by other protest groups, such as those campaigning for animal rights. Whilst both of those to whom we spoke stressed that they did not wish to judge the tactics of other protest groups, reference was made to the tactics of the anti-aviation lobby group Plane Stupid, who threw a pie at Peter Mandelson. This was felt to be the kind of tactic which would not be used by Greenpeace. The following was said in relation to why Greenpeace activists were often easily labelled by the state:

> Our activists look more like the clichéd caricature of 'vandals', climbing on fences and painting on buildings they don't own, than the suited ministers and executives who cause destruction on an epic scale with the stroke of a pen.

This above is indicative of Bob Dylan's oft-quoted lyrics from his song 'Talkin' New York' (1962), in which he speaks about the ability of some to rob others with a fountain pen. The person to whom we spoke with campaigning experience across a plethora of protest groups emphasised the idea that protest which sometimes involved property damage was often pro-social. With reference to the 'common heritage of new social movements, in terms of the focus on the environment, peace and rights', he emphasised that 'We are pro-social in every possible way'. He added, 'I've got convictions that I will never see the benefits for, but they are pro-social and they have benefitted democracy'. He pointed to the work of 'Climate Rush' as a modern-day protest organisation which took the Pankhurst sisters and the suffragettes as an inspiration. This organisation had deliberately broken the window of a government building in order to replicate what the suffragettes did centuries before.

Having considered the relatively routine and even daily destruction of the environment by the state and big business, these could be considered as acts of collateral vandalism because the environment is being destroyed in the pursuit of capitalistic profit and acquisition.

The chapter now moves on to consider the often forgotten vandalism caused by nation-states when they embark on paths of warfare with each other. This again raises the question as to whether the real label of 'anti-social' should be applied to the pathological or 'deviant' young offender with the ASBO and customary electronic tag, or indeed whether acts of warfare are amongst *the* most anti-social acts in the history of mankind.

Warfare as state vandalism

World War II is the most expensive war in human history, and estimated to have cost between $1 and $2 trillion. Staggeringly the property damage alone amounted to in excess of $239 billion (US History, 2014). According to Steen (2008), the looting and destruction of cultural property is inseparably linked with warfare. Famously, the Napoleonic Wars were underpinned by the massive looting of property. In 1797 in Venice, for instance, Napoleon removed the famous winged bronze and lion horses and relocated them in the Arc de Triomphe.

Any account of property destruction during warfare cannot overlook the occurrences of the Great War between 1914 and 1918. During World War I, the cathedral of Reims in France was seriously damaged by German aerial bombing. Additionally, the library at the University of Louvain in Belgium was destroyed by fire. Critically it was this destruction of cultural rather than military targets which could be interpreted as 'state vandalism' because the former contravened the Hague Treaty of 2007, which dictated that such 'historical monuments' should be protected from warfare.

The level and cost of property destruction during World War II was alluded to earlier in this subsection, and between 1939 and 1945 the Germans actively destroyed works of art, churches and monuments in Poland. There was, for instance, the bombing of a monastery that housed the picture of Our Lady of Czestochowa. This place was both a shrine and a place of pilgrimage for Poles. Other synagogues were burnt and totally destroyed, with books and irreplaceable documentation being thrown onto fires. The Nazis also instigated hate vandalism, uprooting headstones from Jewish cemeteries and using them to pave roads (Steen, 2008).

Property destruction during warfare was not confined to the two Great Wars during the twentieth century. During the first Gulf War in the early 1990s, for example, several historical sites were damaged. In attempting to construct military bases, United States forces damaged archaeological sites at Tell al-Lahm and Tell al-Obeid in southern Iraq. At the end of the war, coalition forces including the British encouraged Kurds and Shiites to rebel against Saddam Hussein's government, and this resulted in the looting of the Iraqi National Museum. The more recent Gulf War has once again seen the coalition forces being responsible for the destruction of Iraqi property, according to Steen (2008). Aid workers in southern Iraq complained that they had witnessed accused American soldiers systematically vandalising the ancient city of Ur, which dates back to 4,000 BC and is thought to be the birthplace of Abraham of the Old Testament and the Torah. It was furthermore alleged that American troops spray-painted ruins of the ancient city and took property as souvenirs. In the more recent conflict following the war on terror' in 2006, United States Marines were condemned for damaging the city of Babylon after vibrations from helicopter propeller blades caused the roof of a building to collapse. Indeed one of the activists to whom we spoke passed comment that:

> The second war in Iraq was both immoral and illegal in terms of the citing of there being weapons of mass destruction. This is the greatest form of vandalism in the history of humankind.

Indeed the irony about the second Gulf War is the dubious claim made by both America and Britain that the war was somehow morally justifiable on the grounds that it was going to either prevent or at least reduce mass property destruction and killing – this was done, of course, through the assertion that Saddam Hussein was harbouring his own weapons of mass destruction. According to Prestowitz (2004: 239), the citing of weapons of mass destruction as a reason for military intervention was merely a bad faith excuse to 'demonstrate American power and the willingness to use it'. Reasserting America's prowess as a 'global policeman', 'needed a target, and Saddam was perfect' (ibid.).

As well as the military use of bombing, it is also the use of fire which has historically caused so much damage to both environment and property in countries during times of conflict. In this context, the actions of the lone arsonist determined to light a match and torch his or her old school building as an act of 'revenge' rather pales into insignificance. A notorious example of this was the widespread military practice of burning villages during the Vietnam War (for a fuller discussion on this and related issues, see Belknap, 2002). The war in Vietnam galvanised and focused an entire generation in protest not only against the war itself but against what Dylan described as the 'Masters of War' in his 1963 hit, which surely was directed at the corporate-sponsored US administration that waged this appalling conflict. According to Sumner (1994: 252), 'corporate, militarised America was failing at what it was supposed to do best – social control'. The morality of that war divided society, and intensified and fed resistance on both sides of the Atlantic.

Cohen (1973: 44) asserted that 'the use of property destruction as a form of revenge is an extremely important sub-type of vandalism', but when considering 'state vandalism', this 'revenge' takes on a far more politicised and organised agenda than the spurned girlfriend who enacts revenge of her former lover by keying his beloved car. As well as destruction in the name of vengeance, Cohen's (1973) original notion of 'tactical vandalism' can also be stretched and applied in the context of modern warfare. Cohen (1973: 43) told us that this type of vandalism 'is a conscious tactic used to advance some end other than acquiring money or property' (ibid.: 43).

In relating the above back to the context of the Vietnam War, as American troops were struggling to win the war in Vietnam, locating and destroying the enemy proved more than difficult as the Vietnamese resistance were adept at hiding both themselves and their weapons amongst the civilian population. This can be explained due to demographics in that the majority of the Vietnamese population lived in rural villages and hamlets, and they were able to build a sophisticated network of underground tunnels in which arms, explosives and other light ordinance could be concealed. From an American perspective, therefore, the prevailing logic seemed to be that the most efficient way of eradicating possible enemy hideouts was to raze these very villages to the ground by obliterating them.

Two events stand out in that bloody conflict from the 1960s and 1970s which are pertinent to our contemporary analysis of vandalism. The first was the controversial report filed by Morley Safer for the American news agency CBS in 1965, following his visit to the village of Cam Ne. His report was broadcast to millions of the American public and undoubtedly helped shift public perceptions of the war. The report contained the now iconic image of an American GI holding his Zippo lighter to the thatched roof of a village dwelling and setting it alight. Then-American president Lyndon B. Johnson apparently accused the Canadian reporter of being a 'Communist' who had proverbially 'shat on the American flag' (see Safer, 1991). This is a prime example of both political and hate vandalism, sponsored by the US state. This was driven by hate-motivated revenge, according to Safer, for the loss of US marines caught in a firefight in and near the Cam Ne village. Whilst there will always remain a degree of ambiguity as to the exact nature of events leading to the village's being destroyed (see Moll, 2014), the evidence overwhelmingly suggests that the village was subject to a 'search and destroy' mission by American troops using Zippo lighters to light huts that were as dry as kindling. The specific use of the Zippo as an instrument to start fires was recounted by Private First Class Reginald 'Malik' Edwards, who recalled, 'When you say level a village, you don't use torches. It's not like in the 1800s. You use a Zippo. That's just the way we did it. You went in there with your Zippos. Everybody. That's why people bought Zippos. Everybody had a Zippo. It was for burnin 'shit down' (see Terry, 1984).

The so-called Zippo raids gained further infamy on 16 March 1968 in one of the worst wartime atrocities since the Nazi death camps took place. As frustration and anger spiralled at their own impotence in the face of an unexpectedly highly determined and skilled Vietnamese enemy, US troops marched into My Lai, a village suspected of harbouring Viet Cong troops, sympathisers and weapons. Under express orders to burn, kill and destroy, what followed were four hours of slaughter, resulting in the death of over 500 unarmed Vietnamese men, women and children, according to Vietnamese government sources. Appallingly, it emerged that women had been gang raped, and that the bodies of some of the dead had been subject to further mutilation. Whilst some 26 soldiers were originally charged with the commission of criminal offences surrounding the atrocity, only one of them, namely platoon leader Lieutenant William Calley Jr. was actually convicted. Despite being found guilty for his role in the death of 22 defenceless villagers and despite being handed down a life sentence, in reality Calley served a mere three and a half years under house arrest.

When called before Congress in 1971, helicopter pilot Hugh Thompson said he'd seen GIs setting light to the village with their Zippos as the killing started and then spread. Thompson landed his helicopter between the marauding GIs and a group of cowering Vietnamese civilians, and his efforts are believed to have saved the lives of at least ten Vietnamese civilians. This act of extreme bravery earned Thompson and his crew years of vilification by unknown attackers on the grounds of his lack of 'patriotism'. It wasn't until the late 1980s that Thompson was not only completely vindicated but elevated as the embodiment of the US military (CBS News, 2006). Whilst Thompson had to deal with hate mail, Zippo, founded by George G. Blaisdell in 1932, went from strength to strength as an iconic cultural artefact. In a classic case of objects associated with criminality becoming commodified for capitalistic profit, Buchanan and Edwards (2007) attest the cigarette lighter's history and rise to iconic cultural status, through the practice of the personalised engraving of the lighters, which became common practice during the Vietnam War itself. They chart the image shift of the Zippo from that of a weapon of destruction during war to a more personalised symbol of politics and belief. The engravings found on Zippos were testaments of allegiance, cultural signposts to personal tastes in music and choice of drug. For instance, many were found with marijuana leaves embossed upon the Zippo jacket. Perhaps the most ubiquitous and axiomatic quote found by Buchanan and Edwards (2007) amongst the GIs' Zippos was 'We're the unwilling led by the unqualified doing the unnecessary for the ungrateful'.

A more recent example which helps us to forge a deeper understanding of vandalism in times of war is that from Yugoslavia in the 1990s. It would appear that Yugoslavia's rapid and bloody decent into civil war presented a confusing array of motivations as village after village picked up arms against each other, after having seemingly lived in peaceful coexistence with each other for decades without the worst excesses of violent conflict (see Denich, 1994).

Communism in Eastern European countries gave way after protesters won a long battle for democratic change during the autumn of 1989 and after the so-called fall of the Iron Curtain. Communist Yugoslavia ceased to exist in 1992, and for the next seven years the country would be ravaged by war. Instances of genocide, not seen since World War II would shock the world, and with this war the notion of 'ethnic cleansing' entered the political lexicon. This conflagration was compounded further by the geographical spread of the religious and ethnic diversity of its population, which Denich described as an 'ethnic mosaic' (1994). As with the aforementioned Vietnam War, this conflict embodied more than simply the capturing of strategic locations and the killing of enemies because it involved the destruction of cultural identity through the vandalism of culturally specific artefacts (Chapman, 1994).

Due to the obvious horrors of killing and maiming people in war, the vandalism of cultural artefacts is often overlooked, and it is possible to inadvertently dismiss the massive symbolic effect that both systematised and targeted property destruction has during times of conflict. Indeed, Chapman (1994: 120) summarises the political significance of destroying monuments as thus, 'Cultural identity in this "ethnic shatter-belt", is forged through the association with the monuments and artefacts of past ancestors…. In such a landscape, heavy with ancestral symbolism, a war could hardly be anything but a question of culture'. In taking account of the above, it becomes easy to understand the author's point that the destruction of both people and symbolic property become intertwined and inseparable in many ways. In practical terms the wholesale removal and destruction of people's cultural artefacts went hand in hand with their subjection to imprisonment, rape and ultimately murder. The vandalism of property itself is of such symbolic significance because these very artefacts embodied a nation's connection with an historical past and the landscape of its territory. For this reason, Yugoslavia's civil war witnessed the loss of some of the finest Islamic architecture in

Europe. In Foca, for instance, an act of specifically targeted vandalism saw the oldest mosque in Bosnia, built in 1448, purposefully destroyed (ibid.: 121). As well as the targeting of places of religious worship, acts of vandalism characteristic of hate, saw the targeting of cemeteries for eradication (see also Appleseed, 1994).

Through utilisation of the ethnographic method, Bax (1997) was able to articulate the underlying rationale for the destruction of a local monument whose existence respected the dead, at a place named Surmanci. It was at this location that local Serbs chose to remember where their forefathers were massacred in 1941. This where the Croats fighting for Adolf Hitler applied the Nazi mandate to 'remove' Serbs as well as Jews and Gypsies. One of the interviewees in this ethnography attempted to rationalise efforts to vandalise and ultimately destroy this monument, recalling stunningly, 'We killed the dead, because they kept them alive' (Bax, 1997: 11). The sheer extent of the deliberate and purposeful vandalism of culturally significant buildings, monuments, cemeteries and other such symbolic artefacts during the Balkans conflict has unbelievably been equated to the equivalent of the burning down of every second parish church and cathedral throughout Britain (Appleseed, 1994).

Two decades earlier, Pol Pot's brutal leadership of Cambodia through the years 1975–1979 presided over the destruction and vandalism of representations of modern intellectual thought and other modes of cultural expression. The destruction was devastatingly all embracing. In many ways, life for Cambodians under Pol Pot's Khmer Rouge was not dissimilar to life in Goffman's (1961) 'ideal type' of dystopian 'total institution'. Pol Pot's autocratic regime not only dictated what to wear, eat, sing and with whom to have relationships but most appallingly how they were to die (Robben, 2010). Such was the nature of the exertion of social control over the indigenous people of Cambodia, together with the speed of change, that by 1976 Cambodia was almost completely sealed off in terms of its divorce from the outside world (Railsback, 1990). The mere act of wearing eyeglasses, relatively innocuous in our culture, in 1970s Cambodia, for instance, 'identified' and labelled one as being a member of the educated middle class. From Pol Pot's perspective, these people were members of the 'dangerous' classes and had to be 'eliminated' because they were perceived as a potential political threat. This seemingly innocent act of being bespectacled might have led to summary execution (see Edwards, 2004). One of the most famous of the Western observers was Sydney Schanberg who, writing for the *New York Times*, accurately predicted that the Khmer Rouge would 'kill all educated people, the teachers, the artists, the intellectuals' (cited in Clymer, 2003: 248).

Whilst the atrocities of the holocaust committed in Cambodia have been well documented, as with our previous treatment of the Vietnam War, these historical accounts of the horrors can often overlook the part played by vandalism in paving the way for the annihilation of some of the aforementioned classes of peoples. In June 1970, for example, the site of Angkor, which covers 400 square kilometres and is located in the northwest of the country, was invaded by the Khmer Rouge (Dauge, 1997). This site witnessed the deliberate desecration of many bronze and ceramic sculptures. Soldiers deliberately damaged images of the Buddha as part of the wider censure and denigration of the Buddhist religion, and in certain cases dynamite was used to great effect. According to Dauge (1997: 172), 'the destruction of cultural heritage is used as a means to annihilate a people's identity, to negate its history, memory and beliefs'.

Having considered the often overlooked extent of property destruction during times of warfare, one can see that these social practices can be subsumed under our twin notions of both 'political' and 'hate' vandalism. The vandalism is political because it is committed for a strategic end, ordinarily to gain some territorial advantage or alternatively to prevent some territorial loss, as was the case with the classic 'domino theory', as originally coined by US president Dwight D. Eisenhower on 7 April 1954, which was posited as a reason for America to intervene in Vietnam in order to prevent the spread of the 'red menace' of Communism. The vandalism is similarly of a 'hate' variety because its victims are often said to 'deserve' their fate because they are presented as 'the enemy' who are part of a cancerous problem which needs to be eradicated. Hate vandalism on a massive scale occurs because the victims are presented as being 'subhuman'.

So having looked at the devastating nature of property destruction during times of war and conflict, we now turn our attention to something which on paper celebrates what should be the very best of human nature, creativity and self-expression – namely, sport. As we shall see, 'state-sponsored vandalism' lurks beneath the public image of athletic success and fair play.

State vandalism in the name of sport

One can see what is effectively 'state-sponsored vandalism' occurring under the far more euphemistic name of 'urban regeneration' in post-industrial cities due to their desire to reinvent themselves as entertainment destinations and urban spectacles (Kearns and Philo, 1993; Broudehoux, 2007) in order to generate productive capital. What is often overlooked and not made transparent in terms of its appearance in the public domain is that the political process which oversees such projects is often responsible for the destruction of thousands of properties together with the morally dubious practice of the forced evictions and displacement of significant numbers of individuals each year.

Following the success of London 2012, it is not difficult to see how hosting global 'mega-events' such as the Football World Cup or the Olympic Games is considered as the ultimate prize in boosting both the global visibility and the status of a city, and that the winning of the right to host such events is often the catalyst for large-scale developments which are disruptive to the local population and which impact adversely on property within that geographical area. Broudehoux (2007) suggests that in order to facilitate such developments, the state works to reduce the level of public scrutiny it would normally receive, which in turn enables plans to be 'fast-tracked' through the planning and development stages of the respective projects, this giving a degree of legitimacy to the eviction of thousands of individuals by using the utilitarian 'it's all for the public good' kind of argument. With specific reference to the Beijing Olympics, Ocheje (2007) articulates how this was the process adopted by the Chinese government to evict over 400,000 Beijing residents in order to build the infrastructure and facilities required to host the 2008 Games. In continuing this theme, Ong (2004) reported that government planners regarded the preservation of heritage as an 'obstacle to progress.' Thus amongst other things, the Beijing Olympics resulted in the destruction of the Qianmen neighbourhood (Qing dynasty, 1644–1911), which had been identified as one of 25 areas of Bejjing which was designated for preservation on historical grounds.

One should not overlook the social class issues raised by decisions of various states to destroy property for the purpose of 'development' in the name of 'sport'. Wherever displacement for so-called 'mega' sporting events occurs, those affected tend to be in the poorer parts of cities which house the most disempowered members of that community. States tend to rationalise and justify their actions through 'platitudes about displacement for "urban regeneration" being offered by policymakers and planning practitioners' (Porter, 2009: 395). Porter's argument is underpinned by the offering of a diverse range of empirical data via case studies from London, Glasgow and Vancouver, where displacements have occurred as a result of either Olympic or Commonwealth Games events being held in those aforementioned cities. One of the commonalities across all such cities was the regeneration and subsequent 'gentrification' of the area, which effectively meant the displacement of the households. The scandal is that such displacements are simply often overlooked by the wider resident population because these state actions are not seen in the popular imagination to be acts of vandalism or to be anti-social. One example of this is that research centred upon the hosting of the 2006 World Cup found that a considerable proportion of residents were interested in the potential benefits of urban regeneration rather than having concerns with displacements (Ohmann et al., 2006).

A similar process occurred with the staging of the Sochi Winter Olympic Games in Russia in 2014. With an urban population of about 350,000, Sochi's transformation into an Olympic village also meant knocking down some of the city that was already there. With the games now passed, this did lead to the eviction and forced relocation of some residents. In Rio de Janeiro, the host of the 2016 Olympic Summer Games as well as the 2014 FIFA World Cup, similar displacements have been rising. There have been media reports concerning thousands of evictions in the city, not just in the Olympic zone but in the city's numerous slum areas (Berg, 2011).

The above has explored the devastating levels of state destruction of property caused by routine destruction of the environment, or in more specific and targeted instances of warfare, and in state preparations for global sporting events. In addition, albeit on a lesser scale, one should not forget that the state is routinely involved in damaging a range of property which belongs to private citizens. In Chapter 3, we considered that vandalism is not random and unfathomable, but rather it is targeted against specific cultural objects. You will recall that this chapter chose to focus on the vandalism of motor vehicles committed by private individuals in acts typically against other private individuals. The next subsection turns this equation on its head by considering the routine and 'taken for granted' damage, if not destruction, of the motor vehicle committed by the state against private individuals.

State 'vandalism' of cars

As a measure to regulate and monitor the flow of traffic, it has to be acknowledged that rising bollards are a relatively recent development in the United Kingdom. They are legislated for under Sections 92 (outside London) and 94 (London) of the Road Traffic Regulation Act of 1984. Bollards may be fixed and stationary, or moveable, and are designed so as to prevent vehicles passing at certain times. According to black letter law, rising bollards are lawful if they prevent the passage of vehicles where a traffic order prohibits this (see Department for Transport, 2015). This is the first major point to consider when attempting to assess whether the term 'vandalism' is an appropriate descriptor of what state agencies are practising in the name of traffic regulation and road safety. It is because it is underpinned by the statute book that at first glance, to talk about this being an instance of the state's being 'vandal' or 'anti-social' seems absurd.

This issue has received attention in the national press for the best part of a decade or so. In a *Daily Mail* article which appeared on 19 October 2006, entitled 'Drivers Fail to Beat the Bollards' (Daily Mail, 2006b), it was, for instance, reported that CCTV cameras had filmed a number of 'cheeky drivers' taking on and being defeated by the infamous rise-and-fall road bollards of Manchester. This was following the installation of three-foot-high barriers which rise and sink into the street to allow Metroshuttle buses through. Ironically, it was claimed that these barriers had been installed to help combat the area's high road casualty rate.

In a classic case of the commodification of crime, video footage taken from closed circuit television cameras in Manchester showed the driver of one 4x4 vehicle hitting his head during the impact before his wife dashed out of the car to check on the safety of their toddler strapped in the back seat. In another clip, a white van driver hit his head so violently that the windscreen smashed (Daily Mail, 2006b; YouTube, 2009). In the latter of these two YouTube clips, images of real-life drivers being 'spiked' and injured is played to a style of music depicting comedy and joy. This voyeuristic presentation of 'dumb' drivers ignores some of the very real human consequences of the actions of state agencies in this respect. One has to raise the legal notion of 'proportionality' in this context. Is it proportionate to potentially risk the health and safety of human beings, most notably minors, for the sake of pursuing a traffic regulation and management strategy?

In the lead author's hometown of Burton-on-Trent, a bollard system was introduced in November 2008 which was jointly funded by the Staffordshire County Council and the East Staffordshire Borough Council at an estimated cost of £200,000 (Burton Mail, 2008). This system was designed to block access for vehicles between 10am and 4pm, with access being blocked for vehicles between 10am and 4pm, except for buses, taxis with disabled access, emergency services, High Street residents and licensed traders. Despite a 400-name petition being sent to the then-Burton MP, Janet Dean, the bollard scheme was not scrapped. The irrationality of this state-sponsored vandalism is highlighted by the fact that in the 21 weeks since the project began, 54 drivers had fallen victim to the bollards. It was estimated that in this initial phase after bollard installation, the county council's highways response team spent approximately £10,000 to clean up fuel spillages and broken glass (Burton Mail, 2009a).

In May 2009, a new registered black Peugeot 207 was impaled on a bollard with the front bumper of the car being smashed off, with oil spread over the road. Passenger Pete Colley, from Lichfield, whose wife, Beth, was driving the car at the time, complained that had the vehicle gone forward just a few more inches, the bollard would have smashed up through the footwell and into the legs of his nine-year-old son. He claimed, 'If my wife had driven forward just a few more inches, that could have broken my son's legs'. Despite the potential injury to an innocent young child, then-Staffordshire County Council member Peter Beresford, who represented the Burton division, claimed that motorists were to blame for accidents involving the bollards. In dismissing the potential for injury, he said, 'It's people's bad driving that's causing the problem. Motorists shouldn't tailgate anything. It's simple – if you try and get in, the bollards come up. If people just followed the Highway Code there shouldn't be a problem' (Burton Mail, 2009b). This attempt to further responsibilise private citizens for their 'inattentive' or 'reckless' actions further legitimises the capacity of the state to incur damage and destruction to these offending motor vehicles. By March 2014, Staffordshire County Council revealed that it had spent more than £100,000 in damage repairs and maintenance since 2009 (Burton Mail, 2014). At the time of writing, following a funding row between county and borough councils, the bollards are non-operational at present (Burton Mail, 2015).

So having outlined the argument that the state can indeed be profoundly anti-social and vandalistic, the task remains to begin to make sense of why this may be so.

Theorising the anti-social state

If one draws upon Marxist theory, one can clearly see that law as a set of ideologies is designed to serve the interests of the ruling classes in society. Rather than uncritically accepting state definitions of crime, according to Hirst (1975: 204), the task of critical criminology is 'to question the nature of laws and values as the property of that establishment'. Critical criminology tells us that the application of the criminal law means that it tends to be so-called 'blue-collar' street crimes which are the focus of the state's attention rather than the abuses of power of the state itself. In returning explicitly to the theme of warfare which shaped much of the early thinking in this chapter, according to Cowling (2008: 39), 'Many Iraqis are victims of Tony Blair's war crimes, but it will not show up in the Home Office surveys because the Home Office does not ask the question and its surveys do not extend to Iraq'.

In terms of the notion of 'proportionality', when one considers the amount of property destruction and human misery caused by the examples cited in this chapter, then there would appear to be far more grave issues in the world compared to 'typical' offences of vandalism which may include broken car wing mirrors and stolen traffic cones. In the 1980s, the newly constituted left realists such as Matthews and Young (1992) were right to remind us that low-level vandalism and what we now refer to as 'anti-social behaviour' did tend to be committed by predominantly disempowered working-class individuals, critically against other working-class people. Whilst low-level vandalism and 'anti-social behaviour' have to be taken seriously as and when they blight the lives of working people in communities across the country, the issue remains that they are quite simply 'small beer' compared to the kind of corporate and state-led criminality which so often involves routine property destruction. In espousing the virtues of a radical criminology, Cowling (2008: 205) proclaimed that 'there is every indication that corporate and white-collar crime is much larger and much more damaging than street crime'.

The vandalism and anti-social practices referred to in this chapter are not 'minor' by any stretch of the imagination. Events such as the Vietnam War have shaped history, and the Olympic Games and the World Cup in soccer remain of massive cultural and commercial significance. It is entirely different from the 'exploratory' vandalism of the stone-throwing nine-year-old who randomly throws peddles at the proverbial greenhouse. It is not the same thing as the 'drift' vandalism of the adolescent gang who kick the odd car wing mirrors off as they return home after a Friday night 'session' at their local. The kind of state vandalism articulated in this chapter is most definitely underpinned by sectional political ideology – in the 'serious' cases of war – in terms of what is to be regarded as 'collateral damage' in the pursuit of 'national interest' or in defence of 'national security'. In cases of environmental destruction, it is both political and ideological in the sense that short-term capitalistic profit is clearly thought to be more important than long-term environmental sustainability. In these cases the destruction requires organisational motivation. In the case of war, the property damage is ordinarily driven by the kind of hatred of 'the other' which we explored in Chapter 6, and this 'otherness' is used to legitimate acts of hate vandalism on an enormous scale, which often have a truly global impact. At the other end of the spectrum, the kind of property destruction cited in the case study of the car bollards in the brewery town of Burton-on-Trent, is of a 'collateral' nature, as we explored in Chapter 5.

Having turned the 'common-sense' view of vandalism and anti-social behaviour on its head and in challenging the conventional wisdom which wrongly assumes that the vandal is always a private actor or group of actors who have a grievance against other individuals or the state, this chapter has demonstrated that the destructive acts of the state deserve in some instances to be labelled as both 'vandalistic' and 'anti-social' at least as much if not more so than some of the examples cited in the earlier chapters of this book. Having made this point, Chapter 8 moves on to consider that many vandalisms committed by individuals and collectivities can actually be 'pro-social' in attempting to challenge the 'anti-social' practices of the state.

8
The Pro-Social Political Vandal

In his original typology of vandalism, Cohen (1973: 35) referred to 'ideological vandalism' as that which is perpetrated with the intention of furthering a particular cause or political issue. In referring to a 'science of ideas', the French Enlightenment philosopher and aristocrat Destutt de Tracy (1754–1836) was one of the first to use both the notion and term 'ideology'. His *Eléments d'idéologie* (1817–1818) was foundational in terms of future social scientific work around shared belief systems and culturally taken for granted assumptions (see Hart, 2008). Indeed Emmet (1979: 355) maintained that the 'science of ideas' was the first 'science' and that all other science would spring forth from the pivotal notion of 'ideology', including conceptions of logic, grammar, education and morality. The overarching goal of ideology was to offer some kind of regulation of society.

Ideologies are cognitive belief systems which critically become shared amongst certain socially and culturally identifiable groups of people. These systems of belief exist primarily at the level of discourses about the way in which the world is perceived and social reality is presented. These shared discourses do not always translate into political action – they can remain at the level of thought or speech. It is precisely because vandalism or, more precisely, 'vandalisms', involve *actions* through social practices of physical and material destruction, that we feel that Cohen's (1973) original notion of 'ideological vandalism' needs to be superseded by the more appropriate term 'political vandalism'. This term is more appropriate as vandalism is more than just a thought. It involves action. In his book *Lost People,* the controversial American anthropologist and political activist David Graeber (2007: 13) defined political action as:

> That which is meant to influence others who are not physically present when the action is being done. This is not to say it can't

> be intended to influence people who are physically present; it is to say its effects are not limited to that. It is action that is meant to be recounted, narrated, or in some way represented to other people afterward.

What is interesting about this definition in terms of its application to politically motivated vandalism is, firstly, the notion that politically motivated actions are designed to influence others who could potentially become politicised. Acts of political vandalism tends to be designed to exert pressure on (a) those who are in some way associated with the 'target' – an 'offending' state agency or a business corporation, for example. Alternatively, it could be designed to influence (b) members of the public or a broader audience who were unaware of the political cause being promoted. Additionally it could be undertaken to attempt to raise public awareness and galvanise (c) existing supporters of the cause who may be inclined to get involved in protest or to take their existing protesting practices to a deeper or more committed of participation.

There are many examples both contemporary and historical of the practice of what we have termed political vandalism. We have deliberately chosen to focus on a range of organisations and informal associations of people who have engaged in these activities from the 1970s onwards in order to offer an historical perspective forged over several decades. We begin by revisiting an organisation which we briefly reflected upon in the last chapter in terms of its commitment to environmental protest and which has sometimes resulted in property destruction.

Greenpeace

In order for us to understand acts of political vandalism, they must be located in their socio-political context; therefore, we delve a little deeper here than we did in the last chapter when we briefly looked at some of the responses made by Greenpeace to what it perceived as anti-social and vandalistic actions of the state. To understand the politically motivated acts of vandalism which are periodically and systematically carried out by an organisation like Greenpeace, one has to return to a 1970s United States which was in political turmoil over the rapidly turning tide over the legitimacy of the Vietnam War, which was again discussed in the previous chapter. After US president Richard 'Tricky Dicky' Nixon defied the requests of several countries, including Japan and Sweden, by allowing his Atomic Energy Agency to explode hydrogen bombs on an island off the north coast of Alaska, people began to protest more aggressively against the crimes of the powerful (Marullo and Meyer, 2004). The forerunner to Greenpeace, Stop the Wave was eventually successful in gathering and harnessing an adequate level of public support to persuade Nixon to drop land-based nuclear bomb tests. During this era, an air of optimism arose that political action could both influence and ultimately change society, and bring about a more equitable and morally just world.

Following the Stop the Wave campaign, Greenpeace began to take a stand for positive change through orchestrating action in the areas of climate change, ancient forests, toxic chemicals, genetically modified organisms and nuclear disarmament (Greenpeace, 2014a). Nevertheless, as we observed in the previous chapter, it is an organisation which has often been accused of what Cohen (1973) termed 'ideological vandalism' and whose members have faced criminal damage charges and been willing to go to prison for their beliefs. For example, in 2010, six Greenpeace activists admitted causing criminal damage to a coal-fired power station at Kingsnorth in Kent by daubing the words 'Gordon' in paint down a chimney as a protest against EON's plans to expand by building a bigger coal-fired station next to the present one. On this occasion, the six were acquitted by a jury on the grounds that they were justified in damaging property in order to attempt to prevent wider environmental damage across the world (Clover, 2008). Without doubt this is a very interesting verdict by the jury to which we will refer below.

Since the 1960s, Greenpeace (together with the World Wildlife Fund) has mounted a sustained attack on genetically modified (GM) foods and genetically modified technologies (Huffman et al., 2004), and the campaign group has reputedly pledged to either remove all GM crops from the ground or support those who take action to remove GM crops. As such, Greenpeace is embroiled in a highly controversial and scientifically complex debate with the commercial food industry, various governments and the Royal Society of Medicine, to name just a few. The attack mounted by Greenpeace was on two fronts: firstly, they targeted the possible environmental costs involved, and secondly, they addressed the unknown effects that consuming GM products may have on human beings. At the turn of the millennium, Greenpeace activists were involved in practices labelled as 'vandalism' by the state authorities when they attempted to sabotage a biotech crop field in London, and in 2003 activists sabotaged a GM wheat crop in Germany (see Consumer Freedom, 2014). These are significant incidents when one considers that Greenpeace cofounder Dr Patrick Moore left the organisation in the mid-1980s after it became apparent that the group were becoming more militant. Without credible scientific arguments the organisation lacked the legitimacy to engage with the 'enemy' through direct action, which was, according to Dr Moore, only part of the solution anyway. This is interesting in that many would be charitable in viewing the vandalistic acts of Greenpeace as being politically progressive in terms of serving the 'greater good' and a higher ideal. This public support, however, seems to wane when prominent figures like Moore begin to criticise the tactics of an organisation from within, and there is a real danger that what are inherently 'political' acts of vandalism could be relabelled and ultimately censured by others as merely vindictive or hateful acts, and where an appeal to 'politics' and the 'greater good' is invoked merely as a lame excuse.

During the course of our conversations with members of Greenpeace, the question was posed as to whether the state should have the legitimate power to condemn some of the actions which the organisation takes through recourse to the criminal justice system. Whilst one person who we spoke to at Greenpeace stated that sometimes 'you will have bad laws', there was a degree of acceptance that the state has the right to make laws which prohibit some of the organisation's activities. The notion of needing to 'commit a crime to prevent a greater crime taking place' was raised, and one of the activists noted that whether offences result in a conviction or acquittal had 'a lot to do with the timing of case', clearly suggesting that there is a political dimension to decisions made by juries.

When our discussions turned to the issue of whether the label of 'vandalism' was an appropriate one to be attached to some of the activities engaged in by Greenpeace, an activist recounted a story about a group of middle-class students who had trashed a restaurant. Not only were these people not apprehended and processed through the criminal justice system, but when reporting her outrage at the occurrence to the local newspaper, the waitress from the restaurant was allegedly dismissed. What passes for vandalism, it was suggested, depends very much on the (often politically motivated) eye of the beholder. Much of the so-called vandalism in which Greenpeace was involved was felt to be 'almost incidental', with property damage described as an 'ancillary activity', and it was certainly 'never mindless'. An interesting perception of a disparity between international and domestic law was raised with the view that 'we are often covered by international law but our courts don't comply' being expressed.

The ability to 'take the rough with the smooth' and be willing to accept administered punishment when necessary was acknowledged, with the example of the whitewashing of the gates of Downing Street as a response to the Hutton Report into the issues surrounding the apparent suicide of Dr David Kelly, a former UN weapons inspector in Iraq and acknowledged expert on biological warfare. 'We took the conviction and we needed the photo opportunity', it was said by a Greenpeace member. So sometimes the publicity generated by being processed through the criminal justice system was thought to be beneficial in terms of furthering the aims of the organisation.

When we enquired as to whether the state should have the power to censure some of the things which political protesters do, through recourse to the criminal justice system, a protester who had not only been involved with Greenpeace but also with a whole range of protest movements such as Trident, Earth 1st and Plane Stupid offered a significant comment. 'It is a question of balanced judgements', he said. The legitimacy of the criminal justice system was thus accepted by these protesters within reason, and again there was reference to the use of 'the label'. With specific reference to the Norfolk crops protest, this activist observed that some fellow protesters preferred the term 'decontamination' rather than 'criminal damage', and stressed the importance of the punitive measures being administered being both 'proportionate and accountable'. Importantly the respondent expressed a degree of 'confidence in the jury system' and the inherent notion that one's actions are being judged by one's peers. In the case of the Norfolk crops protest, a not guilty verdict was returned, as we saw above, and this decision had given this activist some confidence that acts of civil disobedience could be protected by juries.

We asked our respondents whether the activities in which they had engaged were in anyway comparable to the type of 'malicious' vandalism described by Cohen (1973), an example of which would be the apparently 'mindless' and deeply anti-social act of smashing up a bus shelter. Interestingly, certain forms of vandalism were seen to be profoundly 'pro' rather than 'anti'-social, and some were accorded the status of works of art, with one respondent being a professed fan of Banksy, the renowned graffiti artist discussed elsewhere in this book. Having said this, acts of what we have referred to as drift vandalism (see Chapter 2), such as 'daubing one's name on a medieval church', were felt to be inappropriate and fully deserving of the label of vandalism, and dealt with appropriately by the criminal justice system.

The discussion then turned to the creative use of the social practice of 'reverse graffiti' by Greenpeace – referred to as 'Cleanpeace' (see Chapter 10 for a fuller discussion of this type of phenomenon) – in terms of their use of a jet washer to get messages across. Whilst arrests have been made for this activity, it was reported that ordinarily people have tended to be released without charge. Those to whom we spoke were keen to stress that 'our credibility and our logo are everything'. They were keen not to allow their ethos of peaceful, non-violent protest to be hijacked by those with other agendas, and they cited the example of an anti-4 by 4 protest, which they believed had gone beyond the goals of a particular Greenpeace campaign and had indeed brought the organisation into disrepute.

The activist with a more diverse range of protest experience commented that the label 'vandalism' was often problematic. For example, his car had been damaged by a mentally ill person, and he had found the label of vandalism to be unhelpful in those circumstances. He felt that he himself had been labelled as a 'terrorist' for being involved in a road camp protest. 'I have been labelled as a domestic extremist', he commented, which he felt was a 'cheap politician's jibe', before observing that 'vandalism has a narrative behind it'.

A second example of political vandalism which sought to be pro-social involved the case of women peace campaigners who staged a protest against the importation of nuclear cruise missiles at the Greenham Common airbase in Berkshire (BBC News, 2000a).

The Greenham Common women

Taking their lead from the Greenpeace movement, in September 1981 the Greenham Common Women's Peace Camp was set up following the decision of some 36 women to take the ten-day march 120 odd miles from their homes in south Wales to Berkshire to voice their protest at the decision of the United States to work with the British government in storing cruise missiles at the air base. The women managed to capture the media spotlight back in the early 1980s, and gained quite considerable public support by chaining themselves to the perimeter fence of the site and demanding the government consult with them to address their protest (BBC News, 1999). By August 1982, some 30,000 women had arrived at Greenham Common, and increasing numbers of them were getting arrested and imprisoned during acts of protest. Some actions which were criminalised, for example, lying down in front of lorries, were dealt with by public order legislation, but some acts were dealt with as cases of vandalism. Offences charged under the Criminal Damage Act 1971 included the threading of paper doves to signify 'peace' into the perimeter fence and the use of bolt croppers to attempt to cut through the wire fencing of the airbase. The protest lasted exactly 19 years, until September 2000.

Once again these protests have to be situated and understood in the political context in which they occurred. The Greenham Common group was protesting at a time when there had been a radical shift from a period of relative political consensus to a period of conflict politics introduced by the first Thatcher administration in 1979 (see Clarke and Newman, 1997). This was a time when very widely supported campaigns for both unilateral and multilateral disarmament were in existence, and there was a wide degree of scepticism about the perceived willingness to engage in the kind of overseas conflict which would lead to considerable loss of both British and Argentinian life in the Falklands Conflict of 1982.

In more recent and so-called postmodern times, partly due to the growth of the Internet and the inherent improvement in the speed of communication, protest which has had a vandalistic component has taken on more of an international dimension.

The carnival against capitalism

On Friday, 18 June 1999, the Global Carnival Against Capital took place, deliberately coinciding with the staging of the Group of Eight (G8) summit in Germany. This was very much intended to be a day of international protest. Indeed the rallying cry of the protesters was 'Our Resistance Is as Transnational as Capital'. The 1999 Carnival was thought to have been inspired by the smaller-scale 'Stop the City' protests that had occurred during the 1980s (see Barker, 1999).

As the protest day grew ever closer, a sign of the forthcoming vandalism was evident in the decision to cancel all annual leave for City of London Police officers on that day. Letters warning about 'major disruption' and the need for vigilance and enhanced security measures were sent to Managing Directors of all companies within London's Square Mile. On the morning of 18 June, London's rush-hour traffic was brought to a standstill by a mass bike ride, and anti-arms trade protesters managed to close a branch of Lloyds Bank with a sit-in on the premises.

After gathering at Liverpool Street Rail Station at noon, carnival masks were handed out, and no fewer than five processions proceeded to commence, with marchers taking different directions across the City. One such procession is believed to have erupted in violence by London Wall, following a collision between a reversing police van and a protester, resulting in the female's sustaining a broken leg. The early afternoon witnessed a group of protesters breaking into the Cannon Bridge building, with significant vandalism occurring in the reception area before the police arrived on the scene to make a number of arrests. A McDonald's building was also trashed by protesters.

By mid-afternoon the protest marches started to merge with an approximate 5,000 people, eventually converging on the London International Financial Futures Exchange (LIFFE). It is thought the vandalism commenced when a fire hydrant was set off, and following this, graffiti messages were sprayed and CCTV cameras were attacked. The police then began to use CS (named after the initials of the inventors Corson and Staughton) spray as well as mounted horses in an attempt to relocate the protesters down Lower Thames Street and out of the City of London. After this, many protesters re-gathered in Trafalgar Square. It was thought that there were similar protests in around 40 countries in cities as diverse as Tel Aviv, Zurich and New York (see Barker, 1999).

Protests against McDonald's

One of the most memorable images from the Carnival Against Capital in 1999 was that of the windows of a McDonald's in London being smashed either by 'legitimate' protesters or by those anarchists who were have assumed to have 'gate-crashed' the protest. This vandalism against a large multinational corporation is part of a patterned set of political protests globally against this company. Back in 2001, a Hindu group known as the Bajrang Dal vandalised a McDonald's in Mumbai, India. Rather than being a generic 'anti-capitalism' protest, this group was expressing dissent at the highly insensitive use of beef flavouring in the chain's US French fries. Hindus, of course, are vegetarians, while cattle are sacred animals in their religion. As protesters charged into the store, they trashed furniture and lights. In a southern suburb of the city, protesters committed acts of vandalism, including smearing cow dung on the restaurant's mascot (Veg News, 2014). Similar scenes occurred in Munich, Germany, in 2008, with an estimated 60 activists departing from a Mayday rally and occupying the largest McDonald's in Europe. Banners with the slogans 'McExploitation', 'McDeforestation', 'McWorkingclassenemy', 'WorldWideResistance' and 'People before profit' were unfurled (Veg News, 2014).

Taking a step back, one can observe the convergence of several lines of argument, resistance and the general disapproval of various ideas which, either fairly or unjustly, seem to result in the apportioning of 'blame' for many of the world's problems at the door of the United

States. Criticism of that country and in particular its foreign policy has a long tradition with writers from the political left, such as Noam Chomsky (see *Rogue States*, 2000, in particular) and Edward Said (2001) have long been significant voices of dissent prepared to challenge the US political establishment. These members of the establishment have been characterized by what Sumner (1994) and others have called the White Anglo Saxon Protestant (WASP) elites. Notwithstanding the current US president, Barack Obama, it has to be acknowledged that in the main, WASP men have dominated America's political, ideological and business expansionist programme with a ruthless degree of continuity post-World War II. Bakan (2004) notes that throughout the 1950s and 1960s, corporations in the United States grew steadily, but the legal framework and social contract which carried through from the Roosevelt era in terms of the politics of the New Deal guarded against some of the most draconian employment conditions by legitimising the role and status of trade unions in negotiating pay and conditions of service for the working classes. As was the case here in Britain, the economic crisis incurred by the Organisation of the Petroleum Exporting Countries (OPEC) oil crisis era – and the virtual quadrupling of oil prices virtually overnight – saw the incremental introduction of neoliberal economic policies and a concerted assault on trade unions and the employment conditions of the workers.

The agenda of the political New Right, in part legitimised by free-market economic theorists such as Ivan Novick, Milton Friedman and Friedrich Hayek facilitated the proverbial 'nail in the coffin' for a Keynesian philosophy of economic management (see Hudson and Lowe, 2004; Sardar and Davies, 2002). US corporations benefitted hugely from this shift in political ideology and from the Reagan administration, corporations such as McDonalds in the early 1980s become one of the truly globally ubiquitous symbols of American cultural imperialism, in terms of the aggressive spreading of pro-capitalist values. With these developments, of course, came their targeting at the hands of the often increasingly incensed political vandals.

Sardar and Davies (2002: vi) articulated the depth of anti-United States hatred induced by both its foreign policies and the perception of environmental disregard demonstrated by the actions of multinational corporations such as McDonald's. The argument that in global terms the rich get richer and the poor get poorer has been echoed by many other notable social commentators such as Noam Chomsky (1998) and George Ritzer (2004), who famously developed a theory of Mcdonaldisation. At the level of popular culture, the work of Michael Moore in terms of his iconic *Bowling for Combine* and *Fahrenheit 9/11* a decade or so ago has to a large extent put the ideas and discourse of the likes of Chomsky and Ritzer and those of that tradition into a 'language' to which the general public can both comprehend and relate. From this perspective of the 'state as criminal', the politically motivated vandalism of protesters and the disempowered whom they purport to represent appear much more justifiable than say the 'irresponsible' actions of the 'drift' vandal.

Rootes (1992) observes that the protest politics of the 1950s and 1960s was mainly a critique of the rising power of the military industrial complex. The post-war United States witnessed the appearance of what Brogan (1985) referred to as the 'warfare' state. This was namely a capitalist economy underpinned by a commitment to technological advancement, which correspondingly required the procurement of arms. Ideological support for a new arms market was sustained by Western paranoia of Communism which was reliant upon the imagined threat to national security from both Mao Zedong's China and Joseph Stalin's Russia. This legitimised a political culture which endorsed government investment in research and development for the arms industries, which were located on the West Coast of the United States. The economies of these pacific seaboard states, in particular California, benefitted massively from the investment in these emerging technological industries. It was no coincidence that student protesters demonstrating against the war in Vietnam and for the civil rights of Black African Americans were met with bullets on those hotbeds of protest, namely the University of California campuses. In the state of California, Ronald Reagan was to become the governor, replacing the liberal almost hippie-like Jerry Brown as part of the subsequent New Right reaction to these liberal/leftist protests and demonstrations.

The United Kingdom also saw the rise of the student demonstrations in the 1960s, the demand for an end to sex discrimination in the workplace and a call for the right to free expression of sexual preferences, although it was spared involvement in Vietnam because of the refusal of the Wilson Labour Government to help out its US ally. Rootes (1992) noted that the culture of deference had been superseded by a British public who had become less compliant in their dealings with establishment agencies of social control, including the public face of the state, the police. Whilst protest subsequent to the 1960s became far more diversified, politically motivated vandalism remained a common thread. Rootes (1992) observed that Britain had lagged behind America by at least two decades in terms of protest against racial inequality, with the early 1980s witnessing the first sustained race riots in places like

Brixton in London and Toxteth in Liverpool. These demonstrations and the resulting clashes with the police were the beginning of a tumultuous decade, overseen by Margaret Thatcher and the New Right, and perhaps recalled most visibly for the clash of the miners with mounted police at Orgreave in the mid-80s during the 15-month-long acrimonious industrial dispute and the notorious poll tax demonstrations of the early 1990s.

Political vandalism has always been inextricably linked to student protest, and this is in many ways unsurprising as we know that those from their teenage years to their early 20s are predisposed to drift vandalism. Some would see the political vandalism of youth as a mere reversal of drift vandalism and an ideologically infused way of 'letting off steam'.

Student riots

Rootes (1992: 177) argued that in generic terms student demonstrations in Britain between the 1960s and the 1990s had been 'decidedly modest by comparison with that of other major Western societies'. This sense of decorum was characterised as a 'favourable disposition towards any but the most orderly and non-violent of protest tactics' (ibid.: 173). This sense of 'respectable' protest would change as the relative prosperity enjoyed under Tony Blair and Gordon Brown's New Labour gave way, with political vandals waking up to the realisation that a relatively long-term artificially sustained economic boom built on the shaky foundations of credit would lead to a meltdown as the banking institutions went into free fall in the latter part of 2008.

The task of the political vandal would be to expose the lies which had for so long sustained financial irregularities, malpractices and, quite simply in many cases, gross financial mismanagement. The false promise of instant gratification and 'consumer happiness' which was facilitated by easy credit was exposed by the time the newly elected coalition government of the Conservatives and Liberal Democrats gained power in 2010. Indeed, a key facet of the whole 2010 general election campaign was the predominance of political discourses which insisted that the national debt was spiralling beyond control, and that government expenditure simply had to be cut across the board. The new Chancellor of the Exchequer, George Osborne, was tasked with cutting government expenditure, and in this disturbing public sector context Lord Browne of Madingly presented evidence that higher education had long been in the receipt of far too much government funding. *The Browne Review* published its findings in October 2010, and with the recommendation of removing the £3,290 per year cap on the tuition fees which universities could then charge students, the battle lines between the government and politically motivated students were drawn. The aforementioned deference to power observed by Rootes (1992) then vanished as quickly as cash out of the Northern Rock bank at the height of the financial crisis. The political vandal had become a rebel with a cause.

Just one month later, in November 2010, students protesting about the substantial increases in fees for those in higher education, and the complete abolition of the Educational Maintenance Award (EMA) for underprivileged students in further education rioted in London, around the Tory Party headquarters at Millbank. In gathering outside 30 Millbank, students chanted anti-Tory and Lib-Dem slogans, with Deputy Prime Minister Nick Clegg being singled out for particular abuse because of his policy reversal and the ditching of his pre-election commitment to oppose the implementation of higher tuition fees through his signing of the Vote for Students pledge (Rayner et al., 2010).

The protest is thought to have turned violent at around 1.30pm with a minority of around two thousand student protesters breaking away from the fifty-two thousand strong main body of marchers with vandalistic intentions of breaking into Tory Party headquarters. During the course of the afternoon, windows were smashed, graffiti was sprayed and protesters went on to destroy furniture and fittings, setting fire to their own placards. A minority gained access to the building's rooftop, with blocks of concrete and a fire extinguisher being hurled at the police below (Hume, 2010). As a result of the violence, an estimated three hundred office workers had to be evacuated from the Millbank building. The head of the National Union of Students, Aaron Porter, was quick to make the assertion that a minority of protesters had 'hijacked' what was intended to be a peaceful and lawful demonstration.

The then-Commissioner of the Metropolitan Police, Sir Paul Stephenson, ordered an urgent inquiry into the failure of his force to contain a protest which led to hundreds of students storming the building which houses the Conservative Party headquarters (Rayner et al., 2010). The violence led to 35 arrests, with ten people needing to be treated in hospital. The Metropolitan Police had adopted a far more low-key approach to dealing with the student protests than might have been expected, choosing to deploy only 225 officers along the route of the one-mile march, with Stephenson admitting, 'this was an embarrassment for London and for us'. The decision to employ this low-key approach may have been partially influenced by the criticism which the force took following the battering to its image after the death of newspaper vendor Ian Tomlinson, who was pushed over by PC Simon Harwood during the Group of Twenty (G20) demonstrations in April 2009 in London.

Following the events in London in November 2010, riots would be a significant part of the political landscape less than 12 months later.

Summer riots 2011

When the lead author spoke with two senior police officers in Nottinghamshire, they significantly pointed to attacks on three of the police stations in the city in August 2011 as evidence of politically motivated vandalism. The stations attacked included Canning Circus, which was firebombed; Meadows, where a police vehicle was set alight outside; and St Ann's, with a 30-strong crowd throwing stones (BBC News Nottingham, 2011). These acts were seen to be 'political' in the eyes of the police officers to whom we spoke, who felt that they were a statement by the disenfranchised. What is interesting is the case in which 'political' vandalism becomes an excuse for more wanton destruction.

At the trial of the group of people accused of the above in April 2012, Nazma Begum told the court she saw a group of youths smashing up cars and standing on them, as she watched from a first-floor window. Her family's BMW was among the cars damaged, with slashed tyres and a smashed windscreen. This is interesting in the sense that one tends to expect politically motivated vandalism to have a specific target to do with a sense of grievance (BBC News Nottingham, 2012). This is no doubt part of the reason why Assistant Chief Constable Paul Scarrott took a view which was far less generous in terms of accepting this vandalism as having any kind of justifiable political motivation. Indeed, he described the damage as 'gratuitous, senseless and wholly unjustified acts of wanton criminality'. He continued, saying, 'I cannot understand this explosion of mindless hooliganism and violence which is scarring our city and causing untold damage, not just to property but to the peace of mind of the law-abiding majority' (BBC News Nottingham, 2011).

Thus, in beginning to try and make sense of political vandalism, let us return to Stan Cohen's (1973) originally typology offered over four decades ago.

From 'ideological' and 'tactical' vandalism to 'political' vandalism

Cohen (1973) was keen to make the distinction between 'ideological' and 'tactical' vandalism, but for the purposes of our contemporary and evolving typology of vandalism we have chosen to collapse the two categories into what we have termed 'political' vandalism. This is because much tactical vandalism is itself inherently political in nature, and likewise political vandalism often requires a strategic approach to tactical planning. Take the following example of tactical vandalism as reported in the local newspaper of the lead author on 7 July 2003 (Burton Mail, 2003). In this case animal rights activists proceeded to damage nine greens at a Burton golf course because one of the club's members was a partner in a guinea pig farm which bred animals for experimentation purposes. Holes were hacked in the greens, and slogans were daubed in paint, forcing the partner of the farm to resign his membership in the golf club (see Burton Mail, 2003). This vandalism was an inherently political act committed by those who would appear to believe that the rights of animals are being trampled on by those whose breed them to be experimented on in the name of attempting to prevent and treat illness in humans.

Whilst those involved in the above example are clearly a politically motivated determined minority, another example of what Cohen would have termed 'tactical' vandalism would be what he (1973: 43–44) referred to as 'the use of window-breaking to be arrested and provided with food and a bed'. A contemporary example of this form of activity would be a case in Japan in which an Osaka man deliberately tried to get himself arrested by taking a cab from the centre of the city to a neighbouring police station. When he refused to pay, he was, to his apparent dismay, 'let off' by the cab driver. Having failed to get himself arrested, he then proceeded to throw a concrete slab through the police station window in a bid to ensure his second attempt at arrest was more successful than his first (Alfista, 2005). Whilst it would be easy to condemn this act as being the 'mindless' act of a 'madman', there are in practice numerous examples of disempowered and marginalised individuals committing such acts to deliberately get themselves a roof over their head for the night. In Portsmouth, New Hampshire, United States, for example, a judge was told by a homeless man that he threw a rock through the window of a local Dunkin' Donuts store so that he would automatically be put in jail and 'have a place to sleep'. Twenty-seven-year-old Jamaine Makepeace caused over $1,000 damage for his act of vandalism, and it was alleged that the rock narrowly missed causing injury to two employees who were working in the area where the glass shattered (Dinan, 2010).

What is interesting about the above cases is that there are many critical criminologists who would argue that such vandalistic acts are indeed inherently political because the capitalist system is itself criminogenic. They would contend that this type of vandalism is political because it is the product of an unjust society provoking a sense of grievance in an embittered individual who has been left metaphorically 'high and dry' by an uncaring political system. Their outrage and the subsequent destruction they commit are both understandable and justifiable in the social situation in which they find themselves.

Theorising political vandalism

It is precisely because of the lack of structural equality in the socio-political order that many critical criminologists would argue that much vandalism is fundamentally political in nature. As Hopkins Burke (2005) reminds us, 'conflict' theorists have endorsed the idea that society is made up of competing groups which inevitably become involved in a struggle to promote their own interests. In criminological terms this was evident as far back as 1938, with the publication of *Culture, Conflict and Crime* by Thorsten Sellin. It is because the accounts of conflict theorists – and certainly the later radical theorists – are theoretically informed by the work of both Karl Marx himself and the neo-Marxist tradition, that vandalism can sometimes be seen as a social practice which is inextricably linked to the struggle for both authority and power within the social structure.

Much of this kind of criminological thinking stems from the wider social theory of writers like Mills (1956), who espoused a pluralist view of how businesses, state organisations and those in civil society operate as power elites in society. Criminologists working in this kind of theoretical tradition, such as Vold (1958), believe that the access of the power elites to scarce resources means they have the power to criminalise those seen to be a threat to existing moral codes and the status quo. This tradition is closely aligned to the work of the labelling theorists which flourished after Becker's (1963) seminal work in the early 1960s. Just one year after the publication of *Outsiders*, Austin Turk (1969) wrote about how so-called rule breakers who challenge the societal norms and values promulgated by the powerful are most likely to be censured and processed by agencies of social control such as the courts and police.

From this perspective it becomes easy to understand why Greenpeace protests, the Greenham common protests and animal rights protests could become such a concern to the establishment.

The radical tradition in criminology was probably at its height in the 1970s, with the publication of *The New Criminology* by Taylor et al. (1973). According to Hopkins Burke (2005: 159), 'Drawing heavily on labelling theory, it was argued that the power to criminalise, make laws and prosecute offenders, or particular groups that are perceived as offenders, was a function of the state'. In applying this perspective to our study of vandalism, we can see why what are essentially principled and morally underpinned acts are condemned as being 'criminal damage' precisely because it is in the interests of the ruling classes to define them in such a way.

One of the criticisms of both the 'conflict' and 'radical' theoretical traditions in criminology is their tendency to overly romanticise the actions of those labelled as criminal, or in our case, 'vandals'. While fighting for a 'cause', politically motivated vandals nevertheless do cause real damage, and they may well put the lives of innocent people at risk, although many will go to great lengths to ensure that this does not happen. Greenpeace protesters, for example, who choose to scale a giant chimney in Sheffield on the grounds that it is an environmental pollutant are not only putting their own live at risk, but they may be a risk to those such as the police and the emergency rescue services who have a duty of care towards them. A second criticism of the radical tradition and specifically of *The New Criminology* (Taylor et al., 1973) was its tendency to over politicise crime. From that perspective, *all* acts of vandalism in Cohen's typology would have to be seen as political, and all would be assumed to be a direct challenge to the social system. One can see the flaw of this kind of approach when we return to the example of people who use the tactic of breaking windows in order to deliberately get put in jail. Are these people *really* making a commentary on the injustices of the global capitalist system? Are they *really* interested in making a genuine contribution to progressive social change? It could be seen to be more likely that these people are simply making a rational choice, albeit in desperate circumstances, to improve *their* lot in the system. They are simply making a decision which will improve their immediate circumstances rather than making a protest or taking a stand on behalf of a particular class or interest group. They are nevertheless in an objective sense the victims of a cruel and heartless social system, and clearly would not be putting bricks through windows in order to get a bed for the night if their social circumstances were much healthier and they could afford suitable accommodation.

Whilst we have acknowledged the above criticisms and limitations of the conflict and radical traditions, there is nevertheless clearly much to be said for these theoretical traditions in terms of how they can inform our understanding of politically motivated acts of vandalism. Not all vandalism is committed in a fit of rage or by those with malice in mind; indeed, some of it may be highly planned and committed by deeply principled people who are well prepared to be punished for their social practices, while the malice and rage can often be fuelled by negative experiences of a deeply unequal society.

The final part of this book assesses vandalistic futures, and we begin in the following chapter with an assessment of the impact of mediated communication on vandalism. The argument is posited that the late-modern focus on virtual as real geographical communities fundamentally challenges the way in which we must assess the vandalisms of both the present and the future.

Part V

Vandalistic Futures

9
Vandalism and Cyberspace

According to Internet Live Statistics (2014), an estimated 40 per cent of the global population has access to the World Wide Web, with much higher levels among the industrialised 'first world'. The pace of social change is considerable with the worldwide figure standing at just 1 per cent only two decades ago. Between the end of the last millennium in 1999 and 2013, global Internet usage has increased tenfold. In usage terms, the first billion was reached in 2005, the second in 2010 and the third billion by the end of 2014.

The Internet is a series of agreed information protocols which allow personal computers to interact with each other across networks, and over the last decade much has been written about the potential of the Internet to facilitate crime (see, for example, Jewkes, 2007; Jaishankar, 2011). Jewkes (2003: 2) observes that as time and space are transcended through computer-mediated images, 'cyberspace opens up new possibilities to the deviant imagination'. With reference to both the social theory of Anthony Giddens (1991) as well as the criminological practice of Bottoms and Wiles (1996), Wall (2007: 32) argues that 'the social orders which bind time and space have become *disembedded* and *distanciated* (emphasis in original)'. Consequently, the Internet marks the rise of the virtual community and the further decline of traditional geographical communities. In some ways Internet-based communities could be characterised by what Richard Sennett (1992: 238) refers to as 'destructive gemeinschaft', while Wall (2007: 33) observes that 'Community, in its satisfying and organic form, is not to be found … . The virtual relationships within online communities contain neither the full panoply of social relationships nor the cohesive or organic expectations of gemeinschaft (community relationships)'. The so-called process of 'globalization' has been speeded up by the Internet, to the point that in the networked world, no island is an island.

It is because we perceive that we are anonymous and disembodied that Internet communication 'can make us feel daring, liberated, infallible' (Jewkes, 2003: 2). Postmodern societies can be characterised by the concepts of 'spectacle', 'narcissism' and 'performance', with the Internet 'providing us with the opportunity both to *present* ourselves and to *invent* ourselves' (ibid.). We perceive that we can be who, what and wherever we want to be in cyberspace, and thus a feeling of 'freedom' is experienced of the type which can rarely if ever occur in the physical world. Jewkes (2003: 3) suggests that 'the net provides a locus for creative authorship of the self', particularly with websites such as 'Friends Reunited' and 'Facebook' offering what DiGiovanna (1995) termed 'a fan club to oneself'. Of course, what is posted on the Net may not be 'real'. In contextualising the contribution to postmodernism made by Baudrillard (1983), Wall (2007: 14) argues that 'mass communications do not give us reality'; rather, they give us what he calls 'the dizzying whirl of reality (le vertige de la réalité)'.

According to Bennie (2007), the novelist and essayist, William Gibson, coined the term 'cyberspace' in his work's *Burning Chrome* (2003) and *Neuromancer* (1984). He is also credited with predicting the rise of reality tv which is with us today with programmes like 'Big Brother' and 'I'm A Celebrity Get Me Out of Here'. Cybercrime and anti-social behaviour manifest themselves in many ways through the use of mediated technologies. One common Internet-based crime is 'hacking'. Furnell (2010: 173) observes that the social practice of hacking is characterised by 'attempting or gaining unauthorised access to IT systems'. A cultural criminological account requires us this phenomenon to be primarily located within its wider social context.

Hacking in a cultural context

According to Clarke, Clawson and Cordell (2003), the appearance of hacking was mirrored in popular culture with the release of a plethora of books and films. Instrumental in inserting the notion of 'hacking' into the popular consciousness was the 1983 film 'War Games'. The film starred Matthew Broderick who played a young hacker called David Lightman who accesses a US military computer set up to predict future outcomes of nuclear war. The hacking committed by Broderick's character nearly leads to the commencement of World War 3. One has to remember that this film had considerable popular appeal because it was released at a time when the Cold War between East and West was still in progress and was viewed by audiences some six years prior to the collapse of the Berlin Wall. Through this popular movie, the idea of cybercrime was effectively becoming inculcated in the minds of the younger generation who were owning their own computers for the first time in history.

A year before the release of 'War Games', the movie 'Tron' appeared in 1982. This US science fiction film starred the computer programmer Jeff Bridges, who becomes abducted inside the software of a computer. Such was its popular appeal that the film was nominated for both Best Sound and Best Costume Design at the 55th Academy Awards. It would lead to further commodification in terms of the appearance of both comic books and video games. A sequel was released far more recently in 2010 with the appearance of 'Tron: Legacy'. Two years later the cult figure Arnold Schwarzenegger would appear in the iconic 1984 classic 'The Terminator'. Such was the impact that Schwarzenegger made in his role as a cyborg assassin transported back from the year 2029 back to 1984 in being programmed to murder, that a sequel followed in 1991 in the form of 'Terminator 2: Judgement Day'. Indeed such was the cult status of these films that 'Terminator 3: Rise of the Machines' appeared in 2003 and was followed six years later by 'Terminator Salvation', the latter starring Christian Bale.

Embedded into the collective conscience of a generation is the 1987 classic 'RoboCop' which was set in a dystopian and crime ravaged Detroit. The film starred Peter Weller as police officer 'RoboCop' Alex Murphy, who after being murdered by a criminal gang, returns to life and considerable action as a cyborg law enforcement officer with some extraordinary superhuman qualities. Once again as with some of the aforementioned movies, this particular enterprise would spawn its sequels, tv series and associated video games which were so universally popular in the 1980s.

The manifestation of cybercrime was reinforced in the collective consciousness into the 1990s with the 1995 release of 'The Net'. This starred Sandra Bullock as software engineer Angela Bennett from California who becomes entrapped in a murky world of computer espionage after telecommuting to San Francisco. The same year saw the release of 'Hackers' which featured the storyline of a child, played by Jonny Lee Miller, being arrested by the US Secret Service on the grounds of his generating a computer virus which causes the crash of well in excess of 1,000 computer systems and resulting in a detrimental drop on the New York Stock Exchange. The film moves on to focus on conspiracies around corporate extortion and traces the activities of a gang of high school hackers at a time when mediated technology was only just beginning to emerge in the 'reality' of wider society.

By the end of the 1990s, as reported at the beginning of this chapter, the world wide web was fare more widely available and beginning to become part of everyday life for many citizens at least in the industrialised world. The science action film 'The Matrix' was to appear in 1999, starring the Canadian actor Keanu Reeves as the computer programmer Thomas Anderson whose double life sees him operating as a hacker by the name of 'Neo'. By now the common narrative of a dystopian future was a familiar one as it had been in some of the films alluded to previously, with life for most humans being depicted as a kind of virtual reality (hence the name 'Matrix') with machines operating to oppress an often unwitting human populace. Once again sequels were to follow with the release of 'The Matrix Reloaded' and 'The Matrix Revolutions', both released in 2003. Video Games were to follow in the form of 'Enter The Matrix' (2003), 'The Matrix Online' (2004) and 'The Matrix: Path of Neo' (2005) as well as a selection of comics to complement both the film and the aforementioned games.

Clarke, Clawson and Cordell (2003) allude to the manifestation of cyber-crime in the collective conscience in the 1980s and 1990s through the phenomenon of 'Cyberpunk'. One of the principle authors in this context is the aforementioned William Gibson whose 'Burning Chrome' and 'Neuromancer' (1984) were alluded to nearer the beginning of this chapter. The former work told the story of Automatic Jack and Bobby Quine, as respective hardware and software specialists who become free lance hackers. The latter work featured the character of Henry Dorsett Case, who as a computer hacker was forced to hustle for an existence in Japan.

Published in the same year as Gibson's 'Neuromancer' (1984) was Stephen Levy's 'Hackers: Heroes of the Computer Revolution'. This book gave Levy the credit for what is now referred to as the 'Hacker Ethic', which is a moral code for a supposedly more progressive way of life. In the book this ethical code was underpinned by numerous principles such as the right to access computers; freedom of information flow and a mistrust of bureaucratic authority. There was a belief expressed that computers could be instrumental in terms of creating works of art. This was allied to the belief that hackers should operate and be judged for their skill and ethical integrity rather than what their social and educational capital happened to be. For some, this offered far more than a simple ethical code for computer usage, it did far more in terms of encouraging people to think of how they might effect a more co-operative and genuinely progressive social order. Real conviction was expressed that computers really could change one's life for the better.

What is significant about these iconic films and books is that they not only embedded into the popular consciousness, the idea that forms of cyber-crime, including hacking, were somehow an appealing form of transgression, but they did much to further the belief that technology could be the solution to human problems. According to Clarke, Clawson and Cordell (2003:5),"The books, films, and television programs of the 1980s also paved a cultural path for the wild speculation, hope and hype that accompanied the 'information superhighway', the name given to the Internet in the early days of its expansion for mass consumption".

We shall further our discussion with a brief history of the concept before reflecting on the notion of hacking as vandalism.

The historical context of hacking

In popular discourse, a 'hack' involves the shortcutting of some kind of system and the term itself is thought to have originated with those with a preoccupation with model trains at Massachusetts Institute of Technology (see CNN, 2003). According to Clarke, Clawson and Cordell (2003) hacking dates back to the late nineteenth century with teenage pranksters misdirecting telephone calls at the expense of unwitting callers at the Bell Telephone Company (see also Slatalla, 2003). A century or so later in the 1970s, such telephone hackers became known as so-called 'phreakers' and their motivation was economically driven in terms of the attempt to make long distance phone calls without incurring cost.

In the twentieth century, the first wave of computer hackers were keen on experimenting with programming in order to make their functioning more diverse and in some ways more efficient. With the mass availability of personal computers in the 1980s and into the 1990s, it is unsurprising that the hacking of this mode of communication became far more prevalent simply due to opportunity. It was at this point that 'hacking' became centred around crimes of acquisition such as pirated commercial software and there was the proliferation of the computer 'virus' which had the ability to cause whole systems to be effectively shut down. Some of these crimes had a distinctively subcultural element in terms of the emergence of groups who could communicate with each other electronically and potentially access sensitive data held by both the agencies of the state and big business. According to CNN (2003) this subcultural element to hacking activity led to power struggles and conflict. Clarke, Clawson and Cordell (2003) maintain that the authorities, particularly in the United States reacted through recourse to the censure of the law and began to pursue criminal prosecutions, through the Federal Computer Fraud and Abuse Act, passed in 1986 which was underpinned by financial sanction against those found guilty plus the threat of imprisonment.

One very high profile case was that of Kevin Mitnick (see Slatalla, 2003). In 1999, Mitnick was convicted of numerous serious crimes associated with hacking. Indeed, at the time of his arrest he achieved a degree of notoriety as the most wanted computer criminal in America. These offences were thought to have originated in his teenage years and he received a custodial sentence in the late 1980s after illegally accessing computer systems at the Digital Equipment Corporation. He continued his criminal activities upon his release from prison, committing a range of offences using computers and cellular mobile phones and he was arrested in 1995. He served five years in jail and was released in 2000. Significantly in more recent years his rehabilitation has seen him benefit commercially from his previous life of transgression. As well as being a public speaker whose services have been frequently requested, he has gone on to author numerous books related to his crimes which saw him wreak havoc on the networks of companies such as Motorola, Nokia and IBM (see Greenberg, 2014). He continues to develop a flourishing security consultancy business. His website mitnicksecurity.com unashamedly asks those worried about falling victim to hacking the questions, 'Worried about being hacked?' and 'How Secure Are You?'. In offering his services around what he terms 'penetration testing', he boldly promotes himself as 'The World's Most Famous Hacker' in leading his co-called 'Global Ghost Team'.

Clarke, Clawson and Cordell (2003) articulate how hacking has continued to evolve in terms of the practice of so-called 'whacking', which is a form of hacking centred around having the ability to connect to unsecured Wireless Action Points. The targeting of these WAPs can be effected often without too much difficulty because of the inability of owners to adequately protect and secure them from such intrusion. In pointing to the work of Quittner (2003) in this realm of cybercrime, Clarke, Clawson and Cordell (2003) point to how the increasing complexity of computer and software systems has in turn witnessed the increasing sophistication of the hacker in terms of the methodology employed to break into systems. The type of crime committed can be of a political nature in terms of the will to merely disrupt systems or it can be of an acquisitive nature, in the sense that sometimes data theft is the object of desire for the hacker.

It is because the motivations to hack are so diverse, it is at this point that Clarke, Clawson and Cordell (2003) point out the notion of 'the hacker' is in fact a label applied by society and a somewhat unhelpful and misleading label at that. It has become a generic 'catch all' term applied by the popular media to make reference to a variety of social practices which target a multitude of systems. They point out that in an attempt to reject this label, many 'hackers' who claim that their motives are benign rather than malevolent, have dissociated themselves from those whose desires are more destructive or based on the pursuit of material gain, by censuring them as 'crackers' (see also Quinlan, 2003).

Before we move on to look specifically at hacking as vandalism in the next section of this Chapter, it is important to acknowledge that hacking is often more than just vandalism. Clarke, Clawson and Cordell (2003) explore the destructive side of hacking through recourse to articulating the types of harm which it can effect. They say that firstly, there are indeed those who may hack for benign reasons. This may be associated with the 'drift' (Matza, 1964) phase of adolescence whereby those seeking to gain access to unauthorised sites are merely doing so out of a sense of curiosity. For these type of hackers their transgressions are really associated with what we have termed in this book 'drift' vandalism and in many ways their desire to hack into the system for the sense of mere achievement or to avoid the boredom of their mundane lives contains an element of childlike playfulness. If what they are doing can be labelled as 'vandalism' it is often unintentionally so and it is of an exploratory nature, rather than being driven by ill intent or even conscious motive. Clarke, Clawson and Cordell (2003) label those who drift into and out of hacking during their younger years as 'script kiddies'. The transgressions of these type of people are often transitory and the majority are unlikely to go on to become career criminals in later life. For Clarke, Clawson and Cordell (2003: 3), "This is generally a benign activity, which is hardly different from that of any other aficionado who wants to learn more about his or her area of interest. It is about the pursuit of knowledge for its own sake and the ability to create and customise the technological fabric that surrounds us".

The above is significant in that Williams (2004) observes that those who inhabit cyberspace are more likely to be young, white, middle-class males rather than the poor, uneducated and disempowered. So once again we find that diverse forms of vandalism may be committed by the privileged in society and not just the impoverished and disempowered.

Secondly, Clarke, Clawson and Cordell (2003) allude to the more malicious side in terms of the intent of those who transgress. It is at this point that 'hackers' can be re-labelled as 'crackers' because their intention is far more destructive than the kind of 'drift; hacker which we have alluded to above. The third typology which they introduce is indicative of far more professional and organized hacking (see also Quinlan, 2003). There is clear intent, often a subcultural element and the desire to gain access is characterized by the specific targeting and highly detailed plan of attack. In targeting government and large corporations, this type of social practice be it labelled 'hacking' or 'cracking' has links to organized criminal networks and what is known in conventional criminological discourses as 'white collar crime'.

We started this chapter by alluding to the massive expansion of the World Wide Web around the time of the New Millennium so it is unsurprising that all forms of hacking or cracking have become a global phenomenon in recent decades as access to this kind of technology becomes readily available to people. So having contextualized the historical emergence of hacking, we now turn our attention more towards a consideration of specific acts of vandalism.

Hacking as vandalism

Williams (2004) observes that 'vandalism' online tends to apply to commercial, governmental or personal websites. He advises us that vandalism within three-dimensional graphical online communities often involves the breaching of security systems to deface and typically destroy homes and public buildings. Common 'crimes' include the posting of 'graffiti' on virtual buildings and monuments, and attaching pornographic images to online architectural structures. Rather than being armed with a brick, ready to smash a window, or a key with which to run down the door panel of a car as in the 'real' or physical world, the vandal takes on the form of the so-called 'hacktivist'. In articulating the difference between 'real-life' and virtual vandalism, Williams (2004: 6) makes the point that 'terrestrial forms of vandalism are material crimes because they have a physical presence'. Unlike real-life vandalism, with the online variant there is no actual physical damage, but that done to commercial, governmental or individual reputations is more profound.

We have discussed that hacking is a practice which involves a vandalistic element, but the motives for engaging in such practices are multiple and highly dependent on the form these take. Some of these are at the low-level end of the spectrum of seriousness undoubtedly, and have an element of mischief as characterised by other, more geographically rooted forms of vandalism in physical communities. Guillot (2014) refers to the case of 19-year-old Jordan Lee Jones, who caused the Metropolitan Police website to crash by 'overloading' it over a number of days. After he slowed down the website, it eventually ground to a halt before being rendered inaccessible to the public. As Jones was reported to have been boasting online about his exploits, one has to assume that this was not the work of a 'professional' looking to acquire anything materially from the activity, and neither would the apparent public proclamations which were made suggest that this young man was engaging in a politically infused act of vandalism. As no operational disruption was caused to the Metropolitan police, this was officially classified as a 'denial of service attack'.

As we have seen above, some forms of hacking can nevertheless be driven by the desire to commit crimes of acquisition. This typically takes the form of 'spyware', which targets either personal or business data. Whilst not technically 'hacking' in the strictest sense of the word, there is additionally the widespread practice of 'phishing', in which messages are sent in an attempt to get people to divulge sensitive financial or personal information. One such case with an acquisitive motivation is that in which Greenpeace estimated that 1.7m cubic metres of timber (£564 million) had been illegally obtained due to trees being felled as a result of the hacking activities of 107 Brazilian logging firms. These firms were alleged to have used hacking to evade the quotas dictated by tree-felling restrictions (Furnell, 2010). According to Williams (2004), hacks in the United States accounted for the loss of in excess of $70 million dollars to business during the previous year, while back in the year 2000, almost two-thirds (64 per cent) of online security breaches constituted defacement or alteration of website content.

As well as being a profoundly anti-social form of acquisitive crime spawning high levels of collateral vandalism, hacking can also be indicative of hate vandalism. 'Crackers' use malicious software, known as 'malware', which can release viruses, worms and so-called 'Trojan Horses', all of which can intentionally disrupt and damage data. One well-known example is the Melissa virus of 1999, which was a mass-mailing macro virus authored by one David L. Smith who resided in New Jersey, United States. After the involvement of the FBI and New Jersey State Police, Smith was sentenced to ten years in prison in December 1999. A year later, a computer virus carrying the seemingly affectionate message 'I love you' was instrumental in disabling computer networks across the United Kingdom. It was estimated that around 10 per cent of businesses in the United Kingdom were affected by the devastating bug, which impacted upon the National Health Service (NHS), the City of London and even Parliament. At the time, Internet Marketing Management's Martin Eddolls described the virus quite simply as 'one of the nastiest' he had witnessed in his professional career (BBC News, 2000b).

As well as targeting individuals, hate vandalism, which utilises the medium of cyberspace, can be escalated to take the form of warfare in terms of the systematic targeting of entire nations and cultures. It is thought that the former intelligence officer Barry Collin (1997) originally coined the term 'cyberterrorism' back in the 1980s. It is known that al-Qaeda has been utilising cyberspace since the 1990s, and by 2003, it was recorded that there were some 65 active websites with affiliations to six Islamic terrorist organisations (Denning, 2010). In the twenty-first century, recruitment and online training manuals are common on websites of terrorist organisations, and furthermore the Jihadist Cyber Attack Brigade proclaimed that in 2008, some 26,000 emails had been sent to people in the Gulf and Arab countries promoting the ideology of Osama Bin Laden. Additionally the GForce Pakistan group announced the formation of what was termed 'Al Qaeda Alliance Online' on a US government website, which it cybervandalised shortly after the atrocities of 9/11. Interestingly, the promotion of forms of 'electronic jihad' by people such as Imam Samudra, who was one of the convicted Bali bombers whose 2002 attack saw the death of 202 people, with a further 240 being injured, represents the deadly alliance between collateral and hate vandalism. The collateral damage was an attempt to prevent the further acquisition of capital by both the United States and the West through the specific targeting of the US stock exchange and the associated websites of multinational banks, which of course facilitate the circulation of capital (Denning, 2010).

We have explored the kind of anti-social cybervandalism driven by hate, but let us not forget that for some, the 'hacker ethic' (Furnell, 2010: 174) to which we alluded above is driven by a more altruistic pro-social code of ethics. This perspective was articulated by 'The Mentor', who attempted to provide a moral justification for hacking in his essay 'The Conscience of a Hacker' in 1986. In this piece the man born Lloyd Blankenship attempted to argue that hacking was about far more than self-interest and asserted that it had an important role in safeguarding the freedoms of the world. In an important twist of commodification, it should be noted that reference to the ideas of 'The Mentor' can be found on T-shirts and in films (see Douglas, 2003). One such example of 'hactivism' which would appear to be pro-social in some senses is that of the Condemned.org group, who attempted to use their technological prowess to fight child pornography in an act of cybervigilantism (see Meikle, 2002). They apparently resorted to hacking only when the relevant law enforcement agencies seemed powerless to take action in closing down servers and websites. Ben

Bidner, who founded and ran the Condemned.org server, was quoted as saying, 'everyone that I have spoken to is so anti-child-pornography that they literally beg me to find something for them to do to help' (Radcliff, 2000: 189).

Many would indeed argue that cyberspace can be used to prevent acts of vandalism and anti-social practices by the state and by multinational corporations. Van Laer and Van Aelst (2010: 321) observe that the Internet 'facilitates and supports (traditional) offline collective action in terms of organisation, mobilisation and transnationalisation'. One such example is the anti-World Trade Organisation (WTO) mobilisations which occurred in Seattle in 1999, where during the barricades and blockages, activists with portable computers continuously updated each other with details of police tactics on the streets (see de Armond, 2001). Additionally on 30 November 1999, a so-called email bomb – whereby hundreds of thousands of people email a focal point at the same time – was sent to the WTO website with the foreknowledge that this would cause the site to overload and crash. In seeing themselves as being profoundly pro-social rather than anti-social, the activist group Critical Art Ensemble (CAE) rejected the label of 'hacker' and embraced the professed and self-referential term of 'electronic civil disobedience' (see Meikle, 2002). The electronic civil disobedience movement seeks to give continuity to the original philosophy of non-violent but disruptive protest undertaken by the likes of Henry David Thoreau in the mid-nineteenth century. In a similar vein the Electronic Disturbance Theater (EDT) established by writer and artist Ricardo Dominguez in the late 1990s created the hacktivistic program of 'FloodNet', which helped facilitate virtual 'sit-ins' in cyberspace in order to protest and to politicise citizens globally. One such use of this kind of tactics was in protesting about the appalling state-sponsored massacre of women and children at a religious ceremony in Mexico in December 1997, known as the Acteal massacre (see Electronic Disturbance Theater, 2014).

As well as the motivation to engage in 'hacking' in order to commit acquisitive crime, which in itself spawns a degree of collateral vandalism, plus regressive hate vandalism and potentially progressive political vandalism, it is impossible to ignore the considerable amount of vandalism posted online by 'drift' vandals. Those adolescents caught up in the drift phase of delinquency and who wish to share their vandalistic practices online have been aided and abetted by the widespread accessibility of YouTube in recent years and it is to this form of social media that we now turn our attention to.

YouTube

YouTube is a popular video-sharing website, which has been in operation since February 2005. It is based in San Bruno, California, and was created by three former employees of PayPal, Steve Chen, Chad Hurley and Jared Karim. YouTube now operates as a subsidiary of 'Google', having been bought for an estimated $1.65 billion in the latter part of 2006. Video blogging, music videos and television and movie clips are all part and parcel of the video content generated by users.

Whilst the majority of YouTube content has been uploaded by individual members of the public, some orthodox media groups, including the BBC, offer a percentage of their material through the site. Users who are unregistered are permitted to watch the videos, while registered users are allowed to upload an unlimited number of videos. The site expanded rapidly, and by the summer of 2006, YouTube announced that around 65,000 new videos were being uploaded daily.

Whilst the video uploading of materials which encourage criminal conduct, consist of pornography or represent defamation and copyright violations is prohibited by the terms of service of YouTube, inevitably a significant proportion of the material does indeed contain some of the above. This is because YouTube does not view videos prior to their being posted online, and it is the responsibility of copyright holders to issue a takedown notice under the provisions of the Digital Millennium Copyright Act. In terms of policing the content on the website, YouTube trusts its users to flag the content of videos deemed to be inappropriate, after which an employee of YouTube will review the video to ascertain whether it is a violation of the terms of service of the site.

YouTube undoubtedly has its place in terms of facilitating political protest, some of which will inevitably result in property damage. In writing about the wave of revolutionary protests which swept the Arab world in the latter part of 2010 – known as the 'Arab Spring' – the Canadian sociologist Philip Howard (2011) noted the perceptive comments of one activist whose commentary on the value of mediated communication was perceptive in that 'We use Facebook to schedule the protests, Twitter to coordinate, and YouTube to tell the world'. This being said, for many the use of mediated technology is not to organise some pro-social political protest, but rather it is about the conveyance of the trivial and banal details of their own private lives.

YouTube provides a readily available online but public forum to share one's transgressions if so inclined. Certain YouTube clips which feature low-level criminality have, for instance, achieved cult status in recent years. One such is the posting of the so-called 'Stupid Burglars' (YouTube, 2007c).

Case study – the Stupid Burglars

The YouTube site contains the video of the so-called 'Stupid Burglars' who at face value appear to be attempting to break into a building containing a computer. Apparently unbeknown to the two youngsters, their exploits were being captured by a closed circuit television camera. One of the youngsters attempts to break into the building by appearing to throw a rock at the window, whilst the other appears to act as the 'lookout'. As the rock is thrown into the window, it appears to rebound off the glass and strikes the 'lookout' on the back of the head, appearing to knock him down unconscious. This appears to occur without the knowledge of his fellow assailant, who has a second attempt at throwing a rock through the window. The rock once again rebounds off the window, and this time strikes its thrower on the head, also appearing to knock him down and rendering him unconscious in the same way as his friend.

What is interesting about this clip on YouTube is the issue of whether or not what one is viewing is 'real'. Did this event really occur? Is what is viewed evidence of a real crime in progress, or is it part of clever stage-managing? Was the apparent attempted burglary 'staged' for effect by those acting out a scenario in an attempt to simulate a burglary? Was the event a real crime in progress whose video footage was manipulated to create a humorous effect at a later date?

Interestingly, among the comments posted about the video footage was that by 'Edjamablake', who provides us with the assessment that 'joke or not, it's fucking funny!! Lol'. In a sense this comment captures the essence of how 'crime' can become simulated in the postmodern world. By 29 August 2014, this YouTube posting had recorded 20,045 viewings. The overwhelming majority of these viewers would be logging on to be titillated or just for a 'cheap laugh'. This clip was presented on the US Lawyershop.com programme as being an authentic 'real' crime. In a postmodern sense, whether the footage is 'real' or not is immaterial as the boundaries between reality and 'hyper-reality' (Baudrillard, 1983) become increasingly blurred. We are meant to log on and laugh at the so-called 'world's most stupid burglars' whether it 'really' happened or not.

A similar clip titled 'Most stupid burglar ever' is posted on the YouTube site which apparently captures 'real' footage of a bungled burglary (YouTube, 2008b). The hapless burglar attempts to scale a building, but an outside CCTV camera captures him falling off. When he is successful in gaining access to the roof of the building, his next move means he has crashed through the ceiling onto the floor of the supermarket which he is attempting to burgle. All the while this apparently 'real' footage is being shown, the viewer is treated to slow motions of these 'highlights' as well as bubbles appearing on-screen to denote a 'break', as in a cartoon clip. The clueless burglar proceeds to 'shop' around the store before attempting to break out of the door. On failing to do this, he then attempts to use a stepladder to make his exit via the ceiling through which he crashed while gaining entry. In falling off the ladder onto a shelf of food, the burglar then appears to realise the 'game is up'. He sits down on a bin and lights a cigarette before lying down on the floor in a position of surrender before allowing the police who are waiting outside to arrest him. Once again, with the inclusion of edited highlights, this 'performance' may be part real and part stage-managed. Again we find a blurring of the boundary between reality and fiction so that wrongly illusion is perceived to be authentic.

Theorising vandalism and posted on YouTube

Acts of drift vandalism or acquisitive burglary which may have a collateral impact and are posted online are examples of 'second-life' criminality (Bakhtin, 1984), and once again can be seen to be characteristic of the decline of community attachment and a sense of social responsibility. According to Williams (2004: 24), 'some individuals feel no allegiance to a wider online social structure, and are possibly therefore free of "respectable" constraints, dissociating their deviant actions with "real" consequences'. Those who engage in vandalism online may be more likely to exhibit the Durkheimian characteristic of 'anomie' precisely because the transient and ever-changing nature of the Internet promotes transitory, superficial and fleeting encounters rather than genuine, sustainable relationships.

The emergence and development of the commodity form in capitalist societies was originally outlined by Karl Marx. In going beyond the creation of use value, the goal of commodity production becomes exchange value in the form of commodities. We can begin therefore to see how the packaging of acts of vandalism in cyberspace is turning 'crime' into a product to potentially be bought and sold.

The Internet has undoubtedly contributed to the destruction of the '*Gemeinschaft*', or organic community. Networks of 'communities' facilitated by the Internet are characteristic of far more fragmentary, or '*Gesellschaft*', social relations (see, for example, Hobsbawn, 2007). Postings about vandalism on YouTube are characteristic of the so-called 'society of the spectacle' (Debord, 1983). Image and simulation are key components of postmodern culture. Rather than living in stable, productive, Gemeinschaft communities, individuals are consuming a world fabricated by other human beings. In individuals' pursuit of gaining voyeuristic thrills by viewing real or apparent crimes on the Internet, a kind of social 'dumbing down' effect occurs across society. Best (1989: 29) argues that 'the spectacle is a tool of pacification and depoliticization: it is a "permanent opium war" (Debord, 1983: 44), which stupifies social subjects and distracts them from ... real life'. The posting of crimes of vandalism on the Internet is further evidence that 'the concrete life of everyone has been degraded into a *speculative* universe' (ibid.: 19). In echoing Marx by observing the commodification of reality, Debord (1983: 68) highlights the, 'falsification of social life'. Thus, to post videos on YouTube of 'real' or apparently real crimes being committed is part of a depressing picture whereby 'the affirmation of all human life' is 'mere appearance' (ibid.: 10). Penfold-Mounce (2009: 13) notes that 'it appears that culture is driven by its fascination with image, simulation and losing its grounding in substance or reality'. YouTube provides titillation by means of distraction from the mundaneness of everyday life, which is why it is so characteristic of postmodern consumer culture. Best (1989: 47) observes that 'within postmodern consumer culture, subjects wear designer jeans yet remain lonely and unhappy; the spectacle is ubiquitous but people are still bored; everyday life is shit *and people know it*' (emphasis in original).

To develop a greater appreciation of the posting of online vandalism, it is necessary to look more in-depth at the postmodern culture of 'celebrity'.

Vandalism on YouTube – connection with the culture of 'celebrity'

To understand the vandalism clips posted on 'YouTube', one has to understand the culture of 'celebrity' which pervades the modern mass media and dominates late-modern societies. YouTube is part of what Theodore Adorno and Max Horkheimer (1997) termed 'the culture industry'. Whereas functionalist social theorists expected the culture industry to provide 'enlightenment', 'reason' and even 'ultimate truth', a more depressing negative picture has emerged. Penfold-Mounce (2009: 7) observes that 'contemporary society has been heralded as bearing witness to and experiencing the emergence and increasing dominance of "celebrity" and "celebrity culture"'. People gain perverse pleasure from watching all things, 'nasty, frightening or disgusting' (ibid.: 4), and YouTube further fuels this desire, which is part of the negative side of human nature. Rather than simply offering enlightenment and emancipation, YouTube provides for quick consumption items of the 'cheap thrill'. The watching of 'crime' or the 'appearance of crime' on YouTube allows viewers a kind of psychological release without actually performing the act themselves. Through identification with those engaged in criminal acts like vandalism, people are able to live vicariously.

We have discussed how YouTube, rather than merely offering a window to some objective 'reality', offers the potential to distort or even pervert reality. Penfold-Mounce (2009: 5) observes that 'in the carnivalesque world, vice and transgression have an energy that perverts reality, creating the spectacle of debauchery'. YouTube facilitates and exacerbates, our 'voyeuristic delight in deviance' (ibid.: 6). Rojek (2001) notes that for the overwhelming majority, 'celebrity' status remains aspirational rather than a lived reality. YouTube, however, seemingly offers the potential for everyone to live out Andy Warhol's maxim about everyone being famous for 15 minutes. 'Celebrity' is fetishized in post-modern societies through YouTube's contribution to a mediated world.

Rojek (2001) identifies three categories of celebrities: (1) *ascribed*, that is, those born into a famous family, for example, royalty; (2) *achieved*, those who achieve fame because of some personal talent or skill, for example, pop star or footballer; and (3) *attributed*, those who are 'famous for being famous', and is what some have called 'the Jade Goody phenomenon'. Thus, Penfold-Mounce (2009: 15) proposes that 'celebrity is gained through manufacturing visibility in the public eye', while Rojek (2001: 21) refers to the majority in this latter category as 'celetoids' as 'they command media attention one day, and are forgotten the next'. Their long-term celebrity status is almost never fulfilled with their sinking back into the world of the obscure as quickly as they shot to 'fame'.

We could thus conceive of the people who post videos on YouTube of themselves vandalising property as being celebrity-seeking. The commission of the act of vandalism is almost incidental to their desire to be noticed and sought after on YouTube. The vandalism is instrumental in the sense that it is a means to the end – the end being the achievement of 'celebrity status'. It is, however, because of the sheer volume of images and 'performances' on YouTube which paradoxically guarantees that these people will never achieve long-standing celebrity status.

Their fame is characteristic of the 'celetoid' status so aptly described by Rojek (2001). There will always be a more ridiculous or 'stupid' vandal or burglar on YouTube. Once the audience have laughed at the clip and perhaps at best shared it in cyberspace with their friends, they will quickly move on to search for their next voyeuristic thrill. The exploits of online vandals' are consumed by the many one minute and then spat out the next.

Lowenthal (1961) argued that 'productive idols' or genuine celebrities with talent were on the decline. We can see how those who post themselves on YouTube while engaging in acts of vandalism could be aptly described as 'destructive idols'. The people in the clips do not present themselves as fully fledged human beings. They are one-dimensional, and rather than being known to us by name, they assume the master status of 'dumb criminal' or 'stupid vandal'. Their 'celebrity' is cheap and perverse. It is amoral in that it seeks attention in any way possible. Crime and 'deviance' are seen as just another way in which to present oneself publicly to achieve the acknowledgement that one is 'real' and really does exist. Penfold-Mounce (2009: 63) observes that 'the culture industry provides a structure in which there are no limitations, regulations or restraint on who becomes a celebrity, allowing even crime and criminals to become celebrated'.

Su Holmes (2005) maintains that the everyday world is saturated by celebrity. Achievement or meritocratic fame is on the decline, and is increasingly being superseded by those who simply become 'known for being known'. Penfold-Mounce (2009: 20) asserts that 'talent is no longer related to status; instead it is about presence'. YouTube is the perfect postmodern vehicle by which the mediocre can involve themselves in 'the performance of some deed to attract initial attention' (ibid.). 'Criminals' and, in our more specific case, vandals, who post online, can become celebrated in a perverse sense for having a mere presence online. Penfold-Mounce (2009: 21) continues, 'in a celebrity culture...the artificial and synthetic are becoming celebrated by being well known rather than becoming famous for greatness'. Mathiesen's (1997) notion of 'synopticism' allows us to see how the 'spectacle' provided by the forum of YouTube, enables the masses to gain a vicarious thrill out of crime solely because of its entertainment value and ability to titillate. Rather than appreciating people as fully rounded and 'real' human beings, criminality and the appearance of criminality encourage people to celebrate images.

The people on YouTube are not only one-dimensional but are perversely caricatures of themselves. Herbert Marcuse famously argued that the machinery of the culture industry creates 'false needs', which are in turn consumed by the masses. Mobile phones, for instance, were once a luxury, but are now considered by many as a necessity, and *everyone* seems to have one. Possession of these needs becomes a 'powerful instrument of domination' (Marcuse, 2002: 9–11), which denies the individual genuine opportunity for choice and the expression of individuality. Penfold-Mounce (2009: 22) notes that it is 'unsurprising that people have shifted from being hero-worshippers to being idolaters of images'. Scott Lasch (1979: 59) had earlier observed that pride and acquisitiveness, the sins of ascendant capitalism, have given way to vanity'. YouTube promotes and actively endorses a carnivalesque culture because the 'celebration of self' (Penfold-Mounce, 2009: 26) is its raison d'être. Those who post themselves appearing to commit crimes are perhaps driven by guilt. The type they experience, however, is perhaps not to do with the apparent commission of a crime, but rather with the guilt that one may feel for not indulging in such activities of hedonistic self-promotion. As Penfold-Mounce (2009: 27) emphasises, 'it is more likely that guilt is experienced in celebrity culture as a result of failure to experience indulgent pleasures arrayed in society'.

YouTube is symptomatic of a 'spectator' society, whereby people log on to be entertained, and deviancy is titillating. Penfold-Mounce (2009: 27) observes that 'to spectate is to watch, to see the unusual, something exciting or glamorous, or even ultimately something disgusting or frightening. Spectacle involves things that are worth seeing and meant to be seen'. This supports Mathiesen's (1997) notion of 'synopticism', whereby the masses watch the few.

In talking about the presence of violence in the classic Roman amphitheatre, Kyle (1998) talked about the thrill of the spectacle's being carried through to late-modern times, a view reinforced by Penfold-Mounce's (2009: 28) observation that 'it is perhaps unsurprising that there is evidence of continued public fascination with spectacular violence and crime'. This is precisely what Debord (1983) meant when he characterised late-modern societies as being inherently 'spectacularist'. The difference between contemporary society and ancient Rome is bound up with the diverse and multifaceted developments in the mass media, so that 'In contemporary society the power and control of the spectacle has expanded to become a mediated controlling event designed specifically to titillate and entertain' (Penfold-Mounce, 2009: 32).

The spectacle of YouTube offers a pornography of deviancy. It is what Penfold-Mounce (2009: 33) terms a 'culture of transparency', but it is very much a perverse kind whereby formerly private social practices are made explicit and posted into the public domain. Lasch (1979) wrote about both the voyeuristic and narcissistic nature of modern societies. This was echoed in the earlier work of Lowenthal (1961: 123) who wrote of the fragmentation of society. Paradoxically, it is the desire to break free from the ordinary and the mundane in everyday life which promotes the use of YouTube, which in turn simply ends up reinforcing just how trivial life can be. The vandal who posts him- or herself on YouTube is part of this voyeuristic and narcissistic culture. Penfold-Mounce (2009: 53) stresses that 'the development of narcissistic personalities who are fixated upon fame and glory is coming to set the tone of both public and individual opinion'. Entertainment and immediate gratification capture the thrill of seeing the vandal in action on YouTube.

The public who view criminal acts on YouTube are able to gain a vicarious thrill through the destructive deeds of the vandal. Penfold-Mounce (2009: 71) explains that 'by imaginatively identifying and resonating with the criminal and letting them act out deviant or criminal behaviour, the majority of the public will not actually perform the act personally, but still experience the same psychological relief'. This virtual exchange is 'mediated by adrenalin' (Brophy, 1986: 8), and is what Penfold-Mounce (2009: 72) calls 'the nervous giggle of amoral delight'.

Having considered how vandalism may manifest itself through cyberspace, this chapter has inevitably gone beyond Cohen's (1973) original typology, which was firmly rooted in 1970s land-based Britain. At that time, cyberspace was more than 20 years in the future. That being said, our final chapter moves on to explore the extent to which some of the types of vandalism articulated in this book have an international application.

10
Vandalism and Anti-Social Behaviour across Late-Modern Societies

It has been a central argument of this book that vandalism is far from random and sporadic, but when it is 'filtered' through the lens of cultural criminology we can see that it is highly patterned and systematic, if not predictable. Vandalism may be predictable to a certain extent, but as we have argued using many examples, it is multifaceted, in places sophisticated and inspirational in others, asinine, repulsive and offensive. The focus of much of this work has been on the United Kingdom – although we have used examples from around the world, in particular, Australia and the United States – but it is now time to systematically cast our gaze towards other countries, to develop a more international and comparative perspective. In doing so, we can see that in some cases the experience of the United Kingdom is repeated in other countries, but in other instances there are marked social and cultural differences in terms of the experience of vandalism.

Methodological issues of international comparison rates of vandalism

In attempting to develop an international perspective on vandalism across societies, one immediately faces a plethora of problems if attempting to do so from a predominantly statistically informed positivist epistemology. One of the primary data sources often utilised to forge a comparative perspective is that of the International Crime Victimization Survey, which collates data from 27 countries. A survey carried out on this scale has inherent problems, making it difficult to ascertain reliable and valid figures for international rates of vandalism. Data is based on different sample sizes from different countries, and some datasets appear to be more longitudinal, gathering evidence over a period of time, whereas others appear to offer more of a 'snapshot'. Even when factoring in differences in reporting and recording procedures, self-report studies reveal that much vandalism is simply ignored at the expense of crimes which are deemed to be more worthy of criminological attention. Van Wilsem (2004: 90) has suggested that 'because of inconsistencies in legal codes and differences in the public's propensity to report crimes to the police across nations and within nations over time, most cross-national studies on crime have concentrated on homicide'. Even where data are available for crimes such as car vandalism (as expressed through the number of people victimised per 100,000 of the population), it tends to be 'collateral' car damage incurred in the process of attempting to steal the vehicle which is recorded, rather than 'political', 'drift', 'hate' or 'exploratory' damage.

The above observations nevertheless do not stop us making cross-cultural comparisons informed by a less positivist and more culturally informed criminological perspective. Rather than do this country by country and risk producing an overly simplistic and misleading caricature of vandalism across societies, we have instead chosen to empirically test the strength of the typology of vandalism, which we have introduced and discussed throughout this book, across cultures. We take as our starting point the 'exploratory' and 'drift' vandalisms we introduced in the second chapter.

Exploratory and drift vandalisms

Labelling theories are highly relevant when discussing international examples of what Cohen (1973) originally referred to as 'play' vandalism, but what we have termed 'exploratory' vandalism, not least because the age of criminal responsibility is a significant variable when one takes an international perspective. For example, in France, the age of criminal responsibility is 13, while in Belgium it is 18. Blaya and Gatti (2010) suggest that vandalism is one of a group of offences – group fighting and shoplifting being the others – in which the age of offending starts 'very young'. More specifically, self-report studies indicate that 19.7 per cent of respondents had vandalised property before the age of 11. This is an interesting finding because there tends to be a popular assumption that the type of low-level vandalism and anti-social behaviour committed in the spirit of play and adventure actually occur much later into adolescence during the 'drift' between childhood and adulthood.

In the case of the Netherlands, the vandalism rate apparently peaked in 1996, according to official statistics. These should nevertheless be treated with caution when one considers the change in policy and practices introduced by the Juvenile Justice Act 1995 in that country. For example, this legislation changed the police practice of dropping charges for petty offences in favour of one of prosecution in virtually every case. Thus, previously 'hidden' petty offences began to appear in the police statistics due to changes in recording practices. Junger-Tas (2004) notes that, despite these increases, the number of offences of vandalism committed by young people remains low and is actually lower than amongst the adult population.

Responses to what we have termed 'drift vandalism' across all age groups within the Netherlands have traditionally allowed charges to be dropped if the offender offers compensation to the victim or attends a diversion scheme such as the HALT programme, which operates in Rotterdam with the objective of reducing the commission of acts of vandalism. Junger-Tas (2004) also observes a shift in emphasis with diversionary programmes targeting children below the age of criminal responsibility, possibly as a response to an increase in delinquency amongst these younger children. For example, a pilot project launched called STOP, for children aged 12 and under, was introduced, which allowed police officers to arrest the children, contact the parents and propose restorative interventions supervised by social workers. Most of the young people who were referred to the scheme were males aged ten and eleven who had committed acts of vandalism or theft-related offences.

Comparing 'exploratory' and 'drift' vandalisms between Britain and other European countries such as France and the Netherlands is to some extent feasible, but it is far more difficult, if not impossible, when one considers the demographics and different criminal justice traditions in the United States. Partly due to the sheer demographic and geographical diversity of the United States, it is perhaps not surprising that the age of criminal responsibility varies in each state. While thirteen states have set minimum ages – ranging from 6 to 12 years – the remaining states rely on common law, which declares that from age 7 to age 14, children cannot automatically be presumed to bear responsibility for their actions, but they can ultimately be held responsible. The evidence suggests that whilst 'exploratory' and 'drift' vandalisms are widely seen to be anti-social behaviours which can have a very negative impact on communities, there is a widespread recognition in most societies that allowances should be made for the diminished responsibilities of childhood when dealing with these transgressions.

After exploring exploratory and drift vandalisms in the second chapter of this book, we moved on in the following chapter to explore the cultural phenomenon, 'targeted' vandalism, which we will now consider from a comparative perspective.

Target vandalism

We retain our earlier focus on Holland, by exploring the cultural preoccupation in that country with 'car tipping'. In July 2009, it was reported that Amsterdam police were deeply perturbed by the emergence of a so-called 'new craze' in which vandals were literally tossing 'Smart'-branded parked cars into the canals of the city (Dutch Amsterdam, 2009). This act of 'car tipping', proverbially known as 'Smart tossing', again parallels the UK experience of alcohol-fuelled vandalism. The tossing of cars into the Amsterdam canals has tended to occur on weekends rather than on other nights of the week, typically when groups of young people are enjoying alcohol and perhaps other substances which have the effect of loosening inhibitions.

The Amsterdam-based newspaper *De Telegraaf* reported a widespread fear of repeat 'copycat' incidents, resulting in extra police patrols of canal-based locations on weekends. One such victim of the car-tipping craze was reportedly awoken by police with the news that his car had been uprooted and pushed into the canal (Dutch Amsterdam, 2009). According to Casper de Jong, this was far from being an isolated incident as 'several weeks ago the same thing happened to my companion's Smart. In both cases the Smart was declared a total-loss' (Soodin, 2009).

From a situational crime prevention perspective, the reason that Smart cars are targeted may well be explained by the fact that a low guard rail is present alongside the majority of canals, but these vehicles are compact enough to be lifted and tossed compared with more conventional vehicles. This would go some way towards explaining the targeting of other compact vehicles such as scootmobiles and Cantra brand cars. Whilst this work has repeatedly emphasised the emotive and experiential aspects of vandalism and the sheer joy of transgression, one perhaps unintended consequence of these acts is the victimisation of largely disempowered groups such as the immobile and disabled.

One of the themes of this work is that in this postmodern age, 'hyperreality' (Baudrillard, 1983) has superseded so-called 'reality'. This raises the issue as to the extent to which this so-called reported 'craze' is actually occurring on a widespread scale or not. On the one hand, *The Sun* reported that Dutch police were worried that the phenomenon will 'catch on' and 'spread' to the rest of Europe, yet on the other hand there are no reliable or even publicly available statistics on just how prevalent the so-called 'craze' is. Indeed, one Smart sales car worker was quoted in the article as saying, 'We're not supposed to talk about this because the police don't want the craze to spread, but we've had quite a few drowned cars returned to us' (Soodin, 2009), which does suggest that a well-educated Dutch police force is fully aware of the concepts of 'moral panics' and 'deviancy amplification' (see Wilkins, 1964; Cohen, 1972).

In an interesting commentary on simulation, under *The Sun* (2009) headline 'Not a Very Smart Place to Park', it was reported that one of these cars which was parked on a ferry in Poole Harbour, Dorset, rolled down a ferry ramp and sank in the sea! The owner of the car, Tony Hearn, had apparently darted off for a toilet stop before running out to see his car bobbing on the waves. The Smart car needed to be rescued by a crane. The events left the owner bemused as he was convinced that he had left his handbrake firmly on. This raises the prospect that the Smart car may have been deliberately targeted by pranksters in an attempt to simulate in the United Kingdom some of the 'car-tipping' antics of their Dutch counterparts.

As we saw in the last chapter, the Internet has been used to promote a more universal and voyeuristic sharing of acts of deviance, and perhaps not surprisingly, the alleged phenomenon of 'car tipping' seems to have spread beyond the boundaries of Europe and into Canada. It was, for instance, reported by Ciara Byrne on a Canadian news video posted on YouTube that an Alberta man in his 40s had been arrested for tipping a Smart car over onto its side on White Avenue, Edmonton, damaging the windows, wing mirrors and panels. Sales manager, Ken Lust, who had himself been a victim of this activity several years ago, said that the targeting of the lightweight and superior gas mileage cars should not be labelled as a mere prank. Lust quite rightly commented that 'it's vandalism, pure and simple. It's no different than having the paint on your shiny car scratched up or the soft top on your convertible slashed'. As recently as 2014, this 'craze' was reported as occurring stateside in San Francisco (Nevius, 2014). Significantly, these recent attacks in San Francisco may not simply represent the drift vandalism of adolescents, as for some, the location of the attacks is thought to represent a more politically motivated form of 'hate' vandalism born of social class. According to *The Guardian* (2014), the attacks *may* be indicative of a wider statement on the increasing social and economic divisions between tech workers in Silicon Valley and the more economically impoverished residents of San Francisco.

To return to the theme of 'hyper-reality' (Baudrillard, 1983), when digging deeper into the origins of the so-called car-tipping 'craze', it has reportedly originated from the phenomenon of 'cow tipping', which involves sneaking up on an apparently upright but sleeping cow and attempting to push it over. Historically, this originated as a prank involving country folk 'setting up' visitors from the cities by giving them an impossible task almost as a rite of passage initiation ceremony. Indeed an academic study by zoologist Dr Margo Lillie at the University of British Columbia found that it would take between two and four people to actually tip a cow over and that even these calculations were irrelevant because cows do not actually sleep standing up anyway (see Malvern, 2005). This was confirmed more recently when Collins (2013) reported that it would take an estimated six people of 'average strength' to achieve this.

In the third chapter, we considered how and perhaps why trains were another target of drift vandalism in our culture, and once again they are a popular target for vandals overseas. This combination of drift and target vandalism can be seen elsewhere in Europe, and has caused considerable concern in Germany, where it was reported that vandalism and graffiti had cost an estimated €50 million of damage to trains in 2011 (The Local, 2011). Commuters are being hit in the pocket in terms of higher ticket prices to cover the costs of rail operators such as Deutsche Bahn, according to the daily newspaper *Mitteldeutsche Zeitung*. As well as felt pen-based graffiti, other common reported types of vandalism included seats being slashed, train windows being broken, bus shelters being destroyed and ticket machines being attacked. Whilst property damage to ticket machines sometimes can be labelled 'collateral vandalism' due to the desire to make an acquisitive gain from the act, rather than being driven by political motivation, much of this vandalism would appear to be being committed by youths in their transitory phase of development between adolescence and adulthood, as is the case in the United Kingdom.

Context vandalism

Through an exploration of the house party phenomenon, we developed the idea in the fourth chapter that conventional vandalisms of the young become normalised in certain contexts, depending on the type of people who engage in its social practice. One of the facets we did not explore in that chapter was the class-based elements of such deviancy, which allows some to engage in criminal social practices yet to escape the full censure of the criminal law.

Oxford University's Bullingdon Club has a reputation for alcohol-fuelled debauchery, dating back more than 150 years (The Independent, 2007). Immortalised in Evelyn Waugh's novel *Decline and Fall* (1928), 'The Buller' was established in the nineteenth century as a hunting and cricket club, and an invitation to join was limited to the alumni of leading public schools such as Eton and Harrow. Members had to be able to afford around £2,000 for royal blue tailcoats with ivory lapels, and new recruits tended to be initiated by means of having their college bedrooms systematically 'trashed'. A common practice of the club was to book a private dining room under an assumed name and to routinely destroy property during and after the meal. Despite the profoundly anti-social nature of these kinds of acts, the censure of the criminal law would normally be avoided because of the willingness of members to compensate the restaurant owners in monetary terms. Savory (2008) observes that:

> The idea is that one gets completely off one's titties in a privately rented hall somewhere before trashing the place and leaving the owner with a large cheque to cover the cost of repairs. All this is done, of course, with a charming nudge-and-a-wink-and-we'll-slip-you-a-fiver-later to the establishment. This, of course, sets one clearly apart from the vulgarities of the proletariat youth and their favoured straightforward fingers-up at authority.

Vandalistic and anti-social practices have always been commonplace in the Bullingdon Club. On 12 May 1894, Christ Church College, Oxford, allowed the club to host a dinner which would end in notoriety (The Times Online, 2008). The all-male Bullingdon members went on a drunken and riotous rampage, and proceeded to smash each and every light in the Peckwater Quad, also destroying doors, blinds and all 468 windows. This episode was reported as far afield as the *New York Times*, which described students as being guilty of committing an all-night 'orgy of destruction'. The club generated further infamy by being banned from meeting within 15 miles of Oxford.

Former member Boris Johnson, currently Mayor of London, admitted to so-called 'dark deeds involving plastic cones and letterboxes' (The Independent, 2007), and in 1987, it was rumoured that member Ewen Fergusson threw a plant pot through the window of a restaurant, causing the burglar alarm to activate, and that the local police arrived on the scene with sniffer dogs. Legend has it that six club members were subsequently apprehended and spent a night in the cells at Cowley police station. Significantly, all were released without charge the following day. Having been one of those arrested, Johnson recalled 'the party ended up with a number of us crawling on all fours through the hedges of the botanical gardens, and trying to escape police dogs... and once we were in the cells we became pathetic namby-pambies'. In a classic statement designed to neutralise his actions, Johnson added that 'The blissful sponge of amnesia has wiped clean the slate of memory' (Gardham, 2007). Johnson's biographer, Andrew Gimson, said about the operation of the Bullingdon Club in the 1980s, 'I don't think an evening would have ended without a restaurant being trashed and being paid for in full, very often in cash. [...] A night in the cells would be regarded as being par for a Buller man and so would debagging (an act of removal of the trousers) anyone who really attracted the irritation of the Buller men' (Hub Pages, 2010).

The propensity of the members of the club for anti-social behaviour resurfaced again in December 2004 when police arrested no fewer than 17 of the club's members for damaging the cellar of a fifteenth-century pub by smashing more than twelve bottles of wine into its walls. On that occasion, four of its members, including Princess Diana's nephew Alexander Fellowes, spent the night in police cells. More recently, the club enjoyed what would become an infamous dinner at the White Hart pub in Oxford in 2005. According to the pub landlord, Ian Rogers, 'All the food and plates had been thrown everywhere and they were jumping on top of each other on the table like kids in a playground'. When confronting members of the club about their behaviour, Rogers claimed, 'they apologised profusely but offered absolutely no explanation'. On another occasion, the Bullingdon Club hired a string band to play at a garden party, but the evening resulted in all instruments being smashed, including a Stradivarius.

In November 2009, a documentary by More 4 depicted what the privileged group got up to when David Cameron and Johnson were members. According to Ronay (2008), 'It's this high-handed brand of yobbishness that has drawn most public opprobrium. It's not so much the damage that causes offence. It's the attitude, the innate sense that position and – more specifically – wealth will always be able to make good any inconvenience suffered by "civilians"'.

In taking the kind of comparative perspective which this chapter is keen to engender, it should be noted that the propensity towards vandalistic and anti-social practices of the upper classes in elite institutions such as Oxbridge and public schools seems to have been mirrored across the Atlantic in the United States. At Yale University, for example, the notorious Skull and Bones society had a reputation for crimes of acquisition in terms of stealing from campus buildings. Members of the society unashamedly called this practice 'crooking'. As well as the routinised theft of property, the society was reputed to have used human remains in its rituals. In 2001, journalist Ron Rosenbaum claimed to have videotaped an initiation ceremony whereby he claimed to have possession of skulls and bones. This modern-day practice seemed to be a re-enactment of an incident during World War I, when, as folklore has it, Prescott Bush (the father of US president George H.W. Bush and the grandfather of George W. Bush) was part of a group which plundered the grave of the Apache warrior Geronimo and brought his skull to their 'Tomb', which was based at New Haven. One of the less tasteful rumours about the secret society was that in terms of ceremonial initiation, new recruits were expected to masturbate in a coffin while recounting their most vivid sexual exploits in order to be rewarded with $15,000. Bush's experience seems not unlike that of David Cameron's, who once famously said of his time in the Bullingdon Club, 'Like many people, I did things when I was young that I should not have done, and that I regret' (Wintour, 2007).

With this in mind it is perhaps unsurprising that in his 1999 electoral campaign autobiography 'A Charge to Keep', George W. Bush was particularly evasive about his previous membership in Skull and Bones, simply stating, 'My senior year I joined Skull and Bones, a secret society, so secret I can't say anything more' (Skull and Cross Bones, 2008). Like the Bullingdon Club at Oxford, it is worth noting that the elite Yale University society has included some of the most powerful and influential men in the twentieth and the twenty-first centuries. Over many years, the Skull and Bones society has evolved as a powerful and interconnected social and political network, with those with associations including presidents, cabinet officers, Supreme Court justices and prominent industrialists, to name but a few (Leung, 2002).

These practices are repeated at other US universities. At the University of Virginia, for example, the 'Seven Society' is reputed to write the number '7' on campus buildings and property. Another group referred to as 'The Noze' has allegedly painted school bridges and dyed the water in school fountains pink. To dismiss these practices as 'harmless fun' or 'pranks' is to miss the symbolic significance of such acts of vandalism. Without revealing motivation or explicit membership, and very often without the reprisal of criminal law, these student societies are sending out the message that they 'own' the property of others and have the right to be 'anti-social' because of who they are (Rinf.com, 2014).

As well as there being comparative parallels in terms of 'context' vandalism, there are also striking ones to be observed between Britain and overseas countries when discussing what we termed 'collateral' vandalism previously in the fifth chapter.

Collateral vandalism

We made reference to 'collateral vandalism' as that which occurs incidentally as part of the commission of an offence of acquisition, and this is of course why Cohen (1973) had originally termed such acts 'acquisitive vandalism'. The fifth chapter discussed acts of vandalism which had occurred during the course of metal theft. As we will see, these activities are not unique to the United Kingdom, and indeed, there is much evidence of collateral vandalism occurring internationally, for example, in Asia.

McCurry (2007) reported that the four main islands that make up Japan's archipelago, have been the site of recent metal thefts. Many of these crimes of acquisition inevitably involve acts of vandalism which are profoundly anti-social in that they cost businesses money and often impact on the emotional well-being of private citizens who are victimised. The sheer diversity of objects targeted for acquisition was notable, with artefacts ranging from incense holders found in graveyards, copper wiring and, the main feature of the news item, a stainless steel slide from a children's playground. The spate of thefts in Japan and across the world have largely been attributed to China's recent rapid economic growth and associated demand for material that it is unable to produce (Wolchover, 2011). This is significant in that it tells us that collateral vandalism is inextricably linked to the profit motive, which drives global capitalism, as we pointed out in Chapter 5. This makes it a mode of vandalism which is materially different from others driven by, for example, boredom (in the case of drift and exploratory vandalism), ideological conviction (in the case of political vandalism) or prejudice (namely hate vandalism). What is interesting is that a country like Japan, traditionally associated with relatively low crime rates, particularly where anti-social behaviour is concerned, has suffered these acts of collateral vandalism to facilitate acquisitive crime. This may be indicative of the fact that things may be changing in Japan with the certainties of the old moral order being under threat with the growth of unemployment and associated social problems. In the case of China, the impact of economic growth upon indigenous natural resources seems to offer support to our conviction that collateral vandalism is an inevitable outcome of some of the contradictions of capitalism and the resultant 'strain' effect on individuals living in this social situation (Merton, 1938). More specifically, following a policy of growth maximisation, China has attracted inbound investment, placing unsustainable demands on housing and economic infrastructure. Ash (2006) has argued that this policy has led to innumerable inefficiencies, including so-called 'blind' factory construction, with little forethought in terms of duplication of industrial spaces. Whilst levels of relative poverty and material consumption may have eased amongst China's population, perceptions of poverty, driven by consumerism and notions of individualism have underpinned changing subjective perceptions of economic status. This is something, of course, which has traditionally been associated with Western consumerist culture (see Hall et al., 2008). Rapid expansion tied to China's nascent capitalist model has driven down already low labour costs, pushing urban unemployment higher. There have been considerable differences in the experiences of China and Japan in the global capitalist economy during the past three decades – China on the rise and Japan at best stagnating – but both have entailed considerable social change and a prevailing sense of anomie (Durkheim, 1933, originally 1893).

An international perspective is necessary in order to understand the roots of collateral vandalism as a social practice. Yoshida et al. (2005) have charted the complexity and associated dimensions of the secondary and scrap metal trade that flows from Japan to China. According to customs data held in China, some 316,200 tons of scrap metal were imported in 2003, having a substantial global impact on ferrous pricing. The majority of scrap metal imported to China is of relatively low-quality metal content. These low-grade items include insulated copper wire, but, critically, the price difference between high-quality and low-quality scrap, especially copper, is relatively small. For example the quoted difference of scrap copper is 84 per cent of the purer product. As China has a growing need for plastic as well, the plastic casing stripped from copper wire can also be recycled for further use. Yoshida et al. (2005) have estimated that China employs upwards of 400,000 individuals for this task, with these workers being paid extremely low wages. Stolen and illegally imported scrap from Japan can find its way into China's legitimate and regulated metal import industries during the separation process, thus 'watering down' the purity levels.

The issue of metal theft is not only an Asian and European problem. In the United States, one of the fastest growing crimes of acquisition is metal theft, be it copper, aluminium, nickel, stainless steel or scrap iron. During the illegal pursuit of copper – which can fetch in excess of $4,000 per ton – collateral acts of vandalism have been committed against gutters, flashings, downspouts, water lines and electrical wiring, with industrial facilities, commercial buildings and construction sites typically being targeted. The stolen metal is then sold to scrap yards and recycling companies. One such high-profile case occurred in January 2012 in which three Port of Baltimore men pled guilty to charges of stealing metal worth US $2.6 million. What is interesting is that the collateral vandalism involved in this case was relatively minor, that is, the cutting of a hole in a fence surrounding a Baltimore warehouse, compared to the far greater crime of acquisition (Recycling International, 2012).

In Chapter 5, we discussed whether rational choice theories were best placed to explain the decision-making of offenders who engaged in acts of vandalism for material acquisition. Whilst perhaps more strongly placed to explain this type of vandalism compared to other types such as exploratory, drift and hate vandalism, there are numerous cases whereby offenders have died or suffered severe injury from electrocution (typically in cutting live wires) during the commission of their crimes, which is indicative of an inability to effectively risk assess their intended target(s). The fact, however, that targets are generally unmanned and tend to exist in isolated places away from densely populated areas offers support to those who advocate routine activities theory as at least a partial explanation of this phenomenon (see Cohen and Felson, 1979).

Having considered some pertinent international examples of collateral vandalism, we now move on to consider worrying trends in hate vandalism across France, Germany, the United States, Japan and Palestine, all of which are anti-social and politically regressive.

Hate vandalism

Racially and religiously motivated attacks have become commonplace in France over a period of time, with it being significant that the country is home to the largest Western European Jewish population. In August 2010, the Union of Jewish Students in France (UEJF) reported that swastikas had been found on the windows and frontages of 12 dozen kosher stores in Paris (Benari, 2010). The incident was described by the UEJF as 'a new demonstration of anti-Semitic hatred'. The attack took place within days of the desecration of more than two dozen graves at a Jewish cemetery near Strasbourg in the northeast of the country. This very same cemetery had been targeted back in January 2010 on International Holocaust Remembrance Day, with the slogan *Juden Raus*

('Jews Out') being daubed across one of the tombstones (Benari, 2010). In July 2014, no fewer than eight synagogues were attacked. In one particularly vicious attack in the Paris suburb of Sarcelles, a 400-strong mob firebombed a synagogue amid chants of 'Death to Jews' (Henley, 2014).

Anti-Semitism has also been an issue in Germany. In April 2010, for example, the former Nazi concentration camp Neuengamme was targeted by vandals who daubed the place with banned images of red swastikas. Situated in southeast Hamburg, the camp and its satellites held over 100,000 prisoners from across Europe between 1938 and 1945, with 42,900 of them dying there. This made it the largest Nazi concentration camp in the northwest of Germany (Voz Iz Neouis, 2010).

The desecrated areas were covered up and kept out of further public view, until cleaning could take place. The International Federation of Resistance Fighters, known as FIR in Germany (an anti-fascist association) stated that this was an act of vindictive vandalism which was politically motivated: 'this makes it clear once again that historical remembrance must go hand in hand with vigilance about current tendencies and actions by the far right (Voz Iz Neouis, 2010).

Attacks on the resting places of the deceased are far from uncommon. Such is the threat of the attacks on Jewish cemeteries. Many synagogues and other institutions often need to be under 24-hour police guard. According to Henley (2014), the conflict in Gaza has unsurprisingly seen a rise in anti-Semitic incidents, which has historically occurred whenever the Israeli-Palestinian conflict becomes inflamed, and predictably in July 2014, Molotov cocktails were thrown into a Jewish synagogue in Wuppertal.

In addition to racist attacks in Germany, it would seem extremely likely that the Far Right may well have been instrumental in attacks of vandalism on war memorials dedicated to gay victims. In 2008, for instance, vandals repeatedly broke a window on Berlin's memorial to gay victims of the Holocaust. The attacks came just months after the perceived controversial installation of the memorial. Prior to the attack, the window on the memorial allowed viewers to observe a video of kissing between a same-sex couple. These attacks obviously have a deeply rooted historical legacy in that due to their sexual orientation alone, it is thought that in excess of 50,000 homosexuals were incarcerated by the Nazis, with around 7,000 murdered in concentration camps. Klaus Wowereit, Berlin's openly gay mayor, led the protests of denunciation of the homophobic attack (DW.DE., 2008).

It appears that hate vandalism is an ever present not just in Europe but in other parts of the world as well.

We observed in Chapter 6 that in September 2009 in Fountain Hills, Arizona, United States, Mike and Michele Jaber and their black friends were the subject of racist vandalism, with the windows of two family cars being daubed with the slogan of the overtly racist Ku Klux Klan (Gonzalez, 2009). This kind of attack has again a deeply situated history in terms of the practice of racial segregation in the United States, in particular prior to the Civil Rights Act 1964, and the appalling legacy of violence against Black people, particularly in the Southern states, carried out by extremist racist organisations, of which the Ku Klux Klan is the most infamous.

More recently in 2013, graffiti artists vandalised a GAP subway poster in New York City which featured a Sikh male model, originally from India. The poster was daubed with comments referring to Sikhs as 'bomb making terrorists', with the racist stereotype that they are 'taxi drivers' also being included. When a senior editor at *Islamic Monthly* enquired as to the location of the desecrated poster, the multinational company GAP responded with a message of solidarity, almost immediately changing its header image on Twitter to that which had so enraged the hate-motivated vandals in New York. This move is thought to have earned GAP much respect globally (Kumar, 2013). Once again, it is perhaps not surprising that this racist vandalism occurred in the very city that witnessed the death and destruction at Ground Zero on 9/11 some 12 years earlier.

In Japan, many people who believe are Buddhists and follow Shinto rites, and this partly explains the clash between the Far Right in Japan and members of the Muslim community which became more prominent in that country during the twentieth century due to the migration of Turks fleeing Russia following the Communist revolution of 1917. Religious intolerance as expressed through vandalism was evident back in 2001, when Pakistani immigrant Ahmed Gondal was targeted by a xenophobic group. Gondal became a symbol of the oppression of Japan's estimated 150,000 Muslims when hate-fuelled vandals ripped up a Koran believed to be stolen from a mosque in north-central Japan and scattered the pages on the road outside of his place of employment. This had been preceded by the abhorrent act of nailing a pig's head to his office door in a clear act of disrespect to the Muslim religion (Schmetzer, 2001). More recently in 2014 in Tokyo, hundreds of copies of Anne Frank's *Diary of a Young Girl* were vandalised across a staggering 32 public libraries in what would once again appear to have been a hate-motivated attack of vandalism. Frank, of course, famously wrote the diary whilst hiding from the Nazis in Amsterdam during World War II, before she tragically died of typhus at the hands of the Nazis, aged just 15, at Bergen-Belsen concentration camp in 1945 (Evans, 2014).

On occasions, we can see instances whereby 'hate' and 'political' vandalism become so intertwined that it is difficult to decide which status is more appropriate. A perfect illustration of this is in Palestine, whereby stone throwing stands between traditional non-violent means of protests, such as sit-ins, the boycotting of Israeli goods and hunger strikes. At the other end of the spectrum of resistance are stabbings and petrol bombings, which have perhaps been more readily reported by the Western media. Stone throwing, ordinarily against military tanks or bulldozers, characterises acts of resistance amongst Palestinian children and youths. Despite their age, however, this type of vandalism does not fit into the playful 'exploratory' category, and nor can it be characterised as the 'drift' variety typified by adolescence. These acts represent 'target' vandalism against the military, and are deeply political acts infused by hate. Stone throwing is a social practice conducted in protest of the Israeli occupation of territories seized from Jordan in the Six Day War of 1967 and occupied since. It is thus a problem that the Israeli government, military and police have had to deal with for almost half a century.

People living in the occupied territories of Palestine have a precarious daily existence in extremely impoverished and marginalised social conditions. Kuttab (1988) describes the process whereby growing up under Israeli occupation soon radicalises these young Palestinians and draws them towards political acts of vandalism, which clearly involves 'hatred' towards their oppressors. Slater (2001) argues that ever since the birth of the State of Israel in 1947, it has practised a policy of revanchism, or expanding its borders in response to an Arab enemy that has been determined to drive it into the sea. Once its borders expanded, there has been an aggressive policy of Israeli expansion and settlement to the considerable detriment of the local Arab population and invariably carried out by the army. Slater (2001: 174) discusses the notorious Plan D, which 'called for the "destruction of villages" (setting fire to, blowing up, and planting mines in the debris), especially those population centres which are difficult to control continuously'.

These policies continue to be implemented as the Israeli government seeks to forcefully expel Arabs from their lands and move them into urban ghettoes. In a particular incident in 2012, nearly 100 people lost their homes and possessions as protesters tried blocking the path of the bulldozers in an effort to protect Bedouin homes (Weiss, 2012).

The throwing of stones at the bulldozers is thus deeply ingrained in the culture of resistance found amongst the oppressed Palestinian population and reproduced over time. Relatively young boys are socialised into this politically infused act of defiance as 'to throw a stone is to be "one of the guys", to hit an Israeli vehicle is to become a hero: and to be arrested and not confess to having done anything is to be a man' (ibid.: 15). Kuttab (1998: 16) has previously described the tradition of stone throwing, which is carried out either individually or as part of a large subcultural demonstration, as a 'small well trained team'.

This stone throwing occurs as acts of hate vandalism in response to fully understandable perceptions of unjust Israeli action. The mounting of incursions into refugee camps by the army results in the sounding of an alarm and in the assemblage of teams of stone throwers who act on the messages of female lookouts giving instruction from visibly privileged vantage points, indicating the position of the hated Israeli troops. The objective is firstly to slow the advancing troops, and secondly to hinder and minimise risks of arrest. Those youths who wear the keffiyehs to obscure their identities from Israeli surveillance are considered to be the most agile, quick and courageous of all the stone throwers. The frequent necessity for them to escape is facilitated by a comprehensive and practical knowledge of the connecting rooftops and back alleyways in the dangerous areas in which they choose to attempt to engage their enemy. Rather than the car vandalism of the drift delinquents of the West, these youths engage in political vandalism by sending burning tyres rolling towards roadblocks with the intention of enticing Israeli soldiers towards the ambush of the stone throwers' vantage points. Nevertheless, the cost of these vandalistic acts is high in that Palestinian casualties are frequent.

Whilst the above has been characterised as both 'political' and 'hatred', there is more than a sense that this vandalism is 'collateral', to return to the part of the typology expressed in Chapter 5 in the sense that it is incidental to widespread death, human suffering and property destruction on a massive scale.

Having considered politically infused acts of hate vandalism, we now take a look at international comparisons in the type of political vandalism which we looked at a little earlier in the book.

Political vandalism

Chapter 8 discussed what we have termed political vandalism of the kind which Cohen (1973: 35) observed was underpinned by 'ideological' justifications. Empirical examples involving the work of Greenpeace, the Greenham Common Women (against cruise missiles), the Carnival Against Capitalism and the more recent students riots were cited amongst others as evidence that vandalism can be committed with the intention of furthering a particular political cause. The following section demonstrates how this has an international application as well as a domestic one.

One such example of political vandalism occurred in Europe over a three-week period in October 2005 in which it was estimated that some ten thousand cars were torched. This social practice was more proverbially referred to as the phenomenon of the so-called 'car-becue'! In addition, approximately one hundred factories and other industrial buildings were vandalised, with the same figure applying to schools, kindergartens and sports centres (Belien, 2005). What is significant about this is that cars were once again a prolific target for the vandals and in another society and for other cultural reasons. Unlike the drift vandalism committed by youths in a transitory stage of development, the same cultural target can be seen to be very much ideologically driven in that it was purported by many to be a response to a failing socialist welfare state. According to the French sociologist Nicole le Guennec, quoted in the Belgian newspaper *De Tijd,* car torching has been commonplace in France for the last 15 years, during which approximately 547,000 cars have been destroyed (Belien, 2005).

This targeting and setting fire to motor vehicles again appears to be systematic and repeated, with over four hundred cars being torched on New Year's Eve 2007, along with some 258 people being arrested. These attacks again appear to be ideologically driven in that they occur predominately in suburban communities which are home to the majority of France's five million strong immigrant community (Foley, 2007). Whilst clearly involving the kind of property destruction which many would find anti-social, some would argue that this was an attempt at political and social protest of the kind which could forge a more inclusive and pro-social future. It is unclear as to the extent to which minority ethnic groups were engaging in politically motivated vandalism as a protest against their living conditions or, alternatively, whether they were the explicit victims of hate crime. One suspects that both motivations may have been at play, and this confirms the difficulty of attempting to articulate any kind of 'ideal-type' model of vandalism. It does nevertheless seem reasonable to speculate that these were clearly attacks by a well-documented, alienated and disaffected youth, again victims of an uncaring global capitalism thesis.

A second pertinent example of political vandalism with an international dimension is that of animal rights protests. Since its first appearance in 1976, the Animal Liberation Front is thought to have been responsible for more than one hundred criminal acts committed in support of its cause. Acts of vandalism often more specifically involving arson, have tended to focus on the destruction of research records and experimental equipment. A number of incidents targeted at universities in California, Arizona and Texas in the late 1980s encouraged the FBI to move from the label of 'vandalism' and to apply the far more serious one of 'domestic terrorism'. This is in no small measure due to state fears about the proliferation of such organisations, with there being in excess of an estimated seven thousand animal rights groups in the United States. The label of 'domestic terrorism' is a response to the perception that the Animal Liberation Front (ALF) has built alliances with other militant groups which have periodically engaged in targeted property destruction such as People for the Ethical Treatment of Animals (PETA) and wider environmental groups such as Earth First (see for example ADL, 2014). The majority may find these kinds of acts to be anti-social, and certainly the censure of acts of political vandalism as 'domestic terrorism' is of course far easier to effect in the political climate of fear post-9/11, with the perception that 'America is under attack' and must continue to guard itself against 'external' and 'domestic' threats to its national security.

As well as organised protests of the kind mentioned above, often politically motivated vandalism may occur as a result of far deeper political and social unrest. Thus, in October 2011, the Anti-Terrorism Court in Rawalpindi, Pakistan, sentenced Mumtaz Qadri to death for the assassination of the former Punjab governor Salmaan Taseer. The fact that supporters of Qadri-branded slogans demanding his release as the 'hero of Islam' indicates that this was a religiously motivated murder. After delivering his verdict of condemnation, Justice Syed Pervez Ali Shah needed a police escort to be protected from a baying crowd which had surfaced to provide moral support for Qadri. In waving the green and yellow flag of the Sunni Tehreek political group founded in 1990, protesters declared the verdict to be politically motivated. Despite a concerted police presence, protesters in Rawalpindi strategically blocked several roads and proceeded to burn tyres and vandalise a memorial commemorating the late Benazir Bhutto, who was the 11th prime minister of Pakistan and who was herself assassinated on 27 December 2007 (Samson, 2011).

As with our above consideration of the Israeli-Palestinian conflict, what is significant about the above example is that it demonstrates that there is a blurring of the boundaries in terms of any attempt to produce a watertight typology of vandalism. Whilst on the surface much of the vandalism referred to above is indeed politically motivated, when one adds the variable of religion into the equation it becomes clear that the underlying motivation is one of hatred. So once again, in effect, one may ask the question as to where does so-called 'political vandalism' end and where does so-called 'hate vandalism' begin?

An interesting international example to be included in any discussion of politically motivated vandalism is that of Japan, a nation which – as we observed above – has typically been considered a 'low-crime' society. In the summer of 2008, a wave of vandalism swept Japan, with vandals reportedly destroying flower displays in a range of cities, including Gunma, Fukuoka, Saitama, Miyagi and Shizuoka (Japan Probe, 2008). An editorial in the *Asahi Shimbun* newspaper conveyed the belief that flower vandalism was a response to an oppressive society, with the issue being the discovery of graffiti in the Zenkoji temple in Nagano Prefecture. This was thought to be a politically motivated response to the temple's being named as the starting point of the Olympic torch relay for the 2008 Beijing Olympics (Japan Probe, 2008).

In 2010, the Yokaren Peace Memorial Museum was vandalised by youths who attacked a number of exhibits thought to honour the sacrifices made by kamikaze pilots who lost their lives during the notorious suicide attacks. Whilst the museum was intended to be a dedication to educating the young as to the atrocities of war, the attack was thought to be politically motivated due to the location of the museum near to what was once the Tsuchiura Air Base facility. This facility had been central to the training of kamikaze pilots (Japan Probe, 2010).

As mentioned, Japan has long been considered a 'low-crime' society (see Braithwaite, 1989), while, in contrast, Van Kesteren et al. (2000) found that crime levels in Japan across a number of offences were either average or even insignificant when compared to other countries. In beginning to untangle the differences in the type of vandalism being committed in Japan, it would appear that one can suggest that drift vandalism of the overwhelmingly 'anti-social' variety, committed predominantly by adolescents in the transitional period between childhood and adulthood, appears to be far lower in Japan when compared to Britain. Earlier in this book, for example, specifically car vandalism was referred to as being a massive target for drift vandals in the United Kingdom, whereas in Japan the risk of victimisation was assessed as being far lower. This is perhaps not surprising in a traditionally more respectful and polite society, in which even rock music audiences sit quietly and applaud in moderation.

Indeed, one of the 'worst' recent incidences of drift vandalism in Japan is thought to be the work of foreign nationals. *Stars and Stripes* reported that the Sullivans School, at Yokosuka Naval Base. was the target of extensive vandalism in 2010. The damage to both school and nearby motor vehicles resulted in nearly four hundred volunteers spending hours cleaning up the mess, according to base officials. Naval Criminal Investigative Service officials questioned two suspects, who were later reported to be the offspring of US naval personnel who were stationed at the Naval base. From the perspective of cultural comparison, it is significant that Japanese adolescents themselves were not thought to be involved in the incident (Slavin, 2010).

Explanations for the low crime rate in Japan are not monocausal but are multifaceted. They do, however, tend to focus upon environmental factors, criminal justice processes and, significantly, wider cultural influences. The work of Komiya (1999: 387), for example, emphasises the cultural influences of *uchi* (inner circle/home) and *yoso* (outer circle/elsewhere), and the impact this has on the legal infrastructure with Japan. Rather than the preoccupation with 'guilt' that pervades Western legal systems, overwhelmingly it is suggested that the Japanese legal system is more concerned with the notion of 'shame'. Latham and Shimura (1967) demonstrates the difference between notions of 'guilt' and 'shame' by referring to the Japanese version of Little Red Riding Hood, in which on apprehension the wolf falls on his knees and begs for forgiveness, whereas in the Western version he is simply killed, with death providing no opportunity for redemption (see also Bayley, 1991; Goold, 2004). 'Shame' tends to be tolerated by the collective culture of which the individual is a part, and because this notion is a central tenet of wider Japanese culture, it has been suggested that this in part accounts for the low crime rates experienced in Japan. In addition, reintegrative shaming works better in communitarian societies such as these (see Braithwaite, 1989).

One of the key ideas that the cultural criminological tradition has given us, arguably from the 'new' criminologies of the 1970s, is that the more a society attempts to regulate behaviours, the more social practices of 'resistance' will occur. As a response to a perceived rise in crime in a park in Toyohashi, late in 2008, the Japanese police installed a camera-hotline-alarm equipped a Coca-Cola vending machine. In what appears to have been an act of politically motivated vandalism, police reported the deliberate cutting of the security camera wiring. The Japanese words for 'surveillance society' had been sprayed in black paint on the side of the vending machine, along with the word 'watch' on the rear of the machine (Lets Japan, 2008). This suggests that while levels of drift vandalism may be lower in the polite society of Japan in comparison to the United Kingdom, because Japanese culture is less tolerant of individual indiscretion, there is a different situation with politically motivated vandalism, which is underpinned by principles of conviction and which are about trying to improve the social order for the collective social good.

Having considered some international comparisons of vandalism in terms of the typology that we have presented in this book and the context in which these acts take place, we will now consider some interesting future manifestations of vandalism.

Future manifestations of vandalism

The notion of what is increasingly being referred to as 'reverse graffiti' is worthy of consideration at this point. Paul 'Moose' Curtis provides one of the most interesting examples, fusing 'vandalism' and environmental politics in one arguably creative act. Using large stencils cut from plywood, Curtis has used these stencils, along with pressure washers – Viennese reverse graffiti artists/campaigners have in recent years used compressed air, which arguably provides a 'greener' and more environmentally friendly method – to create murals on walls made filthy by emissions from motor vehicles. In recent years, this so-called 'reverse' graffiti has caught on and become more culturally embedded with a simple search on YouTube illustrating this phenomenon. One such example which is clearly politically motivated in terms of the global pressure towards using less energy is that of the so-called 'vandal', who enters the Paris underground armed with nothing more than a bucket, cloth and ladder. Continuing to clean rather than destroy the tiles needed to create the desired visual effect, this politically infused actor leaves an image of an electric plug and cable on the wall with a tag line, 'Reduce carbon. Pull the plug on high energy costs'. The video clip credits the production to an organisation, ibm.com/fightcarbon (YouTube, 2012).

When conducted as a form of protest, the social practice of reverse graffiti fits within the typology of political vandalism because of the ideological messages which the works often contain. In addition, some would argue that reverse graffiti is pro-social in the sense that it actually involves cleaning, rather than making walls and other appropriate targets dirty. One may ask in what sense the cleaning of property could be deemed to be anti-social. It is one of the ironies in terms of the ability of the capitalist system to embrace resistance and turn it into productive capital, that further investigation reveals that this and other video clips promoting 'green' issues are in fact being sponsored by IBM, a major multinational corporation (see Bakan, 2004: 4). Cynics would suggest that both IBM and other such multinationals are striving to be seen as 'flexing' their 'green' credentials as seemingly 'responsible' and 'ethical' businesses to neutralise any political criticisms resulting from growing political activism on environmental issues, which has gathered momentum since the 1980s. Aside from green politics, large companies such as Microsoft and Smirnoff have advertised their products in this way, and there are dedicated websites such as www.reversegraffiti.co.uk, which promises an 'environmentally friendly, low cost, high impact advertising solution' for businesses.

There have been numerous instances of the relevant authorities attempting to prosecute those producing this kind of advertisement, but in practice prosecution has proved difficult due to the transient and non-destructive nature of the practice. One such example occurred in Leeds in 2011, when the local authority itself was accused of 'environmental crime' following a 12-month trial regarding city centre pavement adverts (The Guardian, 2011d). Indeed, in a further 'twist', the aforementioned reverse graffiti website actually boasts that the Greater Manchester Police used reverse graffiti for a 'drink safe' campaign which was specifically targeted at students.

A second new phenomenon worthy of consideration is the practice of 'greenwashing', which is actually carried out by big business with the backing of the law. Essentially this entails a business advertising that particular production methods consume less resources, and are less hazardous to the environment and the health of their fellow human beings. This Corporate Environmental Policy (CEP) ordinarily involves either a logo printed on the product or a more public declaration of commitment to such a policy. Significantly these voluntary practices are not ordinarily substantiated by third-party verification. Ramus and Montiel (2005) encourage us to reflect that there is a clear distinction between a public *declaration* of ideological commitment to the so-called green agenda, and the *implementation* of such policies in practice. Indeed it has been alleged that some companies have simply been passing off statements of CEP, which are little more than compliance to legislated regulatory standards rather than being a deep-seated expression of moral conviction. Some would argue that these formal commitments to CEP constitute acts of 'bad faith' in that the profit motive inherent in capitalism which underpins so-called greenwashing practices is clear. As a growing number of politicised citizens globally agree that the environment needs protecting and preserving, cynics would again suggest that by advertising products as green, CEP statements facilitate greater market share, encourage brand loyalty amongst existing customers and thus increase profit margins (Lowenthal, 2001).

This advertising strategy taps into a public conscious that has reframed the notion of 'consumerism' to incorporate criteria for purchasing which considers the ethics of product production and disposal processes. Zinkhan and Carlson (1995) have analysed the effects of green advertising on such customers who are thought to be particularly resistant to corporate ideologies promoted and circulated via the mass media. The study shows that the very people aware of climate change issues and who perhaps are more likely to be enticed to buy greener products are, by their very nature, the least trusting of corporate advertising strategies. It would appear that around 20 years later, both 'politically astute and educated' customers as well as the more 'apolitical but environmentally aware consumers', have been sold the green, responsible and ethical consumer agenda. A radical appraisal of the nature of predatory, expansionist capitalism would have it that any losses incurred in the early stages of the attempt to market green products to suspicious and somewhat reluctant customers were absorbed but ultimately rewarded with greater market share as environmental issues gained political credence and momentum through enhanced exposure in the media.

As we reach a conclusion to this work on vandalism, it is worth reflecting that at its 'best', vandalism can be a highly creative social practice which attempts to forge political progression through resistance to perceived acts of domination. On this note, it is a sobering thought that the appetite and ability of capitalists to 'detoxify' their natural enemies, rebrand, package and sell back to the population have been well documented (Young, 2007; Ferrell et al., 2008; Hall et al., 2008). One of the most easily identifiable cultural examples of this is the emblazoning on T-shirts of the image of Che Guevara, who was a staunch anti-capitalist.

Returning to Paul 'Moose' Curtis and the specific social practice of greenwashing, we can observe the same process. The extent to which capitalism can fuse the politics of resistance and critique into a neatly packaged product that denotes the 'cool individual' who can present as 'anti-establishment', yet whose practices in fact serve the continuation of the status quo, seems to have extended to Curtis's practice. What started out as an innovative and creative form of critique and artistic expression by a leading exponent of reverse graffiti freely admits, 'I've also worked for Transport for London...I have done corporate work – beginning with the launch of Xbox', and then without a hint of irony and typifying the capitalist's indignation in the fullest, says, 'Other people have made money out of what I do without my involvement. I think that's disrespectful' (Moreton, 2011).

Having considered both international examples of the various modes of vandalistic practice outlined in this book and having pointed towards two emerging trends which are likely to be worthy of future attention, we turn now towards offering some conclusions and final reflections on this work.

Conclusions

We will commence this concluding chapter by reviewing the story so far. Thus, we began our tale by looking at how the label 'vandal' has its etymological origins in an East German tribe of that name in the fourth and the fifth centuries who invaded Western Europe, destroying cities, including the so-called sack of Rome in 455. Our first substantive chapter made the point that the implication that 'vandals' are a 'class' or even a 'race' apart, does not square with the evidence that as the most common of all offences in the criminal code, many people will have committed at least one act of vandalism during their life. That first chapter charted how it was only from the nineteenth century onwards that the notion of the 'vandal' was used to describe a social practice – namely that of property destruction – rather than referring to specific group of people with common characteristics.

By exploring the sheer diversity of destructive practices ranging from the routine defilement of property through to graffiti and arson, we began to question the usefulness and value of the generic label of vandalism. We then moved on to consider depictions of 'the vandal' through popular culture in terms of fictional characters like Dennis the Menace and The Smasher. This led to an appreciation that these popular cultural representations have in many ways served to reinforce the stereotype that the vandal is a young, mischievous, often bored and anti-social lone agent.

We then moved on from popular culture to a consideration of political context, which is an important frame of reference for locating any study of vandalism. Nowadays the social practice of vandalism has become conveniently located in discourses around 'anti-social behaviour'. We saw how the notion of anti-social behaviour is very much associated with New Labour, and entered political discourse in the mid-1990s.

Vandalism itself has been subsumed under the broader anti-social behavioural category of 'environmental damage', which is an ambiguous term as it covers a whole plethora of diverse social practices. We considered how it is often convenient for the political elite to do this as it allows for a repoliticisation of the term, thus allowing for its subsequent censure (see Sumner, 1994).

In Part 2 of the book, Cultural Targets and Vandalistic Contexts, we took as our starting point the exploratory and drift vandalisms discussed in Chapter 2. We acknowledged that the former is invariably associated with children under the age of criminal responsibility, whereas the latter tends to be committed in groups during the transient phase of youth or adolescence. An account of how dominant media discourses in this area have traditionally tended to view children as being the proverbial innocents 'at risk' was contrasted with coexisting popular discourses which have tended to caricature 'out of control' and 'feral' children through reference to the so-called Rat Boy phenomenon popularised in magazines. The notion of children under the age of criminal responsibility having 'limited responsibilities' was discussed along with discourses which sought to 'responsibilise' so-called significant others in terms of the families of those responsible. 'Exploratory vandalism' was theorised with reference to the kind of social learning theory advocated classically by Banduru (1977), who in using the notion of the 'imitation of superiors', allowed us to see the how the interplay between social and cognitive factors shapes all kinds of learned behaviour. We made reference to the work of David Matza (1964) and his classic text *Delinquency and Drift* to discuss the kind of anti-social vandalism committed typically, but not exclusively, in groups. We discussed how drift vandals may be relatively law-abiding youths who may be in education or starting out in employment, but who engage in such actions. Through the development of a criminology of 'the prank', we developed an appreciation of how and why this type of property destruction is so appealing for those in the transitory period from childhood to adolescence. The fun element of vandalism is something which cultural criminologists would be keen to remind us is often overlooked by more conventional criminological discourses. In attempting to theorise this mode of vandalism, traditional control theories associated with thinkers like Hirschi (1969) were invoked along with more contemporary developments in control theories which have emphasised gender differences in order to explain why vandalism is a crime more likely to be associated with males rather than females. We began to see in this chapter how apparently 'random' and 'sporadic' acts of drift vandalism can actually involve the targeting of some distinctive cultural targets, such as railways.

Chapter 3 is built on the conviction that vandalism and anti-social behaviour is not 'random' or 'mindless', but is indeed systematic, deeply meaningful and on occasions, targeted. Having explored the centrality of the motor vehicle in Western culture in terms of explicit connotations of social status and more covert connotations of sexual prowess, the chapter highlighted why the motor vehicle, both as a desired object to be acquired or as an object of jealousy to be damaged or destroyed, continues to occupy a central place in youth offending. By exploring how the motor vehicle can be the target of 'collateral', 'political', 'hate' or 'drift' acts of vandalism, the point was made that the same object of vandalism can be targeted for an underlying multiplicity of motives.

Chapter 4 proceeded to debunk the myth that acts of property destruction are unusual aberrations and emphasised that in certain cultural contexts, vandalism and anti-social behaviour are normalised activities in the Durkheimian sense of the word. Using the vehicle of the common cultural phenomenon of the house party, routine destruction and displacement of property appear to be commonplace. The differences between the old industrial world of Stan Cohen's 1973 when he produced his original typology of vandalism and the postmodern world in which mediated technologies exist in order to facilitate the subcultural element of vandalism began to become evident in this chapter. As with many aspects of both exploratory and drift vandalisms, the sheer joy of transgression became evident through reference to the work of Katz (1988), who rejects both positivistic theories on the one hand and theories of rational choice on the other. Katz has reminded us that vandalism and anti-social behaviour (ASB) can be a metaphoric and in some cases a literal sexual 'turn-on'.

Part 3 on Cultural Criminology and Vandalism developed a re-appraisal of what Cohen (1973) originally termed 'acquisitive' vandalism which is inextricably linked to the inherent profit motive which underpins the capitalist mode of production. What we themed throughout this book as 'collateral vandalism' has been described as being 'incidental' in that the vandalism and anti-social aspect of its impact on the victim is a means to an end rather than an end in itself – that end being the generation of profit. We explored one particular manifestation of this, both domestically and internationally, most notably in the United States and in Asia, where what Cohen (1973) would have referred to as the 'junking' of metal occurs. In a global economic system characterised by scarcity, this mode of vandalism is likely to be an ever present. In terms of explanations for this mode of vandalism, whilst many in the cultural criminological tradition have savaged rational choice theories (see Hayward, 2007), it would seem that cost-benefit decision-making is best placed to explain this mode of vandalism rather than other modes because it involves material gain.

Chapter 6 explored how vandalism can be an explicitly political activity. Property damage which is born of prejudice and discriminatory practices is, however, politically regressive and profoundly anti-social and was thus labelled as 'hate' vandalism. It is deserving of a separate label and cannot simply be subsumed under the category of 'malicious' vandalism offered by Cohen back in 1973. Prejudice and discrimination involve much more than mere 'malice'. In light of the global impact of the terrorist atrocities of both 9/11 in New York and Washington and 7/7 in London, this chapter explored both racially and religiously motivated acts of vandalism. One must remember that in the early 1970s, when Cohen originally wrote, Equal Opportunities legislation was yet to be enacted and had indeed not even been conceptualised. In 2012, due to the progress made after the MacPherson Report (1999) into the tragic murder of Stephen Lawrence, issues of diversity remain and are now firmly on the political agenda. This chapter went on to demonstrate, however, that the commission of property damage born of hatred against homosexuals and those with both physical and mental disability continue to be a problem in modern Britain. Unlike the previous chapter on collateral vandalism, this one dispelled the myth that all hate crime is economically motivated because it has existed in times of economic boom and prosperity, and also in times of depression. In addition we found that hate vandalism is not always committed by the most economically marginalised groups in society.

Any cultural criminological contribution to knowledge would not be complete without recourse to a critical tradition of work which has reminded us periodically that the state is a bigger criminal than any individual agent. Indeed this theme was the golden thread of Part IV of the book. Through the examples of routine and often overlooked property destruction caused by states during warfare, in the name of sport or in the name of economic development, Chapter 7 highlighted how the social practices of the collateral, political, hate, drift or exploratory vandal are proverbially 'small beer' compared to the catastrophic, devastating and often irreversible damage caused by the anti-social state in which no legal sanction is incurred.

This theme was developed further in Chapter 8, which explored the plethora of ways in which vandalism, whilst being physically destructive, can attempt to be socially constructive and 'pro' rather than anti-social. We feel that the more explicit term 'political vandalism' should be used to replace Cohen's (1973) original notion of 'ideological vandalism' as the former denotes action, whereas the latter can be restricted to mere thought processes. After exploring specific examples, from Greenpeace to the Student Riots of November 2010, the work of those writing in a neo-Marxist tradition, such as Thorsten Sellin (1938), was invoked to remind us that what is labelled as 'crime' can often be politically progressive. This tradition of critical criminology is something which has been reinvigorated in recent years by those working in a cultural criminological tradition (see Ferrell et al., 2008), and it makes a major contribution to explaining this mode of vandalism. This is precisely because the radical tradition in criminology was undoubtedly at its height in the 1970s, with the publication of *The New Criminology* by Taylor et al. (1973), and it is surely no coincidence that this work was published in the same year as Cohen's seminal contribution on vandalism.

In exploring vandalism and cyberspace, Chapter 9 took us way beyond the geographically situated world inhabited by Cohen in 1973. As well as exploring the engagement in 'hacking' undertaken by individuals in order to commit acquisitive crime which spawns collateral vandalism, we looked at the online continuation of both regressive hate vandalism as well as the extended opportunities for politically progressive vandalism. The activities of so-called 'drift' vandals posting their acts online were appreciated. The capacity of cyberspace to create criminal celebrities intent on grabbing their five minutes of fame was theorised with wider reference to the culture of immediacy and the promotion of celebrity culture at the beginning of the twenty-first century. The appearance in cyber space of these kind of social practices is part and parcel is part and parcel of the hyper-real (Baudrillard, 1983) world of appearance becoming intertwined with reality, which will surely continue in the future.

The final chapter reminded us that there are similarities between countries in terms of vandalistic patterns, as well as marked differences. Whilst keen to make international comparisons, we have deliberately avoided oversimplifications. It does, nonetheless, seem that drift vandalism and anti-social behaviour are likely to continue to be lower in more communitarian societies like Japan in comparison to much of the Western world, when one considers the stigma associated with apprehension and 'control' factors which encourage criminal desistance. Worryingly, despite the efforts of policymakers and social reformers, hate vandalism is highly likely to continue internationally, given the depth of the global economic recession, the failings of neoliberal economics and the subsequent rise of political parties of the extreme Right which are able to attempt to exploit these circumstances. Perhaps encouragingly in some respects, defiant acts of political vandalism, designed to make a protest or to further a particular cause, are also likely to continue in the future due to the sheer indomitability of the human spirit and the ability of the Internet to facilitate the future organisation of such protest, and any future academic analysis of the social practice of vandalism must be ready and willing to explore newer manifestations of the phenomenon such as 'reverse graffiti'.

Communitarianism revisited

In Chapter 1, we observed that the New Labour assault on anti-social behaviour and incivilities – which the party imported from the United States and, in particular, the New York of Mayor Rudy Guiliani and Police Commissioner Bill Bratton (see Hopkins Burke, 1998) – was heavily influenced by the political philosophy of communitarianism, which proposed that the individual rights vigorously promoted by liberals need to be balanced with social responsibilities to the communities in which we live (Hopkins Burke, 2009). We also acknowledged in that chapter that not only was the communitarianism pursued by governments in the United States and United Kingdom authoritarian in its delivery, but we went further and followed Houdt and Schinkel (2013), who have shown how this form of communitarianism operates in combination with neoliberalism with the emphasis on 'responsibility' in communitarianism being compatible with the notion of 'responsibilisation' in neoliberalism, in other words, a neoliberal communitarianism used as a tutelage strategy against the poor and the socially excluded. We thus can observe a repoliticisation of anti-social behaviour and vandalism as a tutelage control strategy in a deeply fragmented society founded on a significantly unequal and forced division of labour characterised by widespread endemic anomie (Durkheim, 1933, originally 1893).

It is indeed the work of Émile Durkheim and his observations on the moral component of the division of labour in society that provides the theoretical basis of radical moral communitarianism which actively promotes both the rights and responsibilities of both individuals and communities, but in the context of an equal division of labour (see Hopkins Burke, 2014a, 2014b). As has been previously argued (Hopkins Burke, 2009), it is this significant latter element that deviates significantly from the orthodoxy promoted by Amitai Etzioni – and that has been embraced and distorted in the United Kingdom by New Labour with its enthusiasm for a strong dictatorial central state apparatus to enforce its agenda – and that provides us with the basis of a genuine moral communitarian way of life founded on notions of consensual interdependency with others whom we all recognise and identify as fellow citizens and social partners, and not as potential legitimate crime targets.

Radical moral communitarianism is thus a variant on the communitarian theme which acknowledges that the earlier orthodox variant – as we have seen – overemphasises responsibilities to the detriment of rights and thus calls for a rebalancing of the two. Thus, individuals have rights and responsibilities, and at the same time so do communities, and it is important to maintain a negotiated balance between the two at both a macro level and a micro level in society.

Hopkins Burke (2014a) identifies essential rights and responsibilities which are highly compatible and closely interconnected and which should be held by all citizens in a society founded on radical moral communitarianism and a substantially more equal division of labour. The first essential right is a return to full-employment policies – no longer perceived to be the fanciful ramblings of an off-the-spectrum political Left, but becoming increasingly popular with economists across the continuum who recognise the failings of neoliberalism to deliver effective capital reproduction strategies – which will lead not only to a more productive and balanced economy but will provide the material and psychological preconditions of other essential rights. The second identified right, the provision of good-quality (invariably rented public-sector) accommodation for all those who need it is also about rebuilding communities by providing a broad mix of interrelated interdependent people from different social backgrounds within a particular geographical neighbourhood. The third right, to be treated with respect by all public servants and with the parallel responsibility to treat each other with respect, is more achievable in a world of full employment and good-quality accommodation in proper communities in which people have self-respect for others and for their contribution to society. The fourth right, the provision of good-quality health care for all citizens with the parallel responsibility to pursue good health, will be more achievable with sensible alcohol and drug policies which decriminalise and medicalise a significant social problem. The fifth right, the provision of good-quality education and the parallel responsibility to engage with this, is also far more achievable in a society with full employment and citizens with good health, and is also highly applicable to the sixth right, which is to live in a crime-free society. The provision of proper alternative rational choices to crime and criminality will lead to a significant reduction in the need to treat and punish miscreants, and in this rebalanced economy provide more resources for highly skilled professionals and practitioners to concentrate their expertise on the very small groups of citizens with real medical or social problems. Clearly central to a radical moral communitarian social strategy will be an enhanced role for an expertise-driven public sector both in service provision but also in wealth creation. Such societies will be more equal and happier, with mutual respect among citizens and less enthusiasm for anti-social behaviour.

References

Access Hollywood (2009) 'Paris Hilton Denies Involvement in Party, Vandalism Incidents' (online). 13 May. Available at: http://www.accesshollywood.com/paris-hilton-denies-involvement-in-party-vandalism-incidents_article_17887#l vzCjuxbyRsY4VS8.99 (Accessed: 6 August 2014).

ACPO (2011) *Total of Recorded Hate Crime from Regional Forces in England, Wales and Northern Ireland during the Calendar Year 2010*. London: ACPO.

ACPO (2013a) *ACPO Recorded Hate Crimes, 2012–13* (online). Available at: http://www.report-it.org.uk (Accessed: 15 July 2013).

ACPO (2013b) *Hate Crime Manual and Tactical Guidance*. London: ACPO.

Adorno, T. and Horkheimer, M. (1997) *Dialectic of Enlightenment*. London: Verso.

Adorno, T.W., Frenkel-Brunswik, E., Levinson, D.J. and Sanford, R.N. (1950) *The Authoritarian Personality*. New York: Harper & Brothers.

Agnew, R. (1992) 'Foundation for a General Strain Theory of Crime and Delinquency', *Criminology, 30*(1), 47–87.

Ahmed, M. (2005) 'Social Services Failing to Commit to Antisocial Behaviour Policies', *Community Care,* 18 April, 15–24.

Akers, R. (1977) *Deviant Behaviour: A Social Learning Approach* (2nd ed.). Belmont, CA: Wadsworth Publishing Company.

Alfista (2005) 'Man Tries Hard to Get in Jail' (online). Available at: http://www.alfista.com/2005/05/05/man-tries-hard-to-get-in-jail (Accessed: 3 December 2009).

Allison, R. (2000) 'Doctor Driven out of Home by Vigilantes', *The Guardian* (online). 29 August. Available at: http://theguardian.com (Accessed: 5 December 2012).

Allport, G.W. (1954) *The Nature of Prejudice*. Reading: Addison-Wesley.

Appleseed, J. (1994) 'Destruction of a common heritage: the archaeology of war in Bosnia and Herzegovina', *Antiquity*, 68(258) (March), 120–127.

Arizona Republic (2009) 'Vehicles defaced with racist words, sexual images' (online). 6 September. Available at: http://wwwazcentral.com/community/ (Accessed: 20 February 2015).

Arizona News (2010) 'Peoria Police: Man Selling $180K in Stolen Hubcaps on E Bay', (online). 4 November. Available at: http://www.azcentral.com/community/peoria/articles/2010/11/04/20101104peoria-stolen-hubcaps-ebay-abrk.html?nclick_check=1#ixzz2v0hNzfYM (Accessed: 15 January 2012).

Ash, R. (2006) 'The Long-Term Outlook for Economic Reform in China', *Asia-Europe Journal*, *4*(2), 177–196.

Association of British Insurers (2009) 'Record Rise in the Costs of Fire Damage' (online). Available at: https://www.abi.org.uk/News/News-Relaeases/200/12/Record-rise-in-the-costs-of *fire-damage* (Accessed: 14 February 2015).

Bakan, J. (2004) *The Corporation: The Pathological Pursuit of Profit and Power*. New York, London, Toronto and Sydney: Free Press.

Bakhtin, M. (1984) *Rabelais and His World*. Bloomington: Indiana University Press.

Banduru, A. (1977) *Social Learning Theory*. New York. General Learning Press.

Barker, J. (1999) 'The Carnival against Capitalism' (online). Available at: http://www.vgpolitics.f9.co.uk/1103.htm (Accessed: 23 January 2012).

Barksy, L., Trainor, J. and Torres, M. (2006) *Disaster Realities in the Aftermath of Hurricane Katrina: Revisiting the Looting Myth* [online]. University of Delaware Disaster Research Centre, Miscellaneous Report 54, Available at: http://www.colorado.edu/hazards/research/qr/qr184/qr184.html (Accessed: 3 October 2011).

Batmanghelidjh, C. (2011) 'Caring Costs – But So Do Riots', *The Independent* (online). 9 August. Available at: http://www.independent.co.uk/voices/commentators/camila-batmanghelidjh-caring-costs-ndash-but-so-do-riots-2333991.html (Accessed: 15 July 2012).

Batson, C.D. and Burris, C.T. (1994) 'Personal Religion, Depressant or Stimulant of Prejudice and Discrimination', in Zanna, M.P. and Olson, J.M. (eds) *The Psychology of Prejudice: The Ontario Symposium, 7*, 131–148.

Baudrillard, J. (1983) *Simulations: Semiotext(e).* Massachusetts: MIT Press.

Baudrillard, J. (1988) *America*, trans. Chris Turner. London: Verso.

Bayer, K. (2009) 'Vandals Slash Car Tyres in Worst Ever Spree' (online). 23 January. Available at: http://www.dailyrecord.co.uk/ (Accessed: 12 February 2012).

Bayley, D. (1991) *Forces of Order: Policing Modern Japan.* Oakland: University of California Press.

Bax, M. (1997) 'Mass Graves, Stagnating Identification and Violence: A Case Study in the Local Sources of "The War" in Bosnia Heregovina', *Anthropological Quarterly, 70*(1), 11–19.

BBC News (1999) 'The women's peace camp' (online) 10 November. Available at: http://news.bbc.co.uk/1hi/special_report/1999/11/99/greenham_common/503679.stm (Accessed: 15 May 2012).

BBC News (2000a) 'Greenham Common Protest Ending' (online). 3 September. Available at: http://news.bbc.co.uk/2/hi/uk_news/908843.stm (Accessed: 15 May 2012).

BBC News (2000b) 'Love Bug Bites UK' (online). 4 May. Available at: http://www.news.bbc.co.uk/2/hi/uk_news/736080.stm (Accessed: 23 November 2011).

BBC News (2001) 'Mentally Ill Abused by the Young' (online). 12 March. Available at: http://webcache.googleusercontent.com/search?q=cache:http://news.bbc.co.uk/2/hi/health/1211814.stm (Accessed: 22 September 2010).

BBCNews(2002a)Availableat:http://www.news.bbc.co.uk/1/hi/england/1972350.stm (Accessed: 23 October 2011).

BBC News (2002b) Available at: http://news.bbc.co.uk/1/hi/scotland/1483423.stm (Accessed: 23 October 2011).

BBC News (2002c) 'Comic's Show Cancelled After Racist Jokes' (online). Available at: http://news.bbc.co.uk/2/hi/uk_news/england/1964321.stm (Accessed: 15 June 2012).

BBC News (2006a) Available at: http:// news.bbc.co.uk/2/hi/uknews/england/1964321.stm (Accessed: 15 June 2012).

BBC News (2006b) 'Children Arrested over Vandalism' (online). 14 July. Available at: https://www.google.co.uk/search?newwindow=1&site=&source=hp&q=(http%3A%2F%2Fwww.news.bbc.co.uk%2F2 (Accessed: 24 October 2011).

BBC News (2007) '"Spiderboy" Jailed for Five Years' (online). 1 March. Available at: http://news.bbc.co.uk/2/hi/uk_news/england/tyne/6410153.stm (Accessed: 15 November 2011).

BBC News (2008) 'Police Probe Theft of Mod Laptop' (online). 19 January. Available at: http://news.bbc.co.uk/1/hi7197045.stm (Accessed: 15 December 2011).
BBC News (2009) 'Homophobic Crime Rise in London', (online) 21 October. Available at: http://news.bbc.co.uk/1/hi/england/london/8316646.stm (Accessed: 16 January 2012).
BBC News (2010a) 'Vandalism Closes Cheltenham Children's Library' (online). 15 April. Available at: http://news.bbc.co.uk/2/hi/uk_news/england/ ... /8623083.stm (Accessed: 23 January 2013).
BBC News (2010b) 'Ferdinand and the Blue Peter Scandal' (online). 21 October. Available at: http://news.bbc.co.uk/sport1/hi/football/983304.stm (Accessed: 22 February 2012).
BBC News (2010c) 'Boy, 10, Arrested After "Stone Throwing" Death Crash' (online). Available at: http://www.bbc.co.uk/news/uk-england-10785830 (Accessed: 15 December 2011).
BBC News (2010d) 'Chile Troops Tackle Earthquake Looters' (online). 1 October. Available at: http://news.bbc.co.uk/1/hi/8542789.stm (Accessed: 8 June 2013).
BBC News (2010e) 'Police Need to Reclaim Streets, Police Chief Warns' (online). 23 September. Available at: http://www.bbc.co.uk/news/uk-11394354 (Accessed: 15 January 2015).
BBC News (2010f) 'Hate Crime Figures Published for the First Time' (online). 30 November. Available at: http://www.bbc.co.uk/news/uk/-11875321 (Accessed: 20 February 15).
BBC News (2011a) 'Plastic Road Signs in Surrey to Deter Metal Thieves' (online). 8 March. Available at: http://www.bbc.co.uk/news/uk-england-surrey-12673455 (Accessed: 15 June 2013).
BBC News (2011b) 'Riots in Tottenham after Mark Duggan Shooting Protest' (online). 7 August. Available at: http://www.bbc.co.uk/news/uk-england-london-14434318 (Accessed: 6 March 2014).
BBC News (2011c) 'London Riots: Tensions Behind Unrest Revealed' (online). 7 August. Available at: http://www.bbc.co.uk/news/uk-14436529 (Accessed: 6 March 2014).
BBC News (2011d) 'Democracy Live- MP Debate England Riots' (online). 11 August. Available at: http://news.bbc.co.uk/democracylive/hi/house_of_commons/newsid_9560000/9560113.stm (Accessed: 21 March 2014).
BBC News (2013a) 'Lead Laid on St Stythians' Church Roof Stolen Hours Later' (online). 16 April. Available at: http:// www.bbc.co.uk/news/uk-england-cornwall-22164206 (Accessed: 15 June 2014).
BBC News (2013b) 'Scrap Dealer Law Aims to Reduce Metal Theft' (online). 1 October. Available at: http:// www.bbc.co.uk/news/uk-24348233 (Accessed: 8 June 2014).
BBC News (2013c) 'Guernsey Holocaust Plaque Racially Motivated' (online). 9 August. Available at: http://www.bbc.co.uk/news/world-europe-guernsey-23630090 (Accessed: 13 April 2014).
BBC News Nottingham (2011) 'Three Nottingham Police Stations Attacked by Gangs' (online). 10 August. Available at: http://www.bbc.co.uk/news/uk-england-nottinghamshire-14469857 (Accessed: 16 May 2012).
BBC News Nottingham (2012) 'Witness "Saw Nottingham Police Station Petrol Bombed"' (online). 19 April. Available at: http://www.bbc.co.uk/news/uk-england-nottinghamshire-17775689 (Accessed: 16 May 2012).

Beard, J.M. (2002) 'Military Action against Terrorists under International Law: America's New War on Terror: The Case for Self-Defense under International Law', *Harvard Journal of Law & Public Policy*, 25, 559.

Becker, H. (1963) *Outsiders: Studies in the Sociology of Deviance*. New York: Free Press.

Becker, G. (1968) 'Crime and Punishment: An Economic Approach', *J.P.E.*, 76 (March–April 1968), 169–217.

Belien, H. (2005) 'France's Toll of Destruction', Available at: http://www.brusselsjournal.com/node/490 (Accessed: 15 August 2013).

Belknap, M. (2002) *The Vietnam War on Trial: The My Lai Massacre and the Court Marshall of Lieutenant Calley*. Lawrence: University Press of Kansas.

Benari, E. (2010) 'France: Kosher Stores Vandalised'. Available at: http://wwwisraelnationalnews.com/News/news.aspx/138916 (Accessed: 15 August 2013).

Bennie, A. (2007) 'A Reality Stranger than Fiction'. Sydney Morning Herald. September 7, Fairfax Media.

Berg, N. (2011) 'Olympic Evictions Come to Russia' (online). 15 September. Available at: http://www.theatlanticcities.com/housing/2011/09/olympic-city-evictions/126/ (Accessed: 12 January 2013).

Best, J. (1989) *Images of Issues: Typifying Contemporary Social Problems*. New York: Aldine de Gruyter.

Blair, T. (1998) *The Third Way: New Politics for the New Century*. London: The Fabian Society.

Blair, T. (2011) 'Blaming a Moral Decline for the Riots Makes Good Headlines But Bad Policy' (online). 20 August. Available at: http://www.theguardian.com/commentisfree/2011/aug/20/tony-blair-riots-crime-family (Accessed: 23 October 2013).

Blaya, C. and Gatti, U. (2010) 'Deviant Youth Groups in Italy and France: Prevalence and Characteristics', *European Journal on Criminal Policy and Research, 16*(2), 127–144.

Bobo, L. (1983) 'Whites' Opposition to Busing: Symbolic Racism or Realistic Group Conflict?' *Journal of Personality and Social Psychology, 45,* 1196–1210.

Boston News Channel (2010) (online). Available at: http://thebostonchannel.com/news/25676003/detail.html (Accessed: 14 March 2012).

Bottoms, A. and Wiles, P. (1996) 'Explanations of Crime and Place', in Muncie, J., McLaughlin, E. and Langan, M. (eds) *Criminological Perspectives: A Reader*, 99–114. London: Sage.

Bowling, B. (1999) *Violent Racism: Victimisation, Policing and Social Context* (Revised Edition). Oxford: Oxford University Press.

Braithwaite, J. (1989) *Crime, Shame and Reintegration*. Cambridge: Cambridge University Press.

Bristol Post, The (2008) 'Vandals are Making cul-de-sac a Misery' (online). 27 August. Available at: www.bristolpost.co.uk (Accessed: 5 January 2014).

Brogan, H (1985) *Longman History of the United States of America*. London: Guild Publishing.

Brophy, P. (1986) 'Horrality: The Textuality of Contemporary Horror Films', *Screen, 27*(1), 2–13.

Broudehoux, A.M. (2007) 'Spectacular Beijing: The Conspicuous Construction of an Olympic Metropolis', *Journal of Urban Affairs, 29*(4), 383–399.

Brown, R. (1995) Prejudice. *Its Social Psychology*. Oxford. Blackwell.

Buchanan, S. and Edwards, B. (2007) *The Vietnam Zippos*. London: Thames and Hudson.
Burton Mail (2003) 'Vandal Attack on Golf Club Greens' (online). 7 July. Available at: http://www.burtonmail.co.uk/burtonmail-news/displayarticle.asp?id=54830 (Accessed: 10 May 2011).
Burton Mail (2008) 'High Street's New System is Up and Running' (online). 11 November. Available at: http://www.burtonmail.co.uk/High-Streets-new-running/story-21488364-detail/story.html (Accessed: 14 April 2014).
Burton Mail (2009a) 'Bollards spear victim every three days' (online). Available at: http://www.burtonmail.co.uk/Bollards-spear-victim-days/story-21487752-detail/story.html (Accessed: 10 January 2013).
Burton Mail (2009b) 'Rising Bollard 'Could Gave Injured My Son' (online). 29 May. Available at: http://www.burtonmail.co.uk/Rising-bollardcould-injured-son/story-21486830-detail/story.html (Accessed: 11 February 2013).
Burton Mail (2014) 'The True Cost of Burton's Rising Bollards is Revealed' (online). 27 March. Available at: http://www.burtonmail.co.uk/true-cost-of-Burton's-bollards-revealed/story-21518356-detail/story.html (Accessed: 12 August 2014).
Burton Mail (2015) 'Burton Bollards Will Stay Out of Action as Council Fails to Reach Decision on their Future' (online). 9 January. Available at: http://www.burtonmail.co.uk/Burton-bollards-stay-action-council-fails-reach/story-25828800-detail/story.html (Accessed: 14 August 2014).
Calder, G. (2004) 'Communitarianism and New Labour', *Social Issues*, *2*(1) (online). Available at: http://www.whb.co.uk/socialissues/vol2gc.htm (Accessed: 23 February 2015).
Cameron, D. (2009) 'Vote for Change' (online). Available at: http://www.conservatives.com/news/speeches/2009/05/David_Cameron_Vote_for_Change_on_4th_June.aspx/ (Accessed: 14 August 2014).
Campbell, D.T. (1965) *Ethnocentric and Other Altruistic Motives*. Lincoln, NE: University of Nebraska Press.
Campbell, B. (1993) *Goliath: Britain's Dangerous Places*. London: Methuen.
Campbell, B.T. and McCandless, D.R. (1951) 'Ethnocentrism, Xenophobia and Personality', *Human Relations*, *4*, 185–192.
CBS News (2006) 'My Lai Hero Hugh Thompson Dies at 62' (online). 6 January. Available at: http://www.cbsnews.com/stories/2006/01/06/ (Accessed: 3 July 2011).
Chakraborti, N. and Garland, J. (2009) *Hate Crime: Impact, Causes and Responses*. London: Sage.
Chapman, J. (1994) Destruction of a Common Heritage: The Archaeology of War in Croatia, Bosnia and Hercegovina. *Antiquity*, *68*(258), 120–126.
Chibnall, S. (1977) *Law and Order News*. London: Tavistock.
Chomsky, N. (1998) *Profit over People: Neoliberalism and the Global Order*. New York: Seven Stories Press.
Chomsky, N. (2000) *Rogue States: The Rule of Force in World Affairs*. New York: South End Press.
Chu, D.C. (2007) 'Religiosity and Desistance from Drug Use', *Criminal Justice and Behaviour*, *34*, 661–679.
Cialdini, R., Borden, R.J., Walker, M.R., Freeman, S. and Sloan, L.R. (1976) 'Basking in Reflected Glory: Three (Football) Field Studies', *Journal of Personality and Social Psychology*, *34*, 366–375.

Clacton Gazette (2010) 'Jaywick: Teenager given ASBO for "Mindless" Vandalism' (online). 4 March. Available at: www.gazette-news.co.uk (Accessed: 4 January 2015).

Clarke, Z. Clawson, J. and Cordell, M. (2003) *'A Brief History of Hacking'* (online). Available at: http://www.steel.lcc.gatech.edu (Accessed: 1 December 15).

Clarke, Ronald V. (ed.) (1987) *Situational Crime Prevention: Successful Case Studies* (2nd ed.). Albany: Harrow and Heston.

Clarke, J. and Newman, J. (1997) *The Managerial State: Power, Politics and Ideology in the Remaking of Social Welfare*. London: Sage.

Clover, C. (2008) 'Greenpeace Kingsnorth Trial Collapse Is Embarrassing for Gordon Brown' (online). 11 September. Available at: http://www.telegraph.co.uk/earth/earthcomment/charlesclover/3351572/Greenpeace-Kingsnorth-trial-col (Accessed: 6 October 2012).

Community Care (2010) 'Disability Hate Crime Figures Reveal Under-Reporting' (online). 1 December. Available at: http://www.communitycare.co.uk/blogs/adult-care-blog/2010/12/disability-hate-crime (Accessed: 17 February 2014).

CNN (2003) 'Timeline: A 40-year History of Hacking' (online). 22 October. Available at: http://www.cnn.com/2001/TECH/internet/11/19/hack.history.idg/?related> (Accessed: 9 January 2015).

Cornish, D.B. and Clarke, R.V. (1986) *The Reasoning Criminal. Rational Choice Perspectives on Offending*. New York: Springer-Wesley.

Clymer, K. (2003) 'Jimmy Carter, Human Rights and Cambodia', *Diplomatic History*, *27*(2), 245–278.

CNN.com 'Timeline: A 40-year History of Hacking' (online). 22 October 2003. Available at: http://www.cnn.com/2001/TECH/internet/11/19/hack.history.idg/?related> [Accessed: 9 January 2015].

Cohen, A. (1955) *Delinquent Boys*. London. Free Press.

Cohen, S. (1972) *Folk Devils and Moral Panics*. London: MacGibbon and Kee.

Cohen, S. (1973) 'Property Destruction: Motives and Meanings', in Ward, C. (ed.) *Vandalism*. New York: Van Nostrand Ueinhold.

Cohen, L. and Felson, M. (1979) 'Social Change and Crime Rate Trends: A Routine Activity Approach', *American Sociological Review, 44*, 488–608.

Collin, B. (1997) 'The Future of Cyberterorrism: The Physical and Virtual Worlds Converge', *Crime and Justice International*, March, 15–18.

Collins, N. (2013) 'Cow Tipping Myth Dispelled' (online). *The Telegraph*. 6 September. Available at: http://www.telegraph.co.uk (Accessed: 8 August 2014).

Comte, A. (1976) *The Foundations of Sociology* (readings edited and with an introduction by K. Thompson). London: Nelson.

Consumer Freedom (2014) (online). Available at: http://www.consumerfreedom.com/news_detail.cfm/headline/2428 (Accessed: 10 August 2014).

Corbett, C. (2003) *Car Crime*. Devon: Willan.

Cornish, D.B. and Clarke, R.V. (1986) *The Reasoning Criminal. Rational Choice Perspectives on Offending*. New York: Springer-Wesley.

Courier, The (2010) 'Vandals Damage Newly Built House for the Disabled' (online). Available at: http://www.thecourier.co.uk/News/Dundee/article/7804/vandals-damage-newly-built-house-for-the-disabled.html (Accessed: 13 July 2012).

Cowling, M. (2008) *Marxism and Criminological Theory: A Critique and a Toolkit*. New York: Palgrave Macmillan.

Crisp, A.H. et al. (2000) 'Stigmatisation of People with Mental Illnesses', *British Journal of Psychiatry, 177*, 4–7.

Crown Prosecution Service (2007) 'Policy for Prosecuting Cases of Disability Hate Crime' (online). Available at: http://www.cps.gov.uk/publications/docs/disability_hate_crime_policy.pdf (Accessed: 8 October 2012).

Crown Prosecution Service (2011) 'Criminal Damage: Legal Advice' (online). Available at: http://www.cps.gov.uk/legal/a_to_c/criminal_damage/#a02 (Accessed: 10 June 2012).

Crown Prosecution Service (2014) 'Guidance on Prosecuting Cases of Homophobic and Transphobic Crime' (online). Available at: http://www.cps.gov.uk/legal/h_to_k/homophobic_and_transphobic_hate_crime. (Accessed: 19 February 2015).

Daily Mail, (2006a) 'Mental Health Prejudice Targeted' (online). 20 March. Available at: http://www.dailymail.co.uk/health/article-380459/Mental-health-prejudice-targeted.html (Accessed: 14 July 2014).

Daily Mail Online (2006b) 'Drivers Fail to Beat the Bollards' (online). 19 October. Available at: http://www.dailymail.co.uk/news/article-411423/Drivers-fail-beat-bollards.html (Accessed: 10 September 2011).

Daily Mail, The (2009) 'Boy 3 Investigated for Vandalism: UKs Youngest Crime-Suspect' (online). 21 September. Available at: http://www.dailymail.co.uk/ ... / Boy-3-investigated-vandalism-UKs-youngest-crime- suspect.html (Accessed: 9 February 2011).

Daily Mail (2013) 'Arson Cases Show Huge Rise' (online). Available at: http://www.dailymail.co.uk/news/article-194485/Arson-cases-huge-rise.html (Accessed: 8 June 2014).

Daily Record (2010) 'New Laws Aim to Crack Down on Scrap Metal Thefts by Ending Cash in Hand Payments' (online). Available at: http://www.dailyrecord.co.uk.co.uk/news/scottish-news/2012/03/14/new-laws-aim-to-crack-down-on-scrap-metal-thefts-by-ending-cash-in-hand-payments-86908–23787973 (Accessed: 9 August 2012).

Daily Telegraph (2007) 'Jail for Saboteur Who Left Rail Firm with £4m Bill' (online). 21 April. Available at: http://www.telegraph.co.uk/news/uknews/1549265/Jail-for-saboteur-who-left-rail-firm-with-4m-bill-html (Accessed: 9 August 2012).

Daily Telegraph (2010a) 'David Cameron Calls for "Full Force of Law" against Student Rioters' (online). 11 November. Available at: http://www.telegraph.co.uk/news/politics/david-cameron/8126495/david-cameron-calls-for-full-force-of-law-against-student-rioters.html (Accessed: 23 June 2013).

Daily Telegraph (2010b) 'Haiti Earthquake Looting and Gun Fighting Breaks Out' (online). 16th January. Available at: http://www.telegraph.co.uk/news/world-news/centralamericaandthecaribbean/haiti/70055/ (Accessed: 12 November 2012).

Dauge, V. (1997) 'Post-war Recovery in Cambodia', *Museum Management and Curatorship, 16*(2), 164–172.

Davies, H. (2010) 'Children at Risk As Vandals Target Flintshire Play Park'. *The Leader* (online). 6 October. Available at: http://www.leaderlive.co.uk/news (Accessed: 24 July 2014).

Debord, G. (1983) *The Society of the Spectacle*. Detroit: Black and Red.

Democracy Now (2011) 'Over 1,000 Arrested in U.K. as Anger over Inequality, Racism Boils Over into "Insurrection"' (online). 10 August. Available at: http://

www.democracynow.org/2011/8/10/over_1_000_arrested_in_uk (Accessed: 10 July 2013).
de Armond, P. (2001) 'Netwar in the Emerald City: WTO Protest Strategy and Tactics', in Arquilla, J. and Ronfeldt, D. (eds) *Networks and Netwars: The Future of Terror, Crime and Militancy,* 201–235. Santa Monica: RAND Corporation.
Denich, B. (1994) 'Dismembering Yugoslavia: Nationalist Ideologies and the Symbolic Revival of Genocide', *American Ethnologist, 21,* 367–390.
Denning, D. (2010) 'Terror's Web: How the Internet Is Transforming Terrorism', in Jewkes, Y. and Yar, M. (eds) *Handbook of Internet Crime.* Devon: Willan.
Department for Transport (2015) (online). Available at: http://www.dft.gov.uk/pgr/roads/tpm/tal/signsandsignals/risingbollards? (Accessed: 24 February 2015).
DiGiovanna, J. (February 1995) 'Losing Your Voice on the Internet' (online). Available at: http://http://aruba.ccit.arizona.edu/~jkandell/james.html, also in P. Ludlow (ed.) (1996) *High Noon on the Electronic Frontier'.* MIT Press. op. cit., 445–457 (Accessed: 12 April 2011).
Dimmer, S. (2013) 'Woman Steals Hundreds of Badges from Cars in Order to Flog Them on Ebay' (online). 12 December. Available at: http://www.mirror.co.uk/news/uk/coventry-car-badge-thief-woman-291784 (Accessed: 2 February 2014).
Dinan, E. (2010) 'Homeless Man Says He Smashed Window to Get Arrested' (online). June 7. Available at: http://www.seacoastonline.com/articles/20100607-NEWS-100609880 (Accessed: 12 April 2012).
Direct Gov (2010) (online) Available at: http://www.direct.gov.uk/en/Motoring/VehicleCrime/DG_10035622 (Accessed: 3 July 2013).
Direct Line (2014) (online) Available at: http://www.directline.com/motor/car-vandalism.htm (Accessed: 6 June 2014).
Disability Rights Commission (2003) Disability Briefing. February 2003. Research and Evaluation Unit.
DJVESTV (2014) 'Man Claims George Zimmerman Threatened to Kill Him' (online). 13 September. Available at: http://www.djdestv.com/2014/09/13/man-claims-george-zimmerman-threatened-kill?session-id=251737cec9e313a7c3b6ab1f77493be4 (Accessed: 30 January 2015).
Doig, A. (2011) *State Crime.* Abingdon: Willan.
Douglas, T. (2003) *Hacker Culture.* Minneapolis: University of Minnesota Press.
Durkheim, E. (1933 originally 1893) *The Division of Labour in Society.* Glencoe, IL: Free Press.
Driver, S. and Martell, L. (1997) 'New Labour's Communitarianisms', *Critical Social Policy, 52,* 27–46.
Dubuis, A. (2013) 'Mapping Crime before It Happens', *Gravesend Reporter* (online). 24 January. Available at: http://www.gravesendreporter .co.uk (Accessed: 6 January 2014)
Duckitt, J. (1994) *The Social Psychology of Prejudice.* Westport, CT: Praeger.
Dunfermline Press (2010) 'Kids as Young as Four Charged with Vandalism' (online). 18 February. Available at: http://www.dunfermlinepress.com/ ... /410308-kids-as-young-as-four-charged-with-vandalism/ (Accessed: 12 October 2012).
Durkheim, E. (1933 originally 1983) *The Division of Labour in Society.* Glemcoe, IL: Free Press.

Dutch Amsterdam (2009) 'Amsterdam Craze: Tossing Smart Cars into Canals' (online). 25 July. Available at: http://www.dutchamsterdam.nl/707-amsterdam-smart-car-11canals (Accessed: 13 June 2011).

DW.DE. (2008) 'Berlin Gay Memorial Vandalised' (online). Available at: http://www.dw-world.de/dw (Accessed: 12 October 2011).

East Anglian Times (2006) 'Vandalism Is Putting Lives at Risk'. Available at: http://www.eadt.co.uk/ ... /vandalism_is_putting_lives_at_risk_1_76608? ... (Accessed: 14 May 2011).

Easton, M. (2011) 'England Riots: The Return of the Underclass' (online). *BBC News*. 11 August. Available at: http://www.bbc.co.uk/news/uk-14488486 (Accessed: 3 June 2014).

Echo News (2010) 'Railway Graffiti Vandal Jailed for a Year' (online). 8 October. Available at: http://www.echo-news.co.uk (Accessed: 18 April 2011).

Edge News (2010) (online) Available at: http://www.edgeboston.com/index.php?ch=news&sc2=news&sc3=&id=103582 (Accessed: 22 October 2013).

Edwards, M. (2004) 'The Rise of the Khmer Rouge in Cambodia: Internal or External Origins?' *Asian Affairs, 35*(1), 56–67.

Electronic Disturbance Theater (2014) (online) Available at: http://www.thing.net (Accessed: 12 August 2014).

Emmet, K. (1979) 'Ideology from Destutt De Tracy to Marx', *Journal of the History of Ideas, 40*(3), 253–368.

Entwistle, J. (2008) 'Amir Khan Launches Hard-hitting Rail Campaign'. *The Northern Echo* (online). 18 July. Available at: http://www.thenorthernecho.co.uk/ ... /3214627 (Accessed: 3 March 2011).

Etzioni, A. (1993) *The Spirit of Community: The Reinvention of American Society*. New York: Touchstone.

Evans, S. (2014) 'Mystery in Tokyo as Hundreds of Copies of Anne Frank's Diary Are Defaced across Public Libraries'. Available at: http://www.dailymail.co.uk (Accessed: 9 August 2014).

Ferrell, J. (1996) *Crimes of Style: Urban Graffiti and the Politics of Criminality*. Boston: Northeastern University Press.

Ferrell, J. (2004) 'Boredom, Crime and Criminology', *Theoretical Criminology, 8*, 287–302.

Ferrell, J., Hayward, K. and Young, J. (2008) *Cultural Criminology: An Invitation*. London: Sage.

Festinger, L. (1954) 'A Theory of Social Comparison Processes', *Human Relations, 7*(2), 117–140.

Fielding, N. (1981) *The National Front*. London: Routledge and Kegan Paul.

Foley, A. (2007) 'Youths Commit Vandalism in France'. Available at: http://imnotemeril.blogspot.com/2007/01/youths-commit-vandalism-in-france.html (Accessed: 2 June 2014).

Fox News (2010) (online) Available at: http://www.fox4kc.com/newss/wdaf-story-ucm-rally-gay-lesbian-vandalism-11101010,0,6814791.story (Accessed: 22 June 2012).

Foucault, M. (1969) *The Archaeology of Knowledge*, trans. A.M. Sheridan Smith. London and New York: Routledge, 2002.

Foucault, M., Hurley, R., Faubion, J. and Rabinow, P. (2001) *The Essential Works of Foucault, 1954–1984*. New York. New Press.

France 24 (2013) 'Predictive Policing: Tackling Crime Before It Happens', *France 24*, 25 February 2013.

Free Library, The (1996) 'Hate Campaign Lover is Jailed' (online). 30 March. Available at: http://www.thefreelibary.com (Accessed: 7 January 2015).

Freud, S. (1905) *Three Essays on the Theory of Sexuality.* Eastford, CT: Martino Fine Books.

Friedrichs, D. (2000) 'State Crime or Governmental Crime: Making Sense of the Conceptual Confusion', in Ross, J.L. (ed.) *Controlling State Crime.* New Brunswick: Transaction Publishers.

Furnell, S. (2010) 'Hackers, Viruses and Malicious Software', in Jewkes, Y. and Yar, M. (eds) *Handbook of Internet Crime.* Devon: Willan

Furness, H. (2013) 'Leaving Heritage Homes Abandoned Is Madness' (online). 5 December. Available at: http://www.telegraph.co.uk/news/uknews/prince-charles/10498995/Leaving-heritage-homes-abandoned-is-madness.html (Accessed: 19 July 2014).

Gable, R.K. (1986) 'Application of Personal Telemonitoring to Current Problems in Corrections', *Journal of Criminal Justice, 14,* 167–176.

Gainsbury, S. and Culzac, N. (2011) 'Rioting Link to Deprivation Revealed', *Financial Times* (online). 4 September. Available at: http://www.ft.com/cms/s/0/236110aa-d716-11e0-bc73-00144feabdc0.html#axzz1X3nspCJu (Accessed: 24 May 2013).

Gardham, D. (2007) 'Cameron as Leader of the Slightly Silly Party' (online). 14 February. Available at: http://www.telegraph.co.uk/news/uknews/1542634/cameron-as-leader-of-the-slightly-silly-party.html (Accessed: 22 May 2011).

Garland, D. (2001) *The Culture of Control.* Oxford: Oxford University Press.

Garside, R. (2009) 'Ministers' Worst Fears Confirmed as the Recession Fuels Crime Surge', *The Times* (online). 23 January. Available at: http://www.timesonline.co.uk/tol/news/uk/crime/article5570002.ece (Accessed: 17 June 2014).

Gatecrasher (2014) (online). Available at: http://www.gatecrasher.com/venues/sheffield/ (Accessed: 18 July 2014).

Gelder, K. (1998) 'Mad Max and Aboriginal Automation: Putting Cars to Use in Contemporary Road Films and Narratives', in D. Thoms, L. Holden and T. Claydon (eds) *The Motor Car and Popular Culture in the 20th Century,* Aldershot, UK: Ashgate, 63. Also see Deloria, 'I Want to Ride in Geronimo's Cadillac'.

Gerstenfeld, P.B. (2004) *Hate Crimes: Causes, Controls and Controversies.* Thousand Oaks, CA: Sage.

Gibson, W. (2003) *Burning Chrome.* New York: HarperCollins.

Gibson, W. (1984) *Neuromancer.* New York: Ace Books.

Giddens, A. (1991) *The Consequences of Modernity.* Stanford: Stanford University Press.

Giddens, A. (1998) *The Third Way: The Renewal of Social Democracy.* Cambridge: Polity Press.

Globe and Mail, The (2008) (online) Available at: http://www.theglobeandmail.com/news/politics/article714755.ece (Accessed: 15 June 2010).

Goffman, E. (1961) *Asylums: Essays on the Social Situation of Mental Patients and Other Inmates.* New York: Anchor Books.

Golden Map (2008) Available at: http://www.swindonweb.com/?m=2&s+625&ss=628&c=4109 (Accessed: 19 May 2011).

Goltz, James D. (1984) 'Are the News Media Responsible for the Disaster Myths? A Content Analysis of Emergency Response Imagery', *International Journal of Mass Emergencies and Disasters, 2,* 345–368.

Gonzalez, N. (2009) 'Vehicles Defaced with Racist Words, Sexual Images'. Available at: http://www.azcentral.com/community/scottsdale/articles/2009/09/06/2009 0906vandals0907.html (Accessed: 12 June 2011).

Goold, B. (2004) 'Idealizing the Other? Western Images of the Japanese Criminal Justice System', *Criminal Justice Ethics*, *23*(2), 14–24.

Graham, J. and Bowling, B. (*1995*) *Young People and Crime*. Home Office Research Study 145. London: Home Office.

Graeber, D. (2007) *Lost People: Magic and Legacy of Slavery in Madagascar.* Bloomington: Indiana University Press.

Green, J. (2011) 'Increasing Public Transport Use with Smart Campaigns' (online). 30 June. Available at: http://dirt.asla.org/2011/06/30/ (Accessed: 15 April 2012).

Green, D.P., McFalls, L.H. and Smith, J.K. (2001) 'Hate Crime: An Emergent Research Agenda', *Annual Review of Sociology, 27*, 479–504.

Greenberg, A. (2014) *'Kevin Mitnick. Once the World's Most Wanted Hacker, Is Now Selling Zero Day Exploits' (online). 24 September. Available at:* http://www.wired.com (Accessed: 1 February 2015).

Greenpeace (2014a) (online) Available at: http://www.Greenpeace.org.uk/about (Accessed: 16 August 2014).

Greenpeace (2014b) (online) Available at: http://www.greenpeace.org.uk/peace/the-crime-of-opposing-war (Accessed: 16 August 2014).

Guardian, The (2001) 'Anger as Spiderboy Gets Cash for Film'. Available at: http://www.newsguardian.co.uk/news/local/anger_as_spiderboy_gets_cash_for_film_I_1600556 (Accessed: 16 March 2010).

Guardian, The (2011a) 'Vandals Ruin Children's Swing' (online). 29 March. Available at: http://www.guardian-series.co.uk/ ... /8939419.WANSTEAD__Vandals_ruin_children's-swing/ (Accessed: 2 September 2011).

Guardian, The (2011b) 'David Cameron's Solution for Broken Britain: Tough Love and Tougher Policing' (online). 15 August. Available at: http://www.theguardian.com/uk/2011/aug/15/david-cameron-broken-britain-policing (Accessed: 10 June 2013).

Guardian, The (2011c) 'Reading the Riots: Investigating England's Summer of Disorder' (online). 14 December. Available at: http://www.theguardian.com/uk/series/reading-the-riots (Accessed: 19 June 2013)

Guardian, The (2011d) 'Pavement Adverts under Fire as Leeds Council Is Accused of "Environmental Crime"' (online). 14 February. Available at: http://www.theguardian.com/leeds (Accessed: 8 May 2012).

Guardian, The (2014) 'San Francisco Pranksters Turn from Cow-tipping to Car-tipping' (online). 9 April. Available at: http://www.theguardian.com (Accessed: 16 August 2014).

Guillot, T. (2014) 'Teenager Hacked into Metropolitan Police's Computer – Causing Force's Website to Crash' (online). 28 August. Available at: http://www.gazettelive.co.uk (Accessed: 14 August 2014).

Hagan, J., Gillis, A. and Simpson, J. (1987) 'Class in the Household: A Power-Control Theory of Gender and Delinquency', *American Journal of Sociology, 92*(4), 788–816.

Hall, N. (2013) *Hate Crime* (2nd ed.). Abingdon: Taylor & Francis.

Hall, S., Winlow, S. and Ancrum, C. (2008) *Criminal Identities and Consumer Culture*. Cullompton: Willan.

Hart, D. (2008) 'Tracy, Destutt de (1754–1836)', in Hamowy, R. (ed.) *The Encyclopedia of Libertarianism*. Thousand Oaks, CA: Sage.

Hastings, M. (2011) 'Years of Liberal Dogma Have Spawned a Generation of Amoral, Uneducated, Welfare Dependent, Brutalised Youngsters', *Daily Mail* (online). Available at: http://www.dailymail.co.uk/debate/article-2024284/UK-riots-2011-Liberal-dogma-spawned-generation-brutalised-youths.html (Accessed: 15 September 2013).

Hayward, K.J. (2002) 'The Vilification and Pleasures of Youthful Transgression', in Muncie, J., Hughes, G. and McLaughlin, E. (eds) *Youth Justice: Critical Readings*. London: Open University Press.

Hayward, K.J. (2007) "Situational Crime Prevention and Its Discontents: Rational Choice Theory Versus the "Culture of Now"', *Social Policy & Administration, 41*(3), 232–250.

Hayes, P. (2012) 'Scrap this Anti-social Meddling in our Lives', *Spiked* (online). 24 May. Available at: www.spiked-online.com/newsite/article/12476 (Accessed: 24 May 2013).

Heining, D. (1998) 'Cars and Girls: The Car, Masculinity and Pop Music', in Thoms, D., Holden, L. and Claydon, T. (eds) *The Motor Car and Popular Culture in the 20th Century,* 96–119. Aldershot: Ashgate.

Henley, J. (2014) 'Antisemitism on Rise across Europe "in Worst Times since the Nazis"' (online). 20 August. Available at: http://www.theguardian.com/society/2014/aug/07/antisemitism-rise-europe-worst-since-nazis: 15 February, 2015).

Hillyard, P. and Tombs, S. (2007) 'From "Crime" to Social Harm?' *Crime, Law and Social Change, 48*(1–2), 9–25.

Hirschi, T. (1969) *Causes of Delinquency*. Berkeley: University of California Press.

Hirst, P.Q. (1975) 'Marx and Engels on Law, Crime and Morality', in Taylor, I., Walton, P. and Young, J. (eds) *Critical Criminology* (1st ed.), 203–232. London: Routledge and Kegan Paul.

Hobsbawn, E. (2007) *Globalisation, Democracy and Terrorism*. London: Little Brown.

Holden, L. (1998) 'More than a Marque: The Car as Symbol: Aspects of Culture and Ideology', in Thoms, D., Holden, L. and Claydon, T. (eds) *The Motor Car and Popular Culture in the Twentieth Century*. Aldershot: Ashgate.

Holmes, Su (2005) *'Starring ... Dyer?': Re-visiting Star Studies and Contemporary Celebrity Culture. Westminster Papers in Communication and Culture (WPCC), 2*(2), 6–21.

Home Office (1997) *No More Excuses: A New Approach to Tackling Youth Crime in England and Wales*. Cm 3809. London: Home Office.

Home Office (2001) *Religious Discrimination in England and Wales*. Research study 220. London: Home Office.

Home Office (2006a) *Vandalism and Criminal Damage- Problem Analysis*. London: Home Office.

Home Office (2006b) *Findings from the 2004–2005 British Crime Survey*. London: Home Office.

Home Office (2013) 'British Crime Survey' (online). Available at: http://www.homeoffice.gov.uk/rds/bcs1.html (Accessed: 16 June 2014).

Hopkins Burke, R.D. (1998) 'The Contextualisation of Zero Tolerance Policing Strategies', in Hopkins Burke, R. (ed.) *Zero Tolerance Policing*. London: Macmillan.

Hopkins Burke, R.D. (1999) *Young Offenders and the Fragmentation of Modernity: Models of Youth Justice.* Scarman Centre for the Study of Public Order. Occasional Paper Series. University of Leicester.

Hopkins Burke, R.D. (2005) *An Introduction to Criminological Theory* (2nd ed.). Cullompton: Willan.

Hopkins Burke, R.D. (2008) *Young People, Crime and Justice.* Cullompton: Willan.

Hopkins Burke, R.D. (2009) *An Introduction to Criminological Theory* (3rd ed.). Devon: Willan.

Hopkins Burke, R.D. (2013) *An Introduction to Criminological Theory* (4th ed.). London: Routledge.

Hopkins Burke, R.D. (2014a) *An Introduction to Criminological Theory* (4th ed.). Oxford: Routledge.

Hopkins Burke, R.D. (2014b) 'The Case for a Radical Moral Communitarianism', *British Journal of Community Justice, 12*(3), 5–18.

Hopkins Burke, R.D. and Pollock, E. (2004) 'A Tale of Two Anomies: Some Observations on the Contribution of (Sociological) Criminological Theory to Explaining Hate Crime Motivation', *Internet Journal of Criminology,* November.

Hopkins Burke, R.D. and Hodgson, P. (2013) 'Responding to Repeat Anti-social Behaviour and Moral Communitarianism'. Paper given to the British Society of Criminology Conference 2013, 'Criminology on Trial', University of Wolverhampton, 1–4 July.

Hopwood, A.J., Mannucci, A. and Sullivan, K.M. (1996) 'DNA Typing from Human Faeces', *Int. J. Legal Med., 108,* 237–243.

Hotten, R. (1999) *Formula One: The Business of Winning.* London: Orion.

Houdt, J.F. van and Schinkel, W. (2013) 'A Genealogy of Neoliberal Communitarianism', *Theoretical Criminology, 17,* 493–515.

Howard, J. (2006) 'Vandalism is Putting Lives at Risk', *East Anglian Times* (online). 11 August. Available at: http:// www.eadt.co.uk/news (Accessed: 15 February 2015).

Howard, P. (2011) 'The Arab Spring's Cascading Effects', *Pacific Standard* (online). 23rd February. Available at: http://www.psmag.com; http://www.alfista.com/2005/05/05/man-tries-hard-to-get-in-jail (Accessed: 14 July 2013).

Available at: http://www.csis-scrs.gc.ca/pblctns/cmmntr/cm21-eng.asp (Accessed: 14 May 2014).

Available at: http://www.communitycare.co.uk/blogs/adult-care-blog/2010/12/disabilityhate-crime-figures-reveal-under-reporting.html (Accessed: 14 June 2014).

Available at: https://www.mitnicksecurity.com/ (Accessed: 31 January 2015).

Available at: http://skinsparty.com (Accessed: 12 May 2014).

Available at: http://www.thefreelibrary.com (Accessed: 21 May 2014).

Available at: http://www.ukpolitics.org.uk/node/3513 (Accessed: 15 May 2014).

Available at: http://www.thefreelibrary.com (Accessed: 21 May 2014).

Hub Pages (2010) (online). Available at: http://hubpages.com/hubpages.com/hub/The-Bullingdon-Club (Accessed: 12 September 2012).

Hudson, J. and Lowe, S. (2004) *Understanding the Policy Process.* Bristol: Policy Press.

Huffington Post (2012a) 'Trayvon Martin Case: Police Chief Bill Lee under Fire with "No Confidence" Vote' (online). 22 March. Available at: http:/www.huffingtonpost.com (Accessed: 3 June 2014).

Huffington Post (2012b) 'Sikh Temple Graffiti Vandalism Leads to Call for Hate Crime Investigation' (online). 8 February. Available at: http://www.huffington-post.com (Accessed: 15 July 2014).

Huffman, W.E., Shogren, J.F., Rousu, M. and Tegene, A. (2004) 'Consumer Willingness to Pay for Genetically Modified Food Labels in a Market with Diverse Information: Evidence from Experimental Auctions', *Journal of Agricultural and Resource Economics, 28*(3), 481–502.

Hughes, G. (1998) *Understanding Crime Prevention: Social Control, Risk and Late Modernity*. Buckingham: Open University Press.

Hume, M. (2010) 'A Respectable Riot' (online). Available at: http://www.spiked-online.com/index.php/site/article/9885 (Accessed: 19 July 2013).

Huxley, A. (1932) *Brave New World*. New York: Crossroad Publishing.

Hybrid Cars (2009) 'Car/Culture Wars: Glen Beck Ridicules Hybrids' (online). 17 September. Available at: http://www.hybridcars.com/hybrid-drivers/car-culture-wars-glenn-beck-ridicules-hybrid-26115.htm (Accessed: 3 September 2014).

Hyde, T. (2013) 'Homophobic Vandals Target Wigan Woman's Home for Second Time with Abusive Graffiti in "Hate Crime"' (online). 4 September. Available at: http://www.mancuanianmatters.co.uk (Accessed: 14 July 2014).

Independent, The (1994) 'Vandals "Caused Death Rail Crash" (online). 27 June. Availabe at: http://www.independent.co.uk/news/uk/vandals-caused-death-rail-crash-1425327.htm (Accessed: 13 July 2010).

Independent, The (1995) Available at: http://www.independent.co.uk/news/riot-police-mop-up-anticar-protestors-1592957.html (Accessed: 10 June 2010).

Independent, The (1997) (online). Available at: http://www.independent.co.uk/news/young-britain-tell-us-your-view-1294899.htm (Accessed: 12 May 2010).

Independent, The (2007) 'The Bullingdon Club class of "87"' (online). 13 February. Available at: http://www.independent.co.uk/news/uk/politics/camerons-cronies-thebullingdon-clubs-class-of-87–436192.htm (Accessed: 15 September 2010).

Independent, The (2011) 'David Lammy: Prejudices of the Few Eclipsed by Civic Pride' (online). 14 August. Available at: http://www.independent.co.uk/voices/commentators/david-lammy-prejudices-of-the-few-eclipsed-by-civic-pride-2337446.html (Accessed: 13 July 2013).

Insurance Daily (2008) (online) Available at: http://www.insurancedaily.co.uk/2008/04/14/aa-reveals-car-vandalism-stats (Accessed: 12 March 2010).

Internet Advert (2014) 'Sports Car-phallic Symbol of Modernity'. Available at: http://www.penis-enlargement.eu/ (Accessed: 22 December 2014)

Internet Live Statistics (2014) (online) Available at: http://www.internetlivestats.com/internet-users/ (Accessed: 20 August 2014).

Jaishankar, K. (2011) *Cyber Criminology: Exploring Internet Crimes and Criminal Behavior.* New York: CRC.

Japan Probe (2008) 'Flower Vandalism and Japanese Society' (online). 22 April. Available at: http://www. japanprobe.com (Accessed: 13 July 2012).

Japan Probe (2010) 'Yokaren Peace Memorial Museum Vandalised' (online). 6 July. Available at: http://www.japanprobe.com (Accessed: 13 July 2012).

Jardine, L. (1998) *Worldly Goods: A New History of the Renaissance.* New York: W.W. Norton Publishers.

Jewkes, Y. (ed.) (2003) *Dot.cons: Crime, Deviance and Identity on the Internet.* Cullompton: Willan.

Jewkes, Y. (2007) *Crime Online.* Devon: Willan.

Johann Hari Gay Issues (2010) (online) Available at: http://www.johannhari.com/2007/12/03/do-the-police-still-have-a-problem-with-homophobia (Accessed: 14 December 2010).

Joke Buddha (2014) (online) Available at: http://www.jokebuddha.com/Hubcap#ixzz1B0cTj2w3 (Accessed: 5 August 2014).

Jones, J.M. (1972). *Prejudice and Racism*. Reading, MA: Addison Wesley Publishers.

Jones, M. (2002) *Social Psychology of Prejudice*. New Jersey: Prentice Hall.

Jordan, B. (1998) 'New Labour, New Community?' *Imprints, 3*(2), 113–131.

Junger-Tas, J. (2004) 'Youth Justice in the Netherlands', *Crime and Justice, 31*, 293–347.

Katz, J. (1988) *Seductions of Crime: Moral and Sensual Attractions in Doing Evil*. New York: Basic Books.

Keane, C., Maxim, P. and Teevan, J. (1993) 'Drinking and Driving, Self-Control, and Gender: Testing a General Theory of Crime', *Journal of Research in Crime and Delinquency, 30*, 30–46.

Kearns, G. and Philo, C. (1993) *Selling Places: The City as Cultural Capital, Past and Present*. Oxford: Pergamon.

Keeble, A. (2014) 'Vandals Trash Disabled Toilet' (online). 4 April. Available at: http://www.northdevongazette.co.uk (Accessed: 4 August 2014).

Kennedy, R. (2013) 'North East Phone Box Scam Gang Sent to Prison' (online). 27 February. Available at: http://www.chroniclelive.co.uk/news/ ... /north-east-phone-box-scam-1724384 (Accessed: 14 June 2014).

Kilmarnock Standard (2009) 'Kilmarnock man damaged car roof by running over it' (online). Available at: http://www.kilmarnockstandard.co.uk/ ... /kilmarnock-man-damaged-car-roof-by- running-over-it-81430–23439666 (Accessed: 13 June 2012).

Komiya, N. (1999) 'A Cultural Study of the Low Crime Rate in Japan', *British Journal of Criminology, 39*(3), 369–391.

Knights, B. (1998) '"The Slide to Ashes": An Antidote to Zero Tolerance', in Hopkins Burke, R.D. (ed.) *Zero Tolerance Policing*. Leicester: Perpetuity Press.

Kumar, R. (2013) 'Here's How GAP Responded to the Racist Vandalism of Their Ad Featuring Sikh Model'. Available at: http://www.dnaindia.com (Accessed: 14 August 2014).

Kuttab, D. (1998) 'A Profile of the Stonethrowers', *Journal of Palestine Studies, 17*(3), 14–23.

Kyle, D. (1998) *Spectacles of Death in Ancient Rome*. London: Routledge.

Latham, B.B. and Shimura, M. (1967) 'Folktales Commonly Told by American and Japanese Children: Ethical Themes of Omission and Commission', *Journal of American Folklore*, January–March, 33–48.

Labour Party (1997) 'Labour Party Manifesto'. Available at: http://www.labour-party.org.uk (Accessed: 14 March 2010).

Lasch, S. (1979) *The Culture of Narcissism*. New York: Norton.

Leaderlive (2010) 'Children at Risk as Vandals Target Flintshire Play Park'. Available at: http://www.leaderlive.co.uk/ ... /children-at-risk-as-vandals-target-flintshire-play- park.aspx) (Accessed: 12 July 2012).

Lets Japan (2008) 'Security Vending Machine Vandalized' (online). 13 October. Available at: http://www.letsjapan.markmode.com (Accessed: 16 June 2013).

Leung, R. (2002) 'Skulls and Bones: Secret Yale Society Includes America's Power Elite' (online). Available at: http://www.cbsnews.com/stories/2003/10/02/60minutes/main576332.shtml (Accessed: 6 June 2012).
Levy, S. (1984) *Hackers. Heroes of the Computer Revolution*. New York: Nerraw Manijaime//Doubleday.
Liverpool Daily Post (2007) 'A City Blazes in Front of the Whole World' (online). 9 July. Available at: http://www.liverpooldailypost.co.uk/liverpool-life-features/liverpool-special-features/2007/07/09/a-city-blazes-in-front-of-the-whole-world-64375–19429599/ (Accessed: 14 June 2014).
Liverpool Echo (2010) 'Tragic Graffiti Couple the Closest Thing to Romeo and Juliet I have Experienced in Court' says Liverpool Coroner' (online). 18 August. Available at: http://www.liverpoolecho.co.uk/liverpool-news/local-news/2010/08/18/tragic-graffiti-couple-the-closest-thing-to-romeo-and-juliet-I-have-experience-in-court-says-liverpool-coroner-100252–270888 (Accessed: 15 June 2014).
Local, The (2011) 'Cost of Train Graffiti and Vandalism on the Rise, Operators Say' (online). 8 July. Available at: http://www.thelocal.de/society/20110708–36157.html (Accessed: 12 September 2012).
London Evening Standard (2010) 'Gatecrashers Invade £1m Kingston House for Boy's Facebook Party' (online) 5 February. Available at: http://www.standard.co.uk/news/gatecrashers-invade-1m-kingston-house-for-boys-facebook-party-6735805.html (Accessed: 15 June 2013).
Lowenthal, L. (1961) *Literature, Popular Culture, and Society*. New York: Prentice Hall.
Lowenthal, M. (2001) 'Don't Be Fooled' (online). Available at: http://www.ecopledge.com (Accessed: 5 March 2012).
Maldon and Burnham Standard (2009) 'Resident Speaks Out about Persistent Vandalism in Burnham' (online). Available at: http://www.maldonandburhamstandard.co.uk/news/localnews/4089183.Resident_speaks_out_about_persistent_vandalism_in_Burnham/ (Accessed: 13 June 2014).
Malvern, J. (2005) 'Cow-tipping Myth Hasn't Got a Leg to Stand on' (online). *London Times*, 5 November. Available at: http://www.timesonline.co.uk/tol/news/uk/article586737 (Accessed: 10 July 2014).
Marcuse, H. (2002) *One Dimensional Man: Studies in the Ideology of Advanced Industrial Society*. London: Routledge.
Marullo, S. and Meyer, D.S. (2004) 'Antiwar and Peace Movements', in Snow, D.A., Soule, S.A. and Kriesi, H. (eds) *The Blackwell Companion to Social Movements*. Oxford, United Kingdom: Blackwell Publishing.
Maruna, S. (2001) *Making Good: How Ex-Convicts Reform and Rebuild Their Lives*. Washington, DC: American Psychological Association Books.
Marsden, S. (2012) 'Britain's Most Prolific Church Lead Theft Gang Jailed' (online). 13 December. Available at: http://www.telegraph.co.uk (online) (Accessed: 4 July 2014).
Mason, R. (2010) 'Forget Stealing Lead off Church Roofs: Copper Thieves Up the Ante with Chainsaws' (online). 3 August. Available at: http://www.telegraph.co.uk/finance/newsbysector/energy/7925566/ (Accessed: 4 July 2014).
Mathiesen, T. (1997) 'The Viewer Society: Michel Foucault's "Panopticon" Revisited', *Theoretical Criminology*, *1*(2), 215–234.

Matthews, R. and Kauzlarich, D. (2007) 'State Crimes and State Harms: A Tale of Two Definitional Frameworks', *Crime, Law and Social Change, 48*, 43–55.

Matthews, R. and Young, J. (eds) (1992) *Issues in Realist Criminology* (Sage Contemporary Criminology). London: Sage.

Matza, D. (1964) *Delinquency and Drift*. New York: John Wiley.

May, T. (2010) 'Speech to Conservative Party Conference' (online). 5 October. Available at: http:// www.ukpolitics.orh.uk/node/3513. (Accessed: 15 February 2015).

McCurry (2007) Available at: http://www.guardian.co.uk/japan/story/0,,2027043,00.html (Accessed: 3 July 2013).

McDevitt, J., Levin, J. and Bennett, S. (2002) 'Hate Crime Offenders: An Expanded Typology', *Journal of Social Issues, 58*(2), 303–317.

McEwen, A. (2012) '80s Revival for Car Badge Theft' (online). 31 March. Available at: http://www.edinburghnews.scotsman.com (Accessed: 24 July 2013).

Meikle, G. (2002) *Future Active: Media Activism and the Internet*. New York and London. Routledge.

Meloen, et al. (1988) 'Authoritarianism and the Revival of Political Racism: Reassessment in the Netherlands of the Reliability and Validity of the Concept of Authoritarianism', by Adorno et al., *Political Psychology, 9*, 413–429.

Merton, R. (1938) 'Social Structure and Anomie', *American Sociological Review, 3*, 672–682.

Merton, R. (1949) 'Social Structure and Anomie: Revisions and Extensions', in Ruth Anshen (ed.) *The Family*. New York: Harper Brothers.

Merton, R. (1957) *Social Theory and Social Structure*. New York. Free Press.

Metropolitan Police Service (2000) *The Investigation of Racist, Domestic Violence and Homophobic Incidents. A Guide to Minimum Standards*. London: MPS.

Miami Student, The (2010) 'Sporadic Vehicle Vandalism Remains Constant Issue' (online). 26 February. Available at: https://miamistudent.net/?p=109817 (Accessed: 4 January 2015).

Mills, C. Wright (1956) *The Power Elite*. Oxford: Oxford University Press.

Mills, H., Skodbo, S. and Blyth, P. (2013) *Understanding Organised Crime: Estimating the Scale and the Social and Economic Costs*. Research Report 73. London: Home Office.

MIND (2007) 'Mind Reveals Alarming Levels of Disability Hate Crime' (online). 29 November. Available at: http://www.mind.org.uk/news/1773 (Accessed: 2 January 2010)

Missing List, The (2009) 'Police Appeal-Stone Thrown Through Train Window Straikes Passenger' (online). Available at: http://themissinglist.co.uk/police-appeal/sone-thrown-through-train-window-strikes-passenger-sundridge-park (Accessed: 14 March 2012).

Moll, B. (2014) (online) Available at: http://www.lbjlib.utexas.edu/shwv/archives/sh95–026.htm (Accessed: 8 August 2014).

Moreton, C. (2011) 'First Person: Paul "Moose" Curtis' (online). *FT Magazine*, 20 May. Available at: http://www.ft.com (Accessed: 5 August 2014).

Morris, N. (2012) '"Predictive Policing" Could Come to UK', *The Independent*, 26 January.

Motoring Bible (2010) http://www.motoringbible.com/articles/accessories/sat-nav-theft-how-you-can-prevent-it.php (Accessed: 23 January 2011).

Mullin, C. (2012) 'Network Rail Campaign to Cut Rail Trespass Deaths', *The Liverpool Echo* (online). 9 May. Available at: http:// www.liverpoolecho.co.uk/ ... /uk ../network-rail-campaign-cut-rail-33443 (Accessed: 7 July 2013).

National Statistics Office (2007) 'Attitudes to Mental Illness' (online). Available at: http://www.dh.gov.uk/en/Publicationsandstatistics/Publications/PublicationsStatistics/DH_076516 (Accessed: 12 June 2011).

New York Times (2012) 'Shooting Focuses Attention on a Program that Seeks to Avoid Guns' (online). 22 March. Available at: http://www.nytimes.com/2012/03/23/us/trayvon-martin-death-spotlights-neighborhood-watch-groups.html?_r=2& (Accessed: 14 May 2013).

National Advisory Group (1999) *Breaking the Chain of Hate: A National Survey Examining Levels of Homophobic Crime and Community Confidence towards the Police Service.* Manchester.

National Travel Survey (2007) *Report Presenting the Results of the National Travel Survey, a Household Survey Designed to Provide a Databank of Personal Travel Information for Great Britain* (online). Department of Transport. Available at: http://data.gov.uk (Accessed: 5 August 2009).

NBC News (2013) 'Potential Trayvon Martin Case Jurors Get Look at Defendant George Zimmerman' (online). 10 June. Available at: http://usnews.nbcnews.com/_news/2013/06/10/18880979-potential-trayvon-martin-case-jurors-get-look-at-defendant-george-zimmerman?lite (Accessed: 6 June 2014).

Nelson, T.D. (2006) *The Psychology of Prejudice* (2nd ed.). Boston: Pearson.

Nevius, C.W. (2014) 'Smart Car Tipping Isn't a Thing, Unless It Is' (online). 9 April. Available at: http://www.blog.sfgate.com/cwnevius (Accessed: 3 August 2014).

News, The (2010) (online) Available at: http://www.portsmouth.co.uk/newshome/A-trail-of-damage-but.6185557.jp (Accessed: 10 July 2011).

NHSA (2014) 'National Head Start Association' (online). Available at: http://www.nhsa.org/ (Accessed: 10 August 2014).

Nicholas, S., Kershaw, C. and Walker, A. (2007) *Crime in England and Wales: 2006–07*. Home Office Statistical Bulletin. London: Home Office.

Northern Echo (2014) 'Warning after Youngsters Throw Stones At Cars' (online). 31 March. Available at: http://www.northernecho.co.uk. (Accessed: 15 February 2015).

Nye, I. (1958) *Family Relationships and Delinquent Behaviour.* New York: John Wiley and Sons.

Ocheje, P.D. (2007) '"In the Public Interest": Forced Evictions, Land Rights and Human Development in Africa', *Journal of African Law, 51*, 173–214.

Office for National Statistics (2013) *Crime in England and Wales. Year Ending June 2013.*

Ohmann, S., Jones, I. and Wilkes, K. (2006) 'The Perceived Social Impacts of the 2006 Football World Cup on Munich Residents', *Journal of Sport and Tourism, 11*, 129–152.

Oldham Chronicle (2010) 'Vandals Trash Children's Garden' (online). 19 May. Available at: http://www.oldham-chronicle.co.uk › News › News Headlines (Accessed: 12 July 2013).

Ong, R. (2004) 'New Beijing, Great Olympics: Beijing and its Unfolding Olympic Legacy', *Stanford Journal of East Asian Affairs, 4*(2), 35–49.

Oxford Mail (1999) 'Stolen Car Badge Haul Found' (online). 27 March. Available at: http://www.oxfordmail.co.uk/archive/1999/03/27/Oxfordshire+Archive/6636671.stolen_car_badge_haul_found\ (Accessed: 10 July 2011).

Oxford Mail (2010) 'Vandals Target Family's Cars' (online). 29 October. Available at: http://www.oxfordmail.co.uk/ (Accessed: 10 July 2011).

Paige, W. (1989) 'The Defacing of Denver', *The Denver Post*, 9 May, 7B.

Patrick, G. (2010) 'Facebook Part House Trashed', *The Sun* (online). 22 February. Available at: http://www.thesun.co.uk/sol/homepage/news/2864021/Facebook-party-house-trashed.html (Accessed: 12 June 2011).

Penfold-Mounce, R. (2009) *Celebrity Culture & Crime*. Basingstoke: Palgrave MacMillan.

Penman, D. (1995) 'Riot Police Mop Up Anti-car Protestors' (online). 24 July. Available at: http://www.independent.co.uk. (Accessed: 16 February 2015).

Perry, B. (2001) *In the Name of Hate: Understanding Hate Crimes*. New York: Routledge.

Pettigrew, T.F. (1958) 'Personality and Socio-cultural Factors in Intergroup Attitudes: A Cross-national Comparison', *Journal of Conflict Resolution, 2*, 29–42.

Phillips, R., Frost, D. and Singleton, A. (2013) 'Researching the Riots', *The Geographical Journal, 179*(1), 3–10.

Pink News (2011) 'Police Figures Show Rise in Recorded Anti-gay and Transphobic Crimes' (online). 9 September. Available at: http://www.pinknews.co.uk/2011/09/09/police-figures-show-rise-in-recorded-anti-gay-and-transphobic-crimes/ (Accessed: 14 June 2013).

Pitch, T. (1995) *Limited Responsibilities: Social Movements and Criminal Justice,* trans. by John Lea. London: Routledge.

Police Oracle (2012) 'Advanced Crime Prediction Model Trialled', *The Police Oracle*, January.

Porter, L. (2009) 'Planning Displacement: The Real Legacy of Major Sporting Events', *Planning Theory and Practice, 10*(3), 395–418.

Post Online (2014) (online) Available at: http:/www.postonline.co.uk/post/feature/2170488/metal-theft-finding-copperbottomed-solution#ixzzluOyBDYk9 (Accessed: 8 August 2014).

Presdee, M. (2000) *Cultural Criminology and the Carnival of Crime*. London: Routledge.

Presdee, M. (2007) 'Young People, Fire and Arson as Resistance', in Brannigan, A. and Pavlich, G. (eds) *Governance and Regulation in Social Life: Essays in Honour of W.G. Carson*. Abingdon: Routledge, Cavendish.

Prestowitz, C. (2004) *Rogue Nation: American Unilateralism and the Failure of Good Intentions*. New York: Basic Books.

Pugh, T. (1988) 'Casle Rock Breaks Out in Graffiti', *Rocky Mountain News*, 21 July, 26.

Pye, C. (2008) 'Fury as Gay Poster Is Vandalised' (online). 20 February. Available at: http://www.lancashiretelegraph.co.uk/news/ (Accessed: 14 May 2013).

Queensland Times, The (2012) 'Race Hate Vandals Hit Cemetery' (online). Available at: http://www.qt.com.au/news/race-hate-vandals-hit-cemetery/1297340/ (Accessed: 14 May 2013).

Quinlan, H. (2003) 'Cyber Terrorism. Online Dictionary Communications' (online). Available at: http://tlc.discovery.com/convergence/hackers/artciles/cyberterror.html (Accessed: 9 January 2015).

Quittner, J. (2003) Hacker Psych 101. 'Online. Discovery Communications' (online). Available at: http://tlc.discovery.com/covergence/hackers/ articles/psych/html> (Accessed: 9 January 2015).

RAC Foundation (2014) 'The Independent Motoring Charity' (online). Available at: http://www.racfoundation.org (Accessed: 14 February 2014).

Radcliff, D. (2000) 'Vigilante Group Targets Child Pornography Sites' (online). 17 January. Available at: http://www.computerworld.com (Accessed: 10 June 2010).

Railsback, Kathryn (1990) 'A Genocide Convention Action against the Khmer Rouge: Preventing a Resurgence of the Killing Fields', *Connecticut Journal of International Law*, *5*, 457–481.

Ramus, C.A. and Montiel, I. (2005) 'When Are Corporate Environmental Policies a Form of Greenwashing?' *Business and Society*, *44*(4), 377–414.

Rayner, et al. (2010) 'Millbank Tuition Fee Protests: "Embarrassed" Metropolitan Police Caught out by Student Riots' (online). 11 November. Available at: http://www.telegraph.co.uk/news/uknews/law-and-order/8124770/Millbank-tuition-fee-protests-embarrassed-Metropolitan-Police-caught-out-by-student-riots.html (Accessed: 17 June 2011).

Reckless, W. (1967) *The Crime Problem*. New York: Appleton.

Recycling International (2012) 'Guilty Pleas over US$ 2.6 Million Metal Theft'. Available at: http://www.recyclinginternational.com (Accessed: 12 June 2013).

Redding, W. (1992) '3 arrested In Random Vandalism; Teens Blame Vandalism For Actions, Police Say', *The Washington Post* (online). 5 March, Available at: http://www.highbeam.com/doc/1P2–994053.html (Accessed: 4 January 2015).

Reuters (2010) 'California Transit Cop Verdict Sparks Looting' (online). 9 July. Available at: http://www.reuters.com/article/2010/07/09/us-california-shooting-idUSTRE66763A20100709 (Accessed: 11 September 2011).

Rinf.com (2014) (online) Available at: http//:www.inf.com/coumnists/news/secret-societies-they-are-not-just-at-yale-they-are-running-a-university-near-you (Accessed: 12 August 2014).

Ritzer, G. (2004) *The McDonaldization of Society*. Revised New Century Edition. London: Sage.

Robben, A. (2010) 'Why Did They Kill? Cambodia in the Shadow of Genocide', *Ethos*, *38*(1), 1–2.

Rojek, C. (2001) *Celebrity*. Guildford and King's Lynn: Biddles.

Rokeach, M. (1960) *The Open and Closed Mind*. New York: Basic Books.

Ronay, B. (2008) 'Young, Rich and Drunk' (online). *The Guardian*. 8 May. Available at: http://www.guardian.co.uk/education/2008/may/09/oxbridgeandelitism.highereducation (Accessed: 3 February 2011).

Rootes, C.A. (1992) 'The New Politics and the New Social Movements', *European Journal of Political Research*, *22*, 171–191.

Ross, M. (2011) 'Blame for Riots Turns to UK Social System', *ABC News* (online). 11 August. Available at: http://www.abc.net.au/news/2011–08–10/society-role-in-london-riots/2833168?section=world (Accessed: 14 August 2014).

Rotter, J.B. (1954) *Social Learning and Clinical Psychology*. New York: Prentice-Hall.

Rundown, The (2005) 'Beyond Traffic Cones: Are Student Pranks Going Too Far?' (online). 1 February. Available at: http://www.therundown.co.uk/features/1107279578. (Accessed: 22 April 2014).

Ryan, Y. (2011) 'From the Arab Spring to Liverpool?' *Aljazeera* (online). 11 August. Available at: http://www.aljazeera.com/indepth/features/2011/08/2011811122931660627.html (Accessed: 12 April 2013).

Said, E. (2001) *Power, Politics and Culture*. New York: Bloomsbury.

Safer, M. (1991) *Flashbacks: On Returning to Vietnam*. St. Martin's Press: Random House.

Samson, R. (2011) *Pakistan: Political Leaders Herald Assassin as 'Hero of Islam'*. Available at: http://www.speroforum.com/a/61397/Pakistan-Political-leaders-herald-assassin-as-Hero-of-Islam (Accessed: 12 May 2013).

Sardar, Z. and Davies, W. (2002) *Why Do People Hate America?* London: Penguin Books.

Savory, Z. (2008) 'A Round of Applause for the Bullingdon Club' (online). 11 November 2008. Available at: http://www.cherwell.org/content/8021 (Accessed: 23 May 2010).

Schactman, N. (2008) 'Russian Coder: I Hacked Georgia's Sites in Cyberwar'. Available at: http://www.cyberwar.com (Accessed: 9 January 2014).

Schmetzer, U. (2001) 'Vandalized Koran Stirs Japan's Muslims'. Available at: http://www.muslimnews.co.uk (Accessed: 15 June 2010).

Schwarz, C. (1988) 'Chambers English Dictionary'. London: Chambers.

SelectaDNA (2014) (online) Available at: http://www.selectadna.co.uk/leadtheft.html?gclid=CJe7Mnxx6QCFUsB4wodNTCBVQ (Accessed: 14 May 2014).

Sellin, T. (1938) *Culture Crime and Conflict*. New York: Social Science Research Centre

Sennett, R. (1992) *The Fall of Public Man*. New York: Norton.

Sergeant, H. (2009) 'Feral Youths: How a Generation of Violent, Illiterate Young Men are Living Outside the Boundaries of Civilized Society'. *The Daily Mail* (online). 19 September. Available at: http://www.dailymail.co.uk/debate/article-1214549/Feral-youths-How-generation-violent-illiterate-young-men-living-outside-boundaries-civilised-society.html (Accessed: 15 February 2015).

Sherif, M., Harvey, O.J., White, B.J., Hood, W.R. and Sherif, C.W. (1961) *Intergroup Cooperation and Competition: The Robbers Cave Experiment*. Norman, OK: University Book Exchange.

Skoda Jokes (2011) (online) 22 April. Available at: http://skoda-jokes.blogspot.com (Accessed: 12 March 2012).

Skull and Cross Bones (2008) (online) Available at: http://www.skullandcross-bones.org/articles/skullandbones.htm (Accessed: 12 March 2012).

Slatalla, M. (2003) 'A Brief History of Hacking' (online). 28 October. *Discovery Communications*. Available at: http://tlc.discovery.com/ convergence/hackers/articles/history.html (Accessed: 9 January 2014).

Slater, J. (2001) 'What Went Wrong? The Collapse of the Israeli-Palestinian Peace Process', *Political Science Quarterly*, *16*(2), 171–199.

Slavin, E. (2010) 'Two Yokosuka Teens Suspected in Base Vandalism' (online). *Stars and Stripes*. 14 October. Available at: http://www.stripes.com (Accessed: 3 July 2013).

Softpedia (2009) '6-Year-Old Boy Learns to Drive from GTA, Takes Car to School' (online). 13 January. Available at: http://www.softpedia.com (Accessed: 16 February 2015)

Soodin, V. (2009) 'Smart Cars Get Dutch Dunking' (online). *The Sub.* Available at: http://www.thesun.co.uk/sol/homepage/news/2556548/Dutch-vandals-chuck-tiny-Smart-cars-in-Amsterdam-canals.html#ixzz0rfXQGdFj (Accessed: 10 July 2013).

South Ayrshire Council (2013) 'Vandals Wreck Signs – A Day After They Went Up' (online). 29 November. Available at: http://www.south-ayrshire.gov.uk (Accessed: 4 January 2015).

South Wales Evening Post (2009) 'Stone Throwing Yobs Showed Breathtaking Stupidity' (online). Available at: http://www.thisissouthwales.co.uk/news/Stone-throwing-yobs-showed-breathtaking-stupidity-inquest-told/article-1085390-detail/article.html (Accessed: 19 May 2011).

Sparks, R. (1992) *Television and the Drama of Crime*. Maidenhead: Open University Press.

Spencer, E. (1992) *Car Crime and Young People on a Sunderland Housing Estate.* Police Research Group Crime Prevention Unit Series Paper No. 40. London: Home Office.

Squires, P. and Stephen, D. (2005) 'Rethinking ASBOS', *Critical Social Policy, 25*(4), 517–528.

Squires, P. (2008) *ASBO Nation: The Criminalisation of Nuisance.* Bristol: Policy Press.

Stallman, R. (2003) 'The GNU Manifesto'. In *The New Media Reader.* Eds. Noah Wardrip-Fruin and Nick Monfort. Cambridge: MIT Press (Accessed: 9 January 2015).

Statewatch (2013) Available at: http://www.statewatch.org/index.php/site/ter.c/analyses/analyses/news/eu-dp.htm?&session-id=174cbb00aad728ba9d8938e42d52f2ed (Accessed: 05 May 2013).

Student Room (2010) 'Have You Actually Stole a Traffic Cone Before?' (online). 11 September. Available at: http://www.thestudentroom.co.uk/showthread.php?t=1402253 (Accessed: 12 August 2014).

Steen, M. (2008) 'Collateral Damage: The Destruction and Looting of Cultural Property in Armed Conflict', *ExpressO* (online). Available at: http://works.bepress.com/matthew_steen/1 (Accessed: 12 June 2012).

Stonewall (2008) 'Homophobic Hate Crime. The Gay British Crime Survey 2008' (online). Available at: http://www.stonewall.org.uk/.../homophobic_hate_crime__final_report.pdf (Accessed: 25 April 2010).

Stonewall (2014) 'History of Lesbian, Gay and Bisexual Equality' (online). Available at: http://www.stonewall.org.uk/at_home/history_of_lesbian_gay_and_bisexual_Equality/default.asp (Accessed: 10 June 2014).

Sturcke, J. (2010) 'Police Under Investigation over Fiona Pilkington Case' (online). 16 March. Available at: http://www.the guardian.com (Accessed: 17 June 2012).

Sumner, C. (1994) *The Sociology of Deviance: An Obituary.* Buckingham: Open University Press.

SunderlandEcho(2007)'HouseTrashPartyGirl:"I"msorry'(online).13April.Available at: http://www.sunderlandecho.com/news?ArticleID=2701454&session-id=c55fd2a154c14c211349bd8ea5bff844 (Accessed: 10 July 2010).

Swindon Advertiser (2011) 'Teenagers in Court for Stealing Car Badges' (online). 1 June. Available at: http://www.swindonadvertiser.co.uk/news/9057957.Teenagers_in_court_for_stealing_car_badges/?ref=twt (Accessed: 15 June 2013).

SWNS (2010) 'Dumped Mistress Pours Paint Stripper Over Lover's Car' (online). 2 September. Available at: http://www.*swns.com/dumped-mistress-pours-paint-stripper-over-lovers-car-021805* (Accessed: 14 April 2011).

Sykes, G. and Matza, D. (1957) 'Techniques of Neutralization: A Theory of Delinquency', *American Sociological Review*, *22*(6), 664–670.

Tajfel, H. and Turner, J.C. (1979) 'An Integrative Theory of Intergroup Conflict', in Austin, W.G. and Worchel, S. (eds) *The Social Psychology of Intergroup Relations*. Monterey, CA: Brooks-Cole.

TalkTalk (2014) 'Most Common Forms of Car Vandalism' (online). Available at: http://www.talktalk.co.uk/ ... /insurance-car-vandalism-most-common-places.ht (Accessed: 9 May 2014).

Tamworth Blog (2010) Available at: http://www.tamworthblog.co.uk/2010/03/22/10000-reward-for-information-on-railway-vandals/ (Accessed: 8 September 2012).

Taylor, I., Walton, P. and Young, J. (1973) *The New Criminology: For a Social Theory of Deviance*. London: Routledge.

TCU (2007) *Faculty Handbook*. Ft Worth, TX: Texas Christian University.

Terry, W. (eds) (1984) *Bloods: An Oral History of the Vietnam War by Black Veterans*. New York: Ballantine Books.

Thames Valley Police (2009) (online) Available at: http://www.thamesvalley.police.uk/yournh-tvp-pol-area-mk-newsitem?id=97777 (Accessed: 12 March 2010).

Times, The (2008) (online) Available at: http://www.timesonline.co.uk/tol/news/politics/article4985718.ece (Accessed: 12 June 2010).

The Sun (2009) 'Not a Very Smart Place to Park' (online). Available at: http://www.thesun.co.uk/sol/homepage/news/2391325/Smart-car-rolls-into-sea-while-driver-is-in-loo.html (Accessed: 13 July 2011).

Thoms, D., Holden, L. and Craydon, T. (1998) *The Motor Car and Popular Culture in the Twentieth Century*. Aldershot: Ashgate.

Thoms, D. (1998) 'Motor in Ownership in Twentieth–Century Britain: A Matter of Convenience or a Marque of Status?' in Thoms, D., Holden, L. and Claydon, T. (eds) *The Motor Car and Popular Culture in the 20th Century*, 96–119. Aldershot: Ashgate.

Times, The (1997) (online) Available at: http://www.the times.co.uk. (Accessed: 12 April 2013).

Times Education Supplement (2000) 'Stopped Dead in their Tracks' (online). 20 October. Available at: http://www.tes.co.uk/article.aspx?storycode=339900 (Accessed: 12 September 2011).

Topping, A. (2011) 'Looting "Fuelled" by Social Exclusion', *The Guardian* (online). 8 August. Available at: http://www.theguardian.com/uk/2011/aug/08/looting-fuelled-by-social-exclusion (Accessed: 12 July 2012).

Trackstar Racing (2014) (online) Available at: http://www.stockcar-racing.co.uk/ (Accessed: 24 August 2014).

Trasler, G.B. (1986) 'Situational Crime Control and Rational Choice: A Critique', in K. Heal and G. Laycock (eds) *Situational Crime Prevention: From Theory into Practice*. London: HMSO.

Travel UK (2010) Available at: http://travel.uk.msn.com/news/articles.aspx?cp-documentid=154132043 (Accessed: 10 July 2013).

Turk, A.T. (1969) *Criminality and Legal Order*. Chicago: Rand McNally.

Urban Dictionary (2014) (online) Available at: http://www.urbandictionary.com (Accessed: 19 August 2014).

US History (2014) (online) Available at: http://www.u-s-history.com/pages/h16 (Accessed: 16 August 2014).

USAF Intelligence Targeting Guide (1998) (online) Available at: http://www.fas.org/irp/doddir/**usaf**/afpam14–210/ (Accessed: 13 June 2010).

Utley, T. (2012) 'What My Liverpudlian Ancestor Tom Could Teach Us About Putting Britain's Whiplash Capital Back on the Path to Honest Toil', *The Daily Mail* (online). 1 June. Available at: http://www.dailymail.co.uk/debate/article-2152954 (Accessed: 16 February 2015).

Uxbridge Gazette (2012) 'Disabled Woman's Mobility Bike Hit by Vandals' (online).16 May. Available at: http://www.uxbrdigegazette.co.uk/west-london-news/local-uxbridge-news (Accessed: 15 March 2013).

Van Kesteren, J.N., Mayhew, P. and Nieuwbeerta, P. (2000) *Criminal Victimisation in Seventeen Industrialised Countries: Key Findings from the 2000 International Crime Victims Survey.* The Hague: Ministry of Justice, WODC.

Van Laer, J. and Van Aelst, P. (2010) 'Cyber-protest and Civil Society: The Internet and Action Repertoires in Social Movements', in Jewkes, Y. and Yar, M. (eds) *Handbook of Internet Crime.* Devon: Willan.

Van Wilsem, J. (2004) 'Criminal Victimization in Cross-National Perspective: An Analysis of Rates of Theft, Violence and Vandalism across 27 Countries', *European Journal of Criminology, 1*, 89.

Varsity (2006) 'Racist Vandalism in Muslim Prayer Room at Anglia Ruskin' (online). 24 February, 1. Available at: http://archive.varsity.co.uk/635.pdf (Accessed: 10 July 2011).

Veg News (2014) (online) Available at: http://www.vegnews.org/vegan_article38.html (Accessed: 6 August 2014).

Vold, G.B. (1958) *Theoretical Criminology.* Oxford: Oxford University Press.

Voz Iz Neouis (2010) 'Former Nazi Concentration Camp Vandalised with Swastikas'. Available at: http://www.vosizneious.com/52577/2010/04/06/hamburg-germany-former-nazi-concentration-camp-vandalized-with –swastikas) (Accessed: 12 December 2011).

Waddington, D. (eds) (1996) *Policing Public Order: Key Issues and Controversies.* Aldershot: Avebury.

Wake, I., Wilmot, I., Fairweather, P. and Birkett, J. (1999) *Breaking the Chain of Hate. A National Survey Examining the Level of Homophobic Crime and Community Confidence Towards the Police Service.* National Advisory Group.

Wall, D. (2007) *Cybercime.* Cambridge: Polity Press.

Wall Street Journal, The (2013) *'Jury Acquits Zimmerman of All Charges'* (online). 14 July. Availableat: http://www.nline.wsj.com/news/articles/SB100014241278873248795045786035627620645O2?mod=WSJ_hpp_LEFTTopStories&mg=reno64-wsj&url=http%3A%2F%2Fonline.wsj.com%2Farticle%2F (Accessed: 23 September 2013).

Waugh, E. (2001, originally 1928) *Decline and Fall.* London: Penguin.

Weber, C (2004) *Imagining America at War: Morality, Politics and Film.* London: Routledge.

Weiss, P. (2012) 'Breaking: Israeli Bulldozer, Soldiers Destroy Entire Bedouin Community near Anata in West Bank'. Available at: http://mondoweiss.net/2012/01/ (Accessed: 13 September 2011).

Westcott, R. (2014) 'Record Number of Deaths on Railway' (online). 2 July. Available at: http://www.bbc.co.uk/news/business-28130579 (Accessed: 12 August 2014).
Williams, M. (2004) 'Understanding King Punisher and His Order: Vandalism in a Virtual Reality Community – Motives, Meanings and Possible Solutions', *Internet Journal of Criminology* (online). Available at: http://www.internet-journalofcriminology.com/Williams%20-%20Understanding%20King%20Punisher%20and%20andhis%20Order.pdf (Accessed: 7 January 2014).
Wilson, P. and Healy, P. (1987) Research Brief. Graffiti and Vandalism on Public Transport. Trends and Issues in Crime and Criminal Justice. Australian Institute of Criminology: Canberra.
Wilson, J.Q. and Hernstein, R.J. (1985) *Crime and Human Nature*. New York: Simon and Schuster.
Wilson, J.Q. and Kelling, G.L. (1982) 'Broken Windows: The Police and Neighbourhood Safety', *The Atlantic Online*, March.
Wintour, P. (2007) 'Tories Back Cameron over Cannabis Claims' (online). *The Guardian*. 11 February. Available at: http://www.the guardian.com. (Accessed: 9 January 2015).
Wilkins, L. (1964) *Social Deviance: Social Policy, Action and Research*. London. Routledge.
Wolchover, N. (2011) 'Weird Metal Thefts in US Driven by Asian Industrial Boom', Available at: http://www.livescience.com (Accessed: 13 September 2012).
World Soccer Talk (2009) Destroying the Myth of Liverpool Fans as Hubcap Stealers and Dole Collectors' (online). 26 January. Available at: http://www.epltalk.com/destroying-the-myth-of-liverpool-fans-as-hubcap-stealers-and-dole-collectors/4172 (Accessed: 3 September 2012).
Wral.com (2011) 'Hundreds Rally at NC State against Homophobic Vandalism' (online). 20 October. Available at: http://www.wral.com/news/local/story/10280700/#VJzrcqjQs7azBytv.99 (Accessed: 14 April 2013).
Wright, P. (2013) 'Prince Charles Decries Historic Buildings Being Abandoned to 'Arsonists and Vandals' at Kenwood House Reopening'. *Ham and High* (online). 5 December. Available at: http://www.hamhigh.co.uk/news (Accessed: 4 December 2014)
Wrong, D. (1961) 'The Oversocialized Conception of Man in Modern Sociology', *American Sociological Review, 26*(2), 183–192.
www.bournemouth.gov.uk (Accessed: 10 August 2014).
www.nottinghamcityhomes.co.uk (Accessed: 10 August 2014).
www.reversegraffifti.co.uk (Accessed: 22 December 2013).
Yoshida, A., Terazona, A., Aramaki, T. and Hanaki, K. (2005) 'Secondary Materials Transfer from Japan to China: Destination Analysis in China. *Journal of Material Cycles and Waste Management, 7*(1), 8–15.
Young, J. (2004) 'Voodoo Criminology and the Numbers Game', in Ferrell, J. et al. (eds) *Cultural Criminology Unleashed*. London: Glasshouse.
Young, J. (2007) *The Vertigo of Late Modernity*. London: Sage.
Young, J. (2009) 'Moral Panic: Its Origins in Resistance, Resentiment and the Translation of Fantasy into Reality', *British Journal of Criminology*, 49, 4–16.
You Tube (2007a) 'The Life and Death of a Supermarket Trolley' (online). 22 October. Available at: http://www.youtube.com/watch?y=UqKyXGBtCKA (Accessed: 20 August 2014).

You Tube (2007b) 'Jake's House Party (Real life skins)' (online). 23 June. Available at: http://www.youtube.com/watch?v+smk7EUWhRw (Accessed: 18 February 2015).

You Tube (2007c) 'Stupid Burglars' (online). 29 October. Available at: http://www.youtube.com/watch?v=GiyV-s0ap4I (Accessed: 18 August 2010).

You Tube (2008a) 'Ye Old Supermarket Trolley Jousting Tournament' (online). 15 June. Available at: http:// www.youtube.com/watch?v=m_d_lYWHZuY (Accessed: 19 August 2014).

You Tube (2008b) 'Most Stupid Burglar Ever' (online). 10 April. Available at: http://www.youtube.com/watch?v=IZIbYiXBzeQ (Accessed: 25 September 2009).

You Tube (2009) 'Drivers Manchester Lose the Battle of the Traffic Bollard' and/or "Dumb Ass Drivers"' (online). 20 October (Accessed: 16 March 2010).

You Tube (2011) 'French Polishers – Classic Yellow Pages TV ad' (online). 1 February. Available at: http://www.youtube.com/watch?v+iKb3J9mctlo (Accessed: 18 February 2015).

You Tube (2012) 'IBM Fight Carbon' (online). 18 July. Available at: https://www.youtube.com/watch?v+RPdv3IGGz4 (Accessed: 30 December 2013).

Zinkhan, G.M. and Carlson, L. (1995) 'Green Advertising and the Reluctant Consumer', *Journal of Advertising,* 16 (Summer), *24*(2), 1–6.

Index

Printed and bound by CPI Group (UK) Ltd, Croydon, CR0 4YY